THE LIBRARY
ST. MARY'S COLLEGE OF MARYLAND
ST. MARY'S CITY, MARYLAND 20686

THE
Canadian
DRAMATIST

VOLUME TWO

Playwrights of
Collective Creation

Theatre Passe Muraille's production of Doukhobors (1971), directed by Paul Thompson. Photo: Theatre Passe Muraille.

THE
Canadian
DRAMATIST

VOLUME TWO

Playwrights of Collective Creation

by Diane Bessai

Series Editor: Christopher Innes

Simon & Pierre
Toronto, Canada

We would like to express our gratitude to the Canada Council, the Ontario Arts Council, and the Ontario Publishing Centre for their support.

Marian M. Wilson, Publisher

This book has been published with the help of a grant from the Canadian Federation for the Humanities, using funds provided by the Social Sciences and Humanities Research Council of Canada.

Copyright © 1992 by Diane Bessai. All rights reserved.
Cover and design copyright © 1992 by Simon & Pierre Publishing Co. Ltd. /
Les Éditions Simon & Pierre Ltée. All rights reserved.

No part of this book may be reproduced or transmitted in any form or by any means, electronic or mechanical, including photocopying and recording, information storage and retrieval systems, without permission in writing from the publisher, except by a reviewer who may quote brief passages in a review.

ISBN 0-88924-227-5
1 2 3 4 5 • 4 3 2 1 0

Canadian Cataloguing in Publication Data

Bessai, Diane, 1931-
   Playwrights of Collective Creation

(The Canadian Dramatist; v. 2)
Includes index.
ISBN 0-88924-227-5

1. Canadian drama (English) — 20th century — History and criticism.*
2. Improvisation (Acting).
   I. Title. II. Series.

PS8163.B47 1992   C812'.5409   C92-093585-0
PR9191.5.B47 1992

Series Editor: Christopher Innes
General Editor: Marian M. Wilson
Editor: Richard Horenblas
Proofreader: Joe Doucet

Printed and Bound in Canada

Order from
Simon & Pierre Publishing Company Limited/
Les Éditions Simon & Pierre Ltée.
P.O. Box 280, Adelaide Street Postal Station,
Toronto, Ontario. Canada M5C 2J4

This book is dedicated to the memory of Frank Bessai (1928-1969).

Acknowledgements

I wish to acknowledge the invaluable assistance of Heather McCallum, formerly of the Theatre Department, Metropolitan Toronto Reference Library, and also of Annette Wengle and Lee Ramsay. At Theatre Passe Muraille over the years, I am grateful to Paul Thompson, Clarke Rogers and Ted Johns for the loan of scripts and the use of additional archival material. Other theatres which have been generous with their records include 25th Street [House] Theatre, Saskatoon; The Globe Theatre, Regina; Rising Tide Theatre, St. John's; Theatre Network, Edmonton; and Toronto Workshop Productions. I am also indebted to Astrid Blodgett, David Barnet, Alan Filewod, Richard Paul Knowles, Donald Kerr, Donald Perkins, Morton Ross, Janis Watkin and to Christopher Drummond for their information and advice. I also wish to thank the University of Alberta for the award of a McCalla Professorship, making the initiation of this work possible; also the University of Alberta English Department for its support, and the graduate students of English 590 in recent years for their interest in Canadian drama. Last but far from least, I thank John, Tom and Carl Bessai for their practical assistance, and Frank M. Bessai for his encouragement.

Diane Bessai

Edmonton, 1992

Contents

Chapter One Collective Creation: Its Background

                and Canadian Developments 13

   1.   Britain and United States 15

   2.   Canada 24

   3.   Paul Thompson and Theatre Passe Muraille 31

Chapter Two Theatre Passe Muraille 49

   1.   Beginning an Underground History of Dissent:

       Doukhobors and *Buffalo Jump* 49

   2.   Community, Present and Past:

       The Farm Show; 1837: The Farmer's Revolt;

       Them Donnellys 63

   3.   Showing West: *The West Show; Far As the Eye*

       Can See 106

Chapter Three Rick Salutin: Playwright

                of Occasion 133

   1.   *Les Canadiens* 137

   2.   *Nathan Cohen: A Review* 145

3. *S: Portrait of a Spy* 155

4. Salutin in Newfoundland 164

Chapter Four   **John Gray's Local Heroes** **179**

1. *18 Wheels* 183

2. *Billy Bishop Goes to War* 186

3. *Rock and Roll* 199

4. *Don Messer's Jubilee* 206

Chapter Five   **Linda Griffiths' Transformations** **217**

1. *Maggie & Pierre* 220

2. *O.D. on Paradise* 225

3. *Jessica* 229

Chapter Six   **Seminal Theatre** **243**

Appendix   **Chronology of Principal Dramatic Works** 252

Endnotes 258

Index 280

List of Illustrations

Frontispiece
Theatre Passe Muraille, *Doukhobors* (1971). Photo source: Theatre Passe Muraille.

12 Blyth Festival, *The Death of the Donnellys* (1979). Photo source: Blyth Festival Theatre Archives, University of Guelph Library. Photographer: Keith Roulston.

48 Theatre Passe Muraille, *The Farm Show* (1972). Photo source: Theatre Passe Muraille Archives, University of Guelph Library.

132 Theatre Passe Muraille, *Les Canadiens* (1978 revival). Photo source: Theatre Passe Muraille Archives, University of Guelph Library.

178 Workshop West Playwrights Theatre, *Billy Bishop Goes To War* (1983 revival). Photo source: Workshop West Playwrights Theatre. Photographer: Gerry Potter.

216 Workshop West Playwrights Theatre, *O.D. on Paradise* (1984 revival). Photo source: Workshop West Playwrights Theatre. Photographer: Gerry Potter.

242 25th Street Theatre, *Paper Wheat* (1977). Photo source: 25th Street Theatre.

Photographs are published with the permission of Theatre Passe Muraille, Blyth Festival Theatre, Workshop West Playwrights Theatre, and 25th Street [House] Theatre. Every effort has been made by the author to seek permissions for photographs from the actors in keeping with the regulations of Canadian Actors' Equity Association. Any errors or omissions should be reported to the publisher.

The Blyth Festival production of *The Death of the Donnellys* (1979), written by Ted Johns and directed by Paul Thompson. From left to right: Kim Vincent, David Pappazian, John Jarvis, Sam Malkin, and Hardee Lineham. Photo: Keith Roulston.

Chapter One
Collective Creation:
Its Background and Canadian Developments

In the annals of English-Canadian theatre history, development during the post-centennial period is likely the liveliest on record. Although many young theatre workers had entered the scene, most regional theatres across the country seemed unreceptive to new Canadian talent and uninterested in the development and performance of new Canadian work. Many of these new workers saw the Canadian theatre establishment during the late 1960s as either the last vestige of British imperialism or the new frontier of American colonization. Feeling like outsiders, they took advantage of alternative funding of the day—grants such as Opportunities for Youth and Local Initiative Programs—to create vibrant new theatre operations run on a shoe string. These so-called "alternative" theatres may be divided roughly into two categories: those concentrating on the development of new playwrights—for example, Tarragon Theatre and Factory Theatre Lab in Toronto—and those working in collective creation. This term refers to actor-improvised plays, created during the rehearsal period, in which theatrical rather than literary values predominate. Of the latter, Theatre Passe Muraille—under the artistic direction of Paul Thompson—was the leading innovator for what became a playmaking process among particular new theatres spread across the country.

Essentially, the collective creators were subversives—like their contemporary American and British counterparts—demystifying the gentilities of "high art" by sharing their themes and performance processes openly with the audience. For this reason, the style of play and performance can be categorized as anti-naturalistic—more often presentational than mimetic. On occasion, this style draws on the theatricality of popular entertainment and often resembles a variety show or a Christmas concert more than a conventional play. The typical structure is a collage of juxtaposed scenes rather than a strictly linear development, comprising dramatic sketch, monologue, song and expressive gesture. The actors perform multiple roles, sometimes portraying inanimate objects as well as people. Through speech and transformational body language, the actors provide the essentials of the scene without much use of props and sets. The result is a type of rough and ready theatre that can be performed almost anywhere—and was: in town halls, school gyms, churches (in either basement or nave), in auction barns and, on one unusual occasion, in a Toronto streetcar. Instead of waiting for an audience to find them, the collective companies set out to create their own audiences by addressing the local public directly on subjects of interest to the lives and traditions of those in neighbouring communities.

The first part of this study analyzes a chronological selection through the 1970s of collective creations at Theatre Passe Muraille under the direction of Paul Thompson. As the most influential Canadian practitioner of collective creation at the time, Thompson was challenged, among other things, by his observation that "the really interesting people are the ones who don't go to theatres."[1] Therefore, he decided to attempt a change. His innovative work with talented actors having a knack for improvisation—and sometimes with writers—resulted in a new kind of Canadian play. These plays deserved critical interest in their own right as performance pieces and were seminal in the cultivation of new audiences for indigenous theatre—in Toronto and elsewhere.

Collective creation at Theatre Passe Muraille was also influential in the development of certain writers for the theatre. There is a paradox here, given that Thompson himself never advocated the primacy of the writer in his collective enterprises and, for some years, was even indifferent to the publication of Theatre Passe Muraille's scripts. For him, theatre is an art serving the performer, not aspiring to be dramatic literature. For him, the play is in the performance, not in the packaging between covers. Yet there is a clear line of descent—the subject of the second part of this study—among certain theatrical workers who have toiled in various capacities on Theatre Passe Muraille's collective creations: Rick Salutin as a writer, John Gray as a composer and musician, and Linda Griffiths as a performer. This suggests that Canadian drama, as well as Canadian theatre, owes more to collective creation than has been acknowledged before.

1. Britain and United States

The roots of collective creation in twentieth-century theatre reach back at least as far as the radical political experiments in non-Aristotelian theatre of Erwin Piscator and Bertolt Brecht in the 1920s. At that time, they were seeking ways to express their sense of the inadequacy of conventional theatre to examine the changing cultural environment of technological mass man.[2] Brecht speaks of organizing "small collectives of specialists in various fields to 'make' the plays; among these specialists were historians and sociologists as well as playwrights, actors and other people of the theatre."[3] Piscator as a director was notorious for his freedom with texts to suit his political intention[4] and was ingenious in his stagecraft for creating new kinds of audience recognition of the changing technological environment of the modern world.

The object, of course, was to reach a new working class rather than a bourgeois audience—an interest transmitted to Joan Littlewood in the 1930s in her attempts to establish a working-class community theatre in Manchester and later in Stratford East, London. In those first years, she directed agitprop theatre, early Brecht, and Piscator's adaptation of *The Good Soldier Schweik*. For the 1940 collective documentary *Last Edition*, about the political crises of the previous decade, she drew on the methods of the American Living Newspaper. This was a form of collective play developed in the U.S. Federal Theatre Project of the mid-1930s, founded by Hallie Flanagan. A documentary type of theatre researched and assembled by "editors," its aims were to develop a factually based theatrical shorthand to explore current issues of public concern—such as agriculture (*Triple-A Ploughed Under*), a public utility (*Power*), and housing (*One Third of a Nation*). As Arthur Arent reports, this involved improvisational techniques for "dramatizing abstraction." In *Power*, for example, the meaning of the term "holding company" was illustrated by the complicated manoeuvres of two actors and a pile of boxes.[5]

For Littlewood, as for Brecht, ensemble playing was a strong priority. In re-forming her resident group after the war as Theatre Workshop, she introduced the company to a rigorous training in the dance techniques of Rudolph Laban, which she adapted to the needs of her actors. In her productions of classics and new plays alike, her aim was to integrate fully the resources of movement, voice, sound and light. Disciplined improvisation was a constant in her rehearsal methods, resulting in what Alan Filewod identifies as her "signature technique of portraying realistic action through mime and sound effects."[6] Her best known work is the ironically titled *Oh What a Lovely War!* (1963), a company creation built on the popular songs of the First World War.[7] This musical combines a pierrot show with Piscator's early technique of using documentary projections as backdrop to satiric versions of factual scenes.

As the basis for establishing a direct link to the community at the Victoria Theatre of Stoke-on-Trent in the 1960s, director Peter

Cheeseman and his company created local documentaries that combined the Living Newspaper's concern for factuality, Joan Littlewood's emphasis on ensemble creativity, and her desire to reach a popular working-class audience. John Elsom notes that

> For the growing regional repertory theatre movement in the 1960s, the local documentaries provided a means of establishing a theatre's identity as part of a town or region, without losing its function as a theatre.[8]

In Britain, local creativity in the theatre was often overshadowed by the transfer systems to and from the West End. The aim of Cheeseman, and those who subsequently took their lead from him—as in Hull, Newcastle and Leeds, for example—was to establish new local theatrical material for audiences who had seldom ventured into the theatre at all. Cheeseman's company worked "to develop a new and special style of acting, which honestly exposed the factual quality"[9] (i.e., *The Staffordshire Rebels*, 1965; *The Knotty*, 1966; *Six into One*, 1968) of local history. In the notable case of a local issue (*The Fight for Shelton Bar*, 1974), the company went out and learned the plant operations they were to depict on stage through combinations of realistic action and mime.

As with Littlewood, popular culture was often an informing principle in this kind of play, providing a way of appealing to its target audiences. The collective improvisation for Alan Plater's *Close the Coalhouse Door*, produced at the Newcastle Playhouse in 1968, drew richly on English music-hall tradition. This documentary musical—about the community experience of the mining industry over the years—filled the theatre with workers both in the Newcastle Playhouse and later in the Nottingham Playhouse. At the Bradford College of Art, Albert Hunt worked collectively with his student Theatre Group to develop a theatre of alternative education. Their *John Ford's Cuban Missile Crisis* (1970), commissioned by radical Bradford University students for the Lenin Centenary celebrations, took its theatrical form as a cartoon version of the American western movie.

In 1966, Hunt had been part of the dramaturgical team assembled by Peter Brook for the Royal Shakespeare Company's collective improvisation, *US*, an English perspective on the events in Vietnam. He later said he preferred a "community core to which our communication could be directed." That had not been the case with the "undefined" audience at the Aldwych Theatre for *US*. For its Lenin Centenary assignment, his company knew it would have an audience of a specific political commitment and therefore chose a subject and popular idiom that would allow "for a cool look at what the Russian Revolution had become."[10] When the play was later performed in a variety of venues—from a north-country village school to a pub to London's Open Space Theatre—Hunt was pleased most by its success with non-theatre-going audiences.[11] In 1974, Red Ladder (a branch of the original AgitProp Street Players formed in London in 1968) moved to Leeds "to establish a cultural presence for socialist theatre" in Yorkshire. With the same kind of audience concerns in mind as theatres in other regions, they collectively developed cabaret-club shows and plays in which they personalized issues relating to past and present working life in the area. Catherine Itsin reports that *Taking Our Time*, an examination of the textile trade in the course of the industrial revolution, reached 10,000 people in West Yorkshire.[12]

In the United States, the specific methods, purposes and degree of collective creation were as varied as the companies working in the mode. Arthur Sainer, writing in 1975, observed that the gradual proliferation of radical ensemble troupes throughout the 1960s was a "disenchantment with commercial theatre" that "paralleled a broader disenchantment with the culture at large." In effect, he was describing the essential attitudes of the American counter-culture when he particularized that disenchantment "with America as a world power, with material well-

Chapter One: Background   19

being, with the ethic of the isolated figure labouring to merit the approval of society."[13] Theodore Shank, in his 1972 investigation of a number of small European and American companies currently practising collective creation, spoke in broader terms of this "one process" group method of devising theatre pieces as the alternative theatre for the alternative society. He surveyed examples of collective theatre of the time as part of an international quest for wholeness "in reaction to the fragmentation of the established society" in a profession traditionally characterized by specialization, competition and internal hierarchies.

In general, the function of such companies was two-fold: through improvisational methods, to stretch the creativity of the individual performer within the group context; and in the process, to explore radical means of engaging or encountering audiences. The latter might occur through personal consciousness-raising experiments or by establishing particular social or political objectives. For all of these, the experimental use of the performance space, indoor or outdoor, was a major factor. The creation of some form of text was a by-product of the collective process—the play emerging as a fluid rather than a fixed entity, a stimulus to group performance rather than an end in itself. The function of the writer—when included in the collective—was similar to that of the director and the performers: to contribute to the group exploration. Established texts, when used, were springboards for ensemble creativity rather than the *raison d'être* of performance as in traditional theatre. Music, movement, non-verbal sound and sometimes visual art—or the use of masks or puppets—became as important as language.[14]

Three American counter-culture ensembles achieved great renown off-off-Broadway: The Living Theatre, founded by Julian Beck and his wife Judith Malina in 1951; The Open Theatre, founded by Joseph Chaikin in 1963; and The Performance Group of Richard Schechner, founded in 1967.[15] Their common features included the exploration of acting techniques that were non-verbal and physically oriented (drawing to some degree on the psycho-physical theories of Jerzy Grotowski of

20 Playwrights of Collective Creation

The Polish Laboratory Theatre); the focus on the presence of the actor rather than the fictional character he traditionally portrays; the collective "confrontation" of classical texts or the creation of radical new versions; and open, often sensational, ritualized interaction with the audience. In this last respect, we see the debt to Antonin Artaud's ideas: for a theatre of cruelty as a therapeutic externalization of latent violence and suffering; and for the return to a theatre of spectacle as well as ritualized sound and gesture.[16] Each of these groups, however, also had its own experimental emphasis.

The dedication of the Becks over the years to a political philosophy of pacifist anarchism led to The Living Theatre's increasing determination to break the barriers between life, theatre and revolution. Beginning in 1964 with *Mysteries and Smaller Pieces* (their first European show following self-exile related to problems concerning tax evasion), the Becks used collective creation along with related innovations of the period—such as onstage improvisation and aggressive interaction between performers and audience. Their production *Paradise Now* (1968), a collective creation, recklessly invited audience participation in the episode called "The Rite of Universal Intercourse" and ended with actors leading spectators out into the street. For their guerrilla-theatre work among the poor of Brazil during 1970 and 1971, they interviewed their research subjects and sometimes invited their direct participation in the collective creation. This work was done for a projected cycle of plays on the origins of violence—*The Legacy of Cain.*

At its most characteristic, The Open Theatre was committed to theatrical exploration through movement and to new body techniques of acting through improvisational exercises—rather than to political awareness and change. Nevertheless, an early phase of their work yielded Megan Terry's *Viet Rock* (1966). This full-length expression of anger against the Vietnam War was improvised from an Open Theatre workshop directed by Terry. The play was unusual at the time because of its experiments in transformational acting, by which the actors not only played multiple roles but also exchanged individual parts.

In the same year, the company produced Jean-Claude van Itallie's *America Hurrah*, a three-play theatricalization of contemporary malaise, which developed in part from The Open Theatre's acting exercises. More typically, however, Chaikin led his company in collective "meditations" on timeless human concerns. These included the Fall of Adam and Eve, based on improvisations from Genesis in *The Serpent* (1967); human response to death in *Terminal* (1969); social conditioning in *The Mutation Show* (1971); and sleep and consciousness in *Nightwalk* (1973). These works grew from the improvisational development of images, non-verbal vocal sound, and physically rendered percussion effects. Although the source of the plays was the actors' improvisations, Chaikin continued to include a participating writer. For example, van Itallie structured the final script of *The Serpent* while Susan Yankowitz provided the words for *Terminal*.

Schechner's environmental theatre, The Performance Group, combined features of the other two but with a special emphasis on creating new spatial relationships. This was done within an extended performance area that would best achieve close interaction between performers and spectators. The famous *Dionysus in 69* combined the company's variation on Euripides' *The Bacchae* with primitive and contemporary rituals as well as with "actuals" (personal interjections by actors) within a design of platforms, scaffolds and towers. The spectators chose their own places within this informal setting and were free at one point to participate in a ceremonial sexual orgy reminiscent of *Paradise Now* (described by the press as a "group grope").

There was a fourth theatre of importance in the radical developments of the period, both at home and abroad. That was Ellen Stewart's prolific Café La Mama, founded in 1961 and "dedicated to the playwright and all forms of the theatre."[17] Tom O'Horgan, now known best for his Broadway productions of *Hair* and *Jesus Christ Superstar*, was a core director of this troupe. He collaborated with the actors of the

La Mama Experimental Theatre Club and with Paul Foster "conjointly" to develop the latter's *Tom Paine*, which premiered at the Edinburgh Fringe Festival in 1967. The play combines text with moments set aside for actor improvisation and reflects the highly physical transformational acting styles of the time.

The influence of this company on director Max Stafford-Clark of Edinburgh's Traverse Theatre was seminal for his experiments in a kind of collective play different from those of the regional theatres. He soon established the Traverse Theatre Workshop, an experimental British fringe theatre that created plays through collaboration by a writer and a group of actors. On one occasion, the creative process included several writers. Most notable was the collective work *Hitler Dances*, done by the company in rehearsal with Howard Brenton. Later, Stafford-Clark became a founding member of Joint Stock, an alternative company whose improvisational workshops in the 1970s led to the creation of plays such as David Hare's *Fanshen* and Caryl Churchill's *Cloud Nine*.[18]

In the 1960s, another type of alternative theatre prevalent in the United States was explicitly political and left-wing. "Our commitment is to change, not to art" was the unequivocal statement of purpose by the San Francisco Mime Troupe in 1971.[19] Since 1962, this company had been performing its *commedia dell'arte* versions of European classics—under the direction of founder Ron G. Davis—in the public parks of the Bay area. The troupe's resolve to reach a new working-class audience through popular forms of theatre was strengthened in 1969 (and continues to this day) with its reorganization into an activist and Marxist collective. Although credited to individual writers—Joan Holden being the principle one—the issue-oriented plays of this troupe reflected the collaborative study and analysis of the whole collective.

Inspired by the example of this group, Luis Valdez established the first Chicano company in 1965—the bilingual (Spanish and English) El Teatro Campesino. Initially, the company's work supported the grape workers' strike in Delano, California. Together, Valdez and the workers devised the brief satiric sketches that they called *actos*. These sketches depicted daily issues in the lives of strikers (*huelgistas*), using the broad gestures of Mexican mime. The company often performed at union meetings, rallies and along picket lines. Later, Valdez broadened the cultural base of the plays, developing a new form he called *mito*, which explored Mayan mythological themes that are part of the Chicano inheritance.[20]

Throughout the 1960s, there was also a strong interest in guerrilla street theatre among left wing students in the United States. Students at many university campuses formed their own "radical arts troupes" under the umbrella of the nation-wide Students for a Democratic Society. Their collectively devised plays were propaganda against the Vietnam War and related issues that they identified as class oppression. In 1968, Henry Peters described the collective genesis of a typical RAT play at Princeton. According to Peters, preparation would begin about 48 hours before the event at which the students were to perform. It took one meeting to create a 10-minute scenario from "nothing" (usually from an idea suggested by one of the actors) and a second meeting to rehearse whatever evolved. The play might be changed and enriched at another meeting or rally.[21]

The Pageant Players, an innovative street theatre active in New York parks and other public places between 1965 and 1970, frequently performed and conducted workshops at campuses to encourage the student theatre movement. According to Michael Brown, spokesman for the Pageant Players, they worked on the principle that art and politics can enrich each other. Their approach was indebted to The Open Theatre and The Living Theatre for movement exercises as the source of images and plots, and to the San Francisco Mime Troupe for its audience-directed energies.[22]

Henry Lesnick identifies two basic principles as governing the American kind of guerrilla street theatre: attempts to "bridge the gulf between players and audience" and efforts "to provide a new model for the relationship between society and social reality."[23] Gradually, the idea of an open and informal relationship to the spectator became firmly imprinted on popular theatre practice, due in large part to the wide-ranging experiments in collective creation of these years.

2. Canada

There are obvious links, both direct and indirect, between the alternative theatre movements outlined above and those that have emerged in Canada. The Canadian terms of protest against conventional theatre institutions were coloured, however, by the peculiarities of Canadian post-colonial circumstances and of geography. After 1967, with a new emphasis on indigenous Canadian culture inspired by the centennial celebrations, cultural politics became an issue in the theatre.

To the casual observer in the early 1970s, the recently established institution of professional Canadian theatre seemed to be thriving. Ever since the creation of the Canada Council in 1957, the founding of new civic theatres in major cities across the country—from Halifax to Vancouver—was an on-going enterprise. Yet even by the late 1960s, a certain disillusionment was setting in, especially among younger and untried Canadian performers and writers. Why this should be so is not hard to determine. Little beyond the fund-raising was explicitly Canadian in these theatres. The "regionals," a collective designation applied scathingly by the young, were conservative and formulaic in their annual subscription programming: one or two classics, a Shakespearean play, and some contemporary successes from Broadway or the West End. As with the Shaw and Stratford festivals, artistic directors were normally sought from elsewhere, as were major performers.

On rare occasions, a new Canadian play might find a slot on a regional second stage. Yet the idea that a regional theatre might reflect a regional culture was decidedly a minor matter. Two notable exceptions were the Manitoba Theatre Centre (MTC), under the direction of its co-founder John Hirsch, and the Globe Theatre in Regina, co-founded and directed by Ken and Sue Kramer. In 1958, the MTC grew out of a union of the long-established Winnipeg Little Theatre (WLT) with Theatre 77, a small new professional company of one season. Hirsch and Tom Hendry, co-founders of the latter, were both Winnipeggers who had served their theatrical apprenticeships with the WLT. Hirsch, the MTC's first artistic director, recalled "the excitement that can come from a theatre that grows out of a community." Although it was dependent on outside professionals in those early years, the MTC tried from the outset to work with the particular interests of its community and region in mind.

For example, the Manitoba Theatre Centre generated new plays, founded and sent on tour its own theatre school, and maintained in its programming—in Hirsch's words—"an organic connection between the audience and what went on stage."[24] By the beginning of the 1970s, however, all this was fading under the pressures of a lack of funding and the need to fill a large new theatre. In Regina in the meantime, the Kramers—who had founded a young people's theatre in 1966 for touring schools in their region—initiated an adult season in 1971 with that "organic connection" very much in mind for their choice of new and established plays. To develop new plays of local interest, they appointed Rex Deverell in 1976 as Canada's first permanent playwright-in-residence.

However, the general direction of theatrical development initiated by the Canada Council was based on the concept of a homogeneous national theatre, not on regional identities. Geography was merely an inconvenience to be overcome. The Council's *Annual Report* in 1961-62 stated: "The essential of a *national* theatre, as we see it, is that it should reach a *national* audience—even if this audience must, for convenience, be broken down into regional audiences...." [emphasis in original] With unconscious centralist irony, the report also speculated that "in a decade or so, a fairly close working relationship might develop among them [the civic theatres outside Ontario and Québec] and with Toronto and Montreal."[25] In theatre parlance, the "regions" in relation to these two cities were already beginning to sound like the British "provinces" in relation to London.

One reason for the rise of alternative theatres in Canada during the 1970s was that regional theatres too often refused to be genuinely regional or, for that matter, national (in the culturally indigenous sense of the term). Cultural colonialism, long a Canadian affliction in relation to both Britain and the United States, was being duplicated within the country itself. Yet paradoxically, the parallel between these Canadian circumstances and those in Britain outside London is instructive. The need, identified by John Elsom, to establish a new theatre's local identity became a concern of Canadian alternative theatres. Yet, it was largely ignored by the Canadian regionals. In its exception to this pattern, the Globe Theatre was the one regional theatre to learn from the changing scene in the British provinces. The Kramers had observed and admired Cheeseman's work at Stoke-on-Trent. For their own collective plays about local subjects, they emulated his insistence on documentary accuracy.[26] (As we will see later in the text, Paul Thompson rejected this principle at Theatre Passe Muraille).

In the 1960s—as already outlined—the term "alternative theatre" usually alluded to radical theatrical trends of the counter-culture, notably in the United States. In Canada, as a protest against conservative cultural dependence in the theatre, alternative theatre became associated with nationalism, Canadian content and experiment. Nevertheless, counter-culture elements hastened the formation of several alternative companies and for a time influenced their productions. At Theatre Passe Muraille, for example, the early improvisational workshops of founder Jim Garrard and his choice of contemporary American plays reflected the new ensemble techniques popular in the United States. Vancouver's Tamahnous Theatre, as Renata Usmiani notes, modelled its adaptation of *The Bacchae* in 1971 on The Performance Group's *Dionysus in 69*. In 1975, Tamahnous developed techniques of ritual and incantation for its collective creation on a native Indian theme, *The Shaman's Cure*.[27] In its second season, 25th Street House Theatre of Saskatoon experimented with theatre-of-cruelty techniques in a production entitled *Sibyl*, directed by Montrealer Alexander Hausvater and based on his adaptation of a novel by Par Lagerkvist.

As already indicated, some alternative theatres in Canada were oriented very specifically to playwright's theatre and the workshopping and premiering of new plays. Yet for many others, collective creation became the solution to a lack of written Canadian material. Of course, there were other good reasons for collective creations. The presence of imported fare and personnel in Canadian theatres reinforced the aversion to the tyranny of the text—a trend initiated by the counter-culture, with its dedication to the creativity of the actor. The challenge of the informal, often improvised, performance space—with its altered relationships between performer and audience—was another important factor. This kind of counter-culture theatre seemed to offer a prescription for the alternative Canadians needed to the establishment institutions that had prevailed for a decade. Alternative theatre provided creative opportunities for new actors, directors and participating writers. It reduced the emphasis on elaborate theatre space with its elitist connotations. Most importantly, it sought direct interaction with a Canadian version of an alternative audience—Thompson's "the really interesting people...who don't go to theatres."

That this was a regional—or often a purely local—enterprise (with all that this implies about content) was its greatest virtue. It didn't happen only in Toronto or Montreal—although, understandably, these densely populated cities were often in the forefront of change. Rather, alternative theatre became a Canada-wide phenomenon from which the country has, fortunately, never entirely recovered. Sometimes, anomalously, alternative theatres were simply protests against the absence of professional theatre in their areas. The Mummers Troupe of St. John's or 25th Street House Theatre are good examples of such protests. At the same time, these two theatres also represent examples of alternative artistic commitment—the one committed to political collective creation, the other to an experimental artists' co-operative in which theatre was initially one component. With the founding of the Mulgrave Road Co-Op in 1977 in the small Nova Scotia community of Mulgrave, the "alternative" designation began to lose its identifying connotations of counter-culture radicalism. In this company—as in the later developments of Edmonton's Theatre Network—the principle of community-related theatre, often through collective creation, was justified in its own right.

George Luscombe, founder of Toronto Workshop Productions (TWP) in 1959, was one important forerunner to the Canadian movement of change. For nearly 30 years, he directed the theatre in a manner that continually challenged complacency in the profession and in the audience. In the early 1950s, he had performed with Joan Littlewood's Theatre Workshop at Stratford East. He returned to Canada, greatly interested in her type of highly disciplined group theatre, with its particular social and political objectives of the working class. Thoroughly trained in the movement techniques of Littlewood and Laban, he used these to develop collaborative methods for making improvisational plays, initially as a basis for training an ensemble of actors. He also applied these methods to the interpretation of established plays—often from Europe's avant-garde repertory—and to the adaptation of prose texts. Luscombe customarily maintained strong directorial control over performance techniques and the new plays evolving from them. While the actors were encouraged to "build characterization," a dramaturge was responsible for writing the dialogue.[28]

In contrast to Luscombe's approach, the most influential type of collective playmaking in Canada during the 1970s was free-form improvisation by the actors—as initiated by Paul Thompson at Theatre Passe Muraille in *Notes from Quebec* (1970). Another contrast was the choice of subject matter. Until *Ten Lost Years* (premiered on Feb. 7, 1974), Luscombe's adaptations rarely focussed on specifically Canadian material. Thus, at an early stage of a nationalistic impulse in theatre,

Toronto Workshop Productions was not considered to be an explicit model for the development of new work.[29] Yet, Luscombe led the way in introducing the idea of an alternative theatre in Toronto. His highly disciplined Littlewood methods of training and production were a revelation in the physical use of the actor and the stage. However, his main influence in Canadian theatre was through the actors who trained in his company. He certainly exercised less influence on the new generation of independent-minded collective creators. Many of the latter, such as Paul Thompson, were characterized by the accessibility of their methods to both experienced and inexperienced performers as well as to the writer.

Thompson joined Theatre Passe Muraille as a stage manager in late 1969, then served as artistic director until 1981. At his own choice, he continued with the theatre as an assistant director until he was appointed director-general at the National Theatre School in 1987. His achievement in developing collective creation at Theatre Passe Muraille is distinguished by its variety of experimentation, "putting Canadian voices and people on stage."[30] Although based at Theatre Passe Muraille in Toronto through the 1970s, where he drew on a core of local actors who developed strong improvisational skills under his guidance, he also moved about the country. On tour, he presented successful productions (*The Farm Show*, summer 1974) and created new shows while encouraging new theatre companies to create their own collective enterprises. Touring also gave him an opportunity to find new talent for his own collective creations.

During this formative period in the growth of new Canadian theatre, Thompson was a key link in a casual network of like-minded theatre groups developing in several parts of the country: the Mummers Troupe, 25th Street Theatre, Theatre Network, and The Mulgrave Road Co-Op. This personal contact was reinforced by Theatre Passe Muraille's seed show programme, by which small amounts of money were given to groups with their own ideas for collective creations. People from elsewhere working in Toronto, like Paul Kelman and *The Edmonton Show*

(1975), were included. In addition, seed shows might travel—such as Clarke Rogers' *Almighty Voice*, which toured the prairies in late 1974 and early 1975.

In the fall of 1974, the national tour of *Ten Lost Years* by Toronto Workshop Productions—adapted from Barry Broadfoot's transcribed interviews of victims of the Great Depression—made a powerful impact[31] wherever it went. This production helped to stimulate audience interest in populist theatre performed in a presentational style. Yet Luscombe's ensemble methods did not operate through practical outreach. On the other hand, Thompson followed up the successful tours of *The Farm Show* and *Almighty Voice* through the prairies by going to Saskatoon with a company of Passe Muraille actors in the summer of 1975. There, he not only created *The West Show* but also introduced the struggling 25th Street Theatre to collective creation by directing it in *If You're So Good, Why Are You in Saskatoon?*. This production eventually led to the theatre's own creation of *Paper Wheat* in 1977. It toured nationally and became the best known collective creation from the prairies. That same year, Thompson and Theatre Passe Muraille worked with writer Rudy Wiebe to develop *Far As the Eye Can See* for its premiere at Edmonton's Theatre 3.

Another kind of outreach closer to home was the creation of Theatre Passe Muraille's own regional audience in southwestern Ontario, although it was never organized on a long-range basis. Beginning with *The Farm Show* in Clinton in 1972, the company often toured through the towns and cities of Huron and Middlesex counties and sometimes beyond with plays created for those audiences as much as for audiences in Toronto. During a tour of *1837: The Farmers' Revolt*, Thompson spotted the potential of the old Memorial Hall in Blyth, Ontario. That building became the home of the Blyth Festival, renowned for its development of new Canadian plays, some of which took shape as collective creations.

3. Paul Thompson and Theatre Passe Muraille

Before his joining Theatre Passe Muraille, Paul Thompson's career provides a characteristic illustration of the unconscious cultural schizophrenia that penetrated English-Canadian theatre in the emerging professionalism during the 1960s. This professionalism was demonstrated by the Stratford Festival, which continued its aspirations as an international showcase. Young Canadians were still going to Europe to satisfy their interests in new theatre. Thompson spent a year in Paris in 1964 after graduating in French from the University of Western Ontario. Until he went to Western, his personal experience of theatre in his home town of Listowel, Ontario was confined to school operettas. (This kind of theatrical was vividly depicted by Alice Munro in 1971 in her novel, *Lives of Girls and Women*, set in the thinly disguised town of nearby Wingham. Such an operetta was also lovingly parodied by Carol Bolt and Theatre Passe Muraille in their collective creation *Buffalo Jump*.) When he first went to university, Thompson joined the wrestling club, only to find that wrestlers had nothing interesting to say. He soon discovered the sociability and creativity of the young theatre crowd, working with English lecturer David Taylor at Huron College where he became friends with future directors Keith Turnbull and Martin Kinch.

In Paris, Thompson attended classes at the Sorbonne and saw as much avant-garde theatre as he could. There, he first learned about the work of Roger Planchon. Two years later, after returning to Canada for an M.A. on Artaud at the University of Toronto, he was accepted as a *stagiare* at Planchon's Théâtre de la Cité de Villeurbanne. The theatre was located in a suburb of Lyons where Planchon, an actor and director, had been developing a theatre for factory workers since 1957. Influenced by Brecht, Planchon was reassessing classics of the French and English theatre for their social and political relevance to contemporary life. During Thompson's two years there, Planchon found the bilingual Canadian useful in staging plays such as Sean O'Casey's *Purple Dust* and

John Arden's *Armstrong's Last Goodnight*. Before returning to Canada, Thompson did a grand tour of European theatres, courtesy of a Canada Council grant. His whole experience of theatre abroad prompted the inevitable question "what has that got to do with me back where I live?"[32]

While he was never able to apply the staging techniques he learned in France to Theatre Passe Muraille, Thompson did make one attempt at "social content à la Planchon." This occurred in 1967 with his production of George Farquhar's *The Beaux' Stratagem* during an abortive stint as professional (i.e., paid) director of an amateur company in Sault Ste. Marie.[33] The main influences on the work Thompson developed later at Passe Muraille were more general, although no less significant: Planchon's receptiveness to the ideas of people working with him, his capacity to surprise both performers and audience, and his focus on "man as a political and social being."[34]

During intervals in Canada over these years, Thompson was alert to some of the new elements emerging at the periphery of Ontario theatre. In the summers of 1965 and 1966, he worked for a time at Keith Turnbull's summer theatre in London, Ontario, where James Reaney's *The Sun and the Moon* and *Listen to the Wind* were premiered. He was excited by shows at Toronto Workshop Productions— particularly by the impressive collective energy on stage. Luscombe was developing this excitement with plays such as Georg Buchner's *Woyzek* and his company's own *Hey Rube!*. After his appointment in Sault Ste. Marie ended, Thompson approached Luscombe as "a really exciting director to be around" but was told that "you've got to be an actor first."[35] Instead, he went to Stratford for two seasons (1968 and 1969) and worked in the new assistant-director programme with Jean Gascon on *Tartuffe* and Douglas Campbell on *La Cenerentola*. Thompson also participated in Stratford's new programme of drama workshops led by Powys Thomas. As a result, he directed young actors in workshop productions of Michael Ondaatje's *The Man with Seven Toes*, José Triano's *The Criminals*, Sam

Shepard's *Red Cross*, and his own adaptation of a separatist theme from Jacques Hébert, entitled *Merde is a four letter word*.

During winters in Montreal, Thompson directed some lunch-time productions at Instanttheatre (soon to become the Centaur). There, he again experimented with a free form theatricalization entitled *I am Coming from Czechoslovakia*, which consisted of literary recollections of Prague, compiled by Mariska Stankova and performed by Walter Massey. By his second season at Stratford, working with Gascon on the revival of *Tartuffe*, he felt like a misfit in an essentially conservative scene. His sense of suffocation was relieved somewhat by the fringe activities of Martin Kinch and John Palmer at their alternative storefront space, provocatively named "The Canadian Place." Productions there included Palmer's *Memories for My Brother*, later revised for Theatre Passe Muraille which Thompson was soon to join.[36]

Ever since 1968, Jim Garrard had been building his "underground" theatre of the counter-culture with mixed success at Rochdale College. Located near the University of Toronto's downtown campus, Rochdale was intended as a highrise experiment in counter-culture living and learning. In hindsight, Garrard's initial "Statement of the Rochdale Theatre Project" reads almost as a blueprint for Thompson's later experiments with collective creation, although it lacks his specifically Canadian commitment. Garrard spoke of the project as "an exploration of the theatre in society and of the educational value for society." Accordingly, Rochdale College would serve "as a laboratory to study the relationship between theatre and environment." Most tellingly, it would be "a theatre free of distinctions between actor and spectator, between 'inside' and 'outside' the theatre, between drama as one art form, music as another, and dancing as yet another."[37] In a contemporary newspaper interview, Garrard spoke of wanting "to make theatre as popular as bowling." To achieve this, an acting ensemble of approximately 15 people "who work well together, who have a dialogue" would be "the resource."[38]

Garrard's workshops at Rochdale—in the first year or so of the theatre's life—used "games, improvisation, non-verbal physical communication, and group awareness."[39] However, instead of attempting its own collective creations, the company chose two American counter-culture plays with improvised and ensemble elements from Ellen Stewart's Café La Mama off-off-Broadway. In December of 1968, the first production—Paul Foster's *Tom Paine*—was staged in the Rochdale basement. That production was followed in May by Rochelle Owens' *Futz*, staged at the Central Library. The show became notorious after the Metro Toronto Police busted the production for nudity.

The following December, the revival of *Tom Paine* was directed by Martin Kinch (soon to become artistic director while Garrard turned to fundraising) in a new space, the church hall at 11 Trinity Square. This production was not received well by Nathan Cohen. *The Toronto Star* reviewer deplored the "forced pseudo-experimental form" of the play and cautioned the company that ensemble playing "means more than taking an ensemble stance."[40] In contrast, Herbert Whittaker had responded quite warmly two weeks earlier to the ensemble work in John Palmer's revised *Memories for My Brother*. In his review, Whittaker praised the production as "played by the agile nude Passe Muraille actors on a pipe structure that conjures up both Russian constructivism and the Living Theatre."[41]

Theatre Passe Muraille's growing reputation as "La Mama of the North" was enhanced considerably in the second half of the 1969-70 season. Martin Kinch directed a double bill of Terence McNally's *Sweet Eros*—daring in its frontal nudity and elaborate in its lighting—and John Lennon's *In His Own Write*. In retrospect, Garrard acknowledged the creative energy of the American draft-dodgers who had contributed to the initial growth of the theatre. Their involvement helped to reinforce the prevailing counter-culture (rather than nationalist) solidarity of the early days.[42]

During that same year, counter-culture theatre was generally strong in Toronto. Ernest J. Schwarz's production of The Performance Group's *Dionysus in 69* ran indefinitely at Studio Lab. George Luscombe's loose-leaf political satire, *Chicago '70*—with new events incorporated as they happened—was a success at Toronto Workshop Productions in the spring and was subsequently invited to New York. The Festival of Underground Theatre at the St. Lawrence Centre included visits from Bread and Puppet Theatre, Le Grand Cirque Magie from Paris, and Jean-Claude Germain's Théâtre du Même Nom from Montreal (performing *Si Aurore m'était contée deux fois*). Several Toronto directors participated in a fringe festival at Global Village. They included Garrard, Kinch and Thompson, who later described his adaptation, *Ubu Raw*, as his farewell to European influences.[43]

Thompson's first work for Theatre Passe Muraille, staged in May of that year, was consistent with the theatre's counter-culture leanings. Entitled *Notes from Quebec*, it is described in Theatre Passe Muraille's records as an adaptation.[44] Actually, the production was a collective creation, freely translated from *Diguidi, Diguidi, Ha, Ha, Ha!*. The script began as collective verbal improvisations by Jean-Claude Germain at Théâtre du Même Nom, where he was co-ordinator and *animateur*.[45] Thompson had admired Germain's play for three actors during the previous year in Montreal. It's a theatrical satire on a contemporary Quebec family in which a father, mother and son speak in monologues about their frustrations and fantasies and then promptly turn into dogs. Renata Usmiani describes the work in its final form as "genuine theatre of liberation."[46] It exemplifies the kind of revolutionary energy in Quebec's collective theatre of the time, which appealed to Thompson.

In *Notes from Quebec*, performed by Danny Freedman, Claire Coulter and Don Steinhouse, Thompson took liberties with the original, retaining the things that worked for his own actors and discarding what did not.[47] In a small way, this marked the beginning for Thompson and Theatre Passe Muraille of a different kind of alternative theatre—with its roots less in the American counter-culture of radical and defiant self-expression and more in the particularities of Canadian culture and politics.

French-Canadian theatre of the period was in many ways different from the English-Canadian. In Quebec, collective creation was not only politically and culturally radical in subject matter but was also taken up as a deliberate political alternative to the literary theatre, whose writers were perceived to have defected to the mainstream.[48] In English Canada, collective creation primarily served the cause of an anti-colonial cultural stance within a theatre whose mainstream, as previously noted, admitted little that was indigenous at all. Playwright James Reaney alluded to this in a general way in 1969 when he wrote, "The tendency in the society in which I lived was to see drama as something somebody else wrote thousands of miles away...."[49] Some five years later, Paul Thompson was more pointed: "to discover yourself is a political act in this country...to learn about your past, to learn what is happening in the country...anything like that is a political act."[50]

One political act, as in the case of *The Farm Show* (1972), was to move into a community in search of people and stories that had never found their way onto a stage before and to play them back to the community involved. The farming audience, Thompson said later, "was great. It was open, it was direct, it recognized things quickly. And therefore, it really challenged the actor...because he wanted to go higher, farther than he needed to in Toronto."[51] Following this production, the strongest and most influential of Theatre Passe Muraille's collective creations were informed by increasingly inventive strategies for direct engagement of the audience through the dramatization of their own lives and traditions.

Thompson's working methods were never highly structured or schematic. Rather, he tailored his direction of Passe Muraille's collective creations to the needs of the subject of the play and to the skills of the particular group of actors involved. However, there are certain governing principles that he always kept in the foreground to make the collective creation accessible to its audience. The most important of these he called "texture work." This is the actor's discovery of a basis for characterization through precisely rendered local language and closely observed gesture.

One of his complaints against Canadian theatre of the day was its "movie-acting" style. In a 1973 interview with Ted Johns, later a member of the company, he noted that

>...to do a small-town character, everybody's trying to be Paul Newman in *Hud* instead of going out to a small town and sitting in the corner drugstore, finding out how people really are there, catching their rhythms and building off that.[52]

His insistence that his actors develop an ear for the "richness in the way people speak"[53] and, by extension, for the many different accents throughout Canadian society is one of his contributions to indigenous Canadian theatre. Naturally, this was an important influence on the performer/writers who emerged from the Passe Muraille experience. Whenever Thompson auditioned actors, he asked for at least five different regional Canadian accents.

Another aspect of texture work in the process of building dramatic character lies in the actor's discovery of a specific social base for his creation. In the handling of contemporary themes, this creative energy comes in part from the personal contact with people in particular communities but also from the "amazing confidence that comes out of dealing with things that you know." Thus "to feed off the source material" refers to the actor's ability to find his or her own connections to the material according to the experience of growing up and living in this country.[54] This can also be useful in dealing with historical subjects. For *Them Donnellys* in 1974, for example, what helped in the characterization was the actors' own experience of being "energetic young boys growing up in a small town."[55] Rick Salutin records that the actors' resentments against British imperialism in the contemporary theatre were a source of energy at one point in the development of *1837*.[56]

For the actor, the physical realization of an idea, theme or character— "how to fill the spaces around him with images"—is as important as textures of language because the company is "always working in a theatre sense." In rehearsals, Thompson has noted, his actors "work with certain techniques and play with visual things, or with sound, or with words to see what kind of possibilities we have for describing the experience we're dealing with."[57] Thompson would introduce improvisational exercises to stimulate energy, invention and ensemble cohesion along a particular line that had thematic and emotional relevance to the play. Examples include his hide-and-seek improvisation of harassed chaperones at a teenage dance in *The Horsburgh Scandal*, or the Sobrania rituals in *Doukhobors*, or the performance of images based on pictures in *1837*. Or he would suggest improvisational scenarios for further exploration of character.[58] At moments of high energy, the ideas feed each other "and at some point you want to put two of them together to see what happens." Once the actors begin playing them in a sequence, the performance "starts to develop its own rhythms." At this point, the director (or writer) assumes the role of editor,[59] shaping segments and putting them together.

For Thompson, the defining element of a successful collective creation was that the actor, through his or her improvisational explorations, became the "medium" for the material that went into the play.[60] Writers who have worked well in Thompson's collectives are those who, like the director, could stimulate and respond to the creative work of the actors. Like the director, the writer required an instinct for the right time to edit and shape the drama that was emerging through the explorations of the actors. Playwright Frank Moher makes this point in a diary he kept of his participation in Passe Muraille's version of *The Studhorse Man*[61] by Robert Kroetsch.

An essential element of most of Passe Muraille's collective creations during the 1970s was their reliance on factual sources, either the researched variety of the history plays or the personal company investigations of the community collectives. This factual element has often led to the critical designation of these plays as documentary drama. Early on, Thompson himself invited comparison with documentary when he spoke of the "living community portrait or photograph...based on all sorts of traditions of documentary that we have in this country—like the work of the CBC and the NFB." The elements in common that he noted on this occasion were "the really interesting people" you meet and "all sorts of rich dynamics" that come from people telling their own stories rather than relying on a plot.[62]

While the identification with documentary seems more like hindsight than an initiating motive, there is a general resemblance of the community plays to John Grierson's view of documentary film as "the creative interpretation of actuality."[63] However, film analogy is not very useful when applying Thompson's theatrical procedure for interpreting the audience back to itself. This is due to the fact that, in Thompson's kind of collective creation for the stage, the dynamics originate in the discovery processes of live actors, not in the more detached artistry of camera eye and cutting room. While the twentieth-century concept of documentary drama has its source and analogies in film, this type of play—even in its purest form—does not attempt to emulate that medium literally.[64]

Passe Muraille's community collectives are closest to documentary drama when they allude to their own discovery process. Examples of this exist in the onstage action such as *The Farm Show*'s "Round the Bend" or "Bale Scene" sequences or in theatrical gestures found in sequences such as "Man on a Tractor" or "Jesus Bus." In essence, such plays become documentaries of the performers' personal encounters with and re-invention of that factual material. This is the point at which myth-making begins. Fact is really the springboard of an audience's encounter with the material of the play and is not the object of enquiry for its own sake.[65] More than a mirror reflection, such a play becomes an "adaptation" of the community, created as the company's expression of the requirements of performance that will engage that community artistically.

In Passe Muraille's collective creations, the authenticating style of presentational stage documentary prevails. The individual performers establish their roles as actors who are playing a number of parts in on-stage transformations (generally speaking in the manner initiated by the ensemble experiments of companies such as The Open Theatre). There is direct address to the audience—either as character, actor or narrator. The speaker may present him or herself as an on-the-spot witness, identify sources of information, or tell about himself as if responding to an interview. There may be reinforcing back projections or maps—a tradition that goes back to the Living Newspaper, to Joan Littlewood, or to Erwin Piscator. Physical realities or abstract concepts are conveyed through the body language of mime. This has clear links to the actuality being defined or demonstrated—as in the work of Cheeseman or Littlewood or the Living Newspaper. The play is shaped in an episodic way. The performers use song as a bridge between scenes or as a narrative frame for an individual scene.

The early history plays at Theatre Passe Muraille—particularly *1837*— appear to work in reverse to the community plays in matters of fact. Here, historical fact is—at least implicitly—the subject of enquiry for corrective purposes. This is suggested by Rick Salutin's observation in his introductory diary of the production: "what nonsense the way we learned it."[66] The use in this play of caricature, parody and the stylistic shaping of facts certainly points to the type of political documentary play that, in Peter Weiss's words, "takes sides."[67]

Despite the obvious resemblances to documentary drama,

Thompson later denied that his plays were documentaries. He asserted that documentary "is a dead end as far as theatre is concerned" because "you can end up 'handcuffed to history.'"[68] The obvious model he could have followed, if he had wanted to, was that of Peter Cheeseman. The British director visited Toronto in June of 1972 to lecture on his work at the Victoria Theatre, Stoke-On-Trent, and to show a film about his making the local historical documentary, *The Staffordshire Rebels*.[69] But Cheeseman's basic premise—that the play must serve the historical documents with absolute, objective fidelity—and his strict use of the actor to expose the factuality were hardly compatible with Thompson's approach. As director of *Doukhobors*, Thompson advised his actors to work only on the material they remembered.[70]

Thompson never shied away from inventing either characters or scenes when the history play seemed to call for it. Some of his best effects came from the freedom of his improvisational sessions with actors. Shortly after staging *1837*, he stated that—even with the admitted restrictions of historical fact— "in the end, you create the character and what he says. And you can make your own statement through what you create." He called this "mythologizing" history.[71]

Some years later, he spoke in the same vein of the theatre's obligation to write history in "current language," for which "you must fashion the information to the audience."[72] By their very nature, the history plays cannot effect the same direct interaction with their audience as the community plays. Yet the "current language" of their re-invention of history approaches that intention. This originates in the company's agreed-upon perspective on the past and in its stylistic explorations of the research. In Passe Muraille's plays, these are rooted very much in the physical actuality of stage imagery— in contrast to what Thompson has referred to negatively as "informational acting."[73]

The actual process of creating a collective play has been documented in some cases—notably in Rick Salutin's published journal on the development of *1837*, and to a lesser extent by Betty Jane Wylie concerning *The Horsburgh Scandal* and Rudy Wiebe regarding *Far as the Eye Can See*. Basically, the procedure is based on improvisation or "jamming" in the jazz sense, and depends on what Thompson refers to as the actors "trying to spark...off each other."[74] While at some point the writer might introduce some written material, it would not necessarily be absorbed into the final script. More usually, the written work derived from the jamming process itself, although this varies from play to play. The whole company was engaged in the research, either in its written sources or through personal contact with the subjects of investigation.

A production might begin with little more than a title—perhaps only enthusiasm for a particular idea. For example, Rick Salutin came to Passe Muraille with the suggestion for a play about William Lyon Mackenzie. Although his own political view, to which the company responded positively, of the Upper Canada rebellion of 1837 prevails in the final script, his notes on the project make it clear that the actors were discovering the material they could perform best. This discovery had much bearing on the final shape of the work. On the other hand, the "needs" of the writer did not necessarily coincide with the way the play was shaping up. He or she might have ended up as the glorified secretary of the project, as in the case of Betty Jane Wylie with *The Horsburgh Scandal* (1976).

As Thompson recognized early, the printed form of a collective creation, where it exists at all, is something of an anomaly. In an interview, he once remarked: "The whole importance of my kind of theatre is to take us back to some kind of first-hand experience. To go into printing that, [sic] makes it again a second or third-hand one."[75] As he expressed it on the same occasion, the "real Farm Show experience was sitting through the show." Nevertheless, the accessibility of this work and some of the other plays in book form has considerably enlarged the critical reputation of Theatre Passe Muraille as a seminal force of the 1970s in the development of indigenous Canadian theatre.

The messy business of recovering the script from performance

Chapter One: Background 43

tapes of poor quality and the inevitable carton of notes is a familiar nightmare to editors preparing a collective creation for publication. Only when the dialogue is clarified by stage directions by someone who actually was involved in the collective, either as performer or writer, does the printed text begin to approximate the reality of the original performance. Even then, there can be no textual equivalent to the physicality of the language performed on the stage. In essence, the resulting "text" needs to be read as the notation of a performance piece rather than as a conventionally scripted play.

If the characterization sometimes seems overblown or the structure unbalanced, the reader needs to remember that the collective tends to take on a life of its own and to reflect elements that were important to the actors at the time of creation. Nevertheless, these published records and the often rough transcripts of collective creations, preserved in the archives of theatres involved in this type of playmaking, are an important indication of the vitality of collective creation. The particular choice of plays in the discussion that follows is based not only on the availability of text but also on the importance of the work to Theatre Passe Muraille's playmaking process or to its wider influences.

By definition, the collective theatre is not in itself a writer's theatre. Yet part of its wider influence mentioned above concerns the growth of individual playwrights who developed their craft at various alternate theatres. Before he went to Theatre Passe Muraille with his idea for a play about the Upper-Canada rebellion of 1837, Rick Salutin had written only one stage work. This was *Fanshen*, his adaptation from William Hinton's study of the Maoist revolution in the Chinese community of Long Bow, which George Luscombe produced at Toronto Workshop Productions in 1972 just as Salutin wrote it. This production was in contrast to Luscombe's usual method of his ensemble's developing the final text. In 1975, British playwright David Hare also wrote a (better known) play called *Fanshen*, based on the same source and initiated in a workshop at Joint Stock.

Salutin's strong involvement as participating writer in *1837*—first staged in 1973—led him to continue in collectives at several times over the next years: first at Theatre Passe Muraille and then in Newfoundland with the Mummers Troupe and Rising Tide Theatre. His response to the work of actors was usually positive, since he was able to bring his own writer's point of view to bear. From this kind of experience, he was able to draw on elements that combine in his scripted plays—as will be discussed later in this study. For a time, Carol Bolt welcomed the collective process at Theatre Passe Muraille, which resulted in the re-working of *Buffalo Jump* in 1972 and the development of *Pauline* (for which no text is extant) the following year. Betty Jane Wylie, with several plays already written, appears to have had a less salutary experience as participating writer on *The Horsburgh Scandal* (1976). In addition, novelist Rudy Wiebe, with better prospects for genuine collaboration, found his participation in *Far As the Eye Can See* (1977) more satisfying than his expectations.

Ted Johns joined Theatre Passe Muraille in 1973 as an actor, participating in the further development of *The Farm Show* and *1837*. He also helped develop new works such as *Under the Greywacke* (1973), *Oil* (1974), *Them Donnellys* (1974), *The West Show* (1975), and subsequent plays such as *The Horsburgh Scandal* and *Far As the Eye Can See*. In March of 1974, Theatre Passe Muraille premiered his one-man show, *Naked on the North Shore*, based on his genial observations of the Labrador community of Old Fort, where he taught school in 1968. This play, a favourite of audiences far and wide, has toured frequently and was revived at the Edmonton Fringe Festival in 1987. In January of 1977, he participated in Theatre Passe Muraille's collective creation, *He Won't Come in from the Barn*, whose collective authorship was attributed to an imaginary "Andrew McKeever." Johns rewrote this play in 1981 for the Blyth Festival, once more performing Elmer, an old farmer from southwestern Ontario who is dead set against progress. Other works of popular appeal (*The School Show* in 1978, *St. Sam and the Nukes* in 1980, and *Garrison's Garage* in 1984) were also written for the Blyth Festival. Of particular interest to the present study is Johns' partial rewriting of Passe Muraille's *Them Donnellys*. Under Thompson's direction, the production became a hit with audiences at the Blyth Festival in the summer of 1979.

John Gray began his theatre career in 1971 as founding artistic director of Tamahnous Theatre. In 1975, he began to direct for Theatre Passe Muraille. His association with Thompson and his actors led to composing his musical, *18 Wheels*, which premiered at Theatre Passe Muraille in February, 1977. That association also influenced his writing *Billy Bishop Goes to War*—premiered at the Vancouver East Cultural Centre in November of 1978—with actor Eric Peterson, a Passe Muraille veteran. These musicals—as well as *Rock and Roll*, premiered at the National Arts Centre in March of 1981, and *Don Messer's Jubilee*, premiered at the Neptune Theatre, Halifax, in January of 1985—reflect some of Passe Muraille's important principles of audience engagement. The latter was Theatre Passe Muraille's most significant contribution during the 1970s to a developing Canadian theatre.

Much of the work of actor and writer Linda Griffiths is derived from her experience in collective creation. She began as a performer at 25th Street Theatre in its first collective, *If You're So Good, Why are You in Saskatoon?*, directed initially by Paul Thompson in 1975. That was followed by the first version of *Paper Wheat*, directed by Andras Tahn in 1977, and its sequel, *Generation and 1/2*, directed by Guy Sprung in 1978. She joined Passe Muraille for *Shakespeare for Fun and Profit* in 1977 and *Les maudits anglais*, developed with writer Garry Geddes in 1978. Thompson directed both plays. Her work in the latter provided the spark for her brilliant one-person show, *Maggie & Pierre*, directed by Paul Thompson in 1979. Her second play, *O.D. on Paradise*—written (rather than improvised) with Patrick Brymer—premiered at 25th Street Theatre (in association with Theatre Passe Muraille) during the spring of

1982. This was followed in the autumn by the first collective version of *Jessica* with writer Maria Campbell and director Paul Thompson. After several more years of work by Griffiths on the play, *Jessica: A Transformation* premiered at Theatre Passe Muraille in 1986 under the direction of Clarke Rogers.

As the title of this study indicates, the following analysis recognizes two kinds of "playwright." In the collective creations of Theatre Passe Muraille, discussed in the first part of this study, all participants are "wrights" in the older sense of the word meaning craftsmen or makers. Through their collaborative creative activity during the rehearsal process, the play is made; thus they can be called "playwrights." The three playwrights who are discussed individually in the second part are playwrights in the more traditional sense, although their work demonstrates various influences from collective creation. Essentially, they are creative "writers" of plays that in some manner reflect either the creative process or product of "wrighters." The latter term was coined by Richard Schechner in his analysis of the playmaking processes of Megan Terry in her work with The Open Theatre. Schechner subtitled his essay "The Playwright as Wrighter."[76] The term could apply equally well to Jean-Claude van Itallie, Howard Brenton and Caryl Churchill, to name only a few. That it should also apply in Canada is a point often neglected in the study of contemporary Canadian drama.

Theatre Passe Muraille's production of *The Farm Show* (1972), directed by Paul Thompson. From left to right: Anne Anglin, Miles Potter (up), Paul Thompson and Fina MacDonell in the scene "Man on a Tractor." Photo: Theatre Passe Muraille.

Chapter Two
Theatre Passe Muraille

1. Beginning an Underground History of Dissent: *Doukhobors* and *Buffalo Jump*

Paul Thompson selected the Doukhobor experience in Canada as his first major effort at giving "current language" to Canadian history. This was an odd choice in one respect: neither he nor his actors at Theatre Passe Muraille could claim a direct knowledge of Doukhobor society.[1] Using books and newspapers as their source materials, the actors improvised freely, drawing also on consultations with a social worker at Toronto's Rochdale College who had worked among the Doukhobors in the Kootenays.[2] The play was not intended to be authoritative in the documentary sense, but rather "what we knew about them as people living in Ontario."[3]

This approach provided the actors with a double focus. They could intersperse their own sympathetic depiction of the sufferings of the Doukhobors with the negative responses of the Canadian public, who resented the Doukhobors' refusal to assimilate. After being victimized by

Czarist Russia, the Doukhobors later suffered as a result of the Canadian government's broken promises. Instead of opening up these questions factually and objectively—as Peter Cheeseman advocated—Thompson used projections of documentary photographs and scene headings that clarified history. The resulting play is an impressionistic or selective depiction based on the actors' discoveries in rehearsal of what they could express individually and collectively about Doukhobor history.

Some members of the cast responded personally to the Doukhobors' communal lifestyle, others to the anarchic element both in Doukhobor society and, as Thompson noted, "even in the show." One actor discovered personal roots in the Russian material. When they began *Doukhobors*, the predominant image in Thompson's own mind was a boyhood memory of blurry newspaper photographs of naked bodies. Nudity on stage was a problem for some in the company—one actress quit on that account—and Thompson reported once appearing nude at rehearsal in order to put the performers at their ease.[4]

Theatre Passe Muraille's affiliation with Rochdale had some bearing on the choice of the Doukhobor theme, in so far as the play explores a communal pacifist society and locates the source of radical protest in oppressive institutional structures. Thompson was aware of the potential for popularity—especially because of the nudity—among counter-cultural audiences who had come to *Sweet Eros* and *In My Own Write*. Nevertheless, the play warns against cheap analogies between the Doukhobors and the hippy generation. This occurs specifically in brief contemporary parodies depicting an absurd American poet-in-residence at York University who is himself inclined to making such connections (34). Knowing that Theatre Passe Muraille's audiences were used to stage nudity, Thompson deliberately played against this by emphasizing non-salacious nudity in its unglamourous physical variety.

Another important element was the resonance of the Doukhobor story—the fact that it "happened here" in Canada and that

It's all tied up with the problem of
assimilating, which all newcomers have
to face. It's one of the strongest themes
in Canada and one that is really worth
investigating. Should you change and
how much? ("General Notes," 3)

When Thompson described the Sons of Freedom as "the FLQ of the Doukhobors," he was making a connection to the contemporary situation in Quebec. Perhaps he was also suggesting that the play's sympathies draw on the energies of anti-authoritarian feeling that followed after Trudeau invoked the War Measures Act. On the protest level, the play exposes political injustice suffered by the Doukhobors, exemplified specifically in "The Oath of Allegiance" and "The Land Race" scenes (13-16). In this respect, *Doukhobors* falls inevitably into documentary's critical stance. It offers a challenge, for example, to the hostile analysis by Simma Holt in her study, *Terror in the Name of God*.

In contrast, Passe Muraille's play borrows from this study for its concluding monologue, "Fred Davidoff's Life Story."[5] The published text of *Doukhobors*, assembled by Connie Brissenden from audio tapes with added descriptions of the stage action and various production notes by Paul Thompson, is presented as a record of what the Passe Muraille company performed on stage to guide further productions. While there is no substitute for the performance itself, the text with accompanying notes provides an indication of the method of performance, although the dialogue (mostly fixed rather than improvised) appears to predominate more than was the actual case in performance.

The play is built on chronologically arranged episodes—often self-contained, occasionally overlapping—that combine narration with non-verbal illustrative action. Beginning with Peter Veregin and ending with Fred Davidoff, several Doukhobor characters recount in monologues highlights of their national history or personal experiences. From time to time, these narratives alternate with the outside perspective of Canadian police and other citizens. Occasionally, a monologue becomes a dialogue, or else one side's brief expressions of concern in the conflict intersect with the other side's responses. Some passages are identified specifically as official reports or first-hand reminiscences taken from books, but most seem to be actors' improvisations based on their source materials. However, the dramatic interest lies less in the verbal exposition of historical events than in the interaction of words and what the company identified as the expressive gestures and sounds of characteristic Doukhobor experience. The latter became the ritualized stage patterns of the play and the source of its primarily theatrical, rather than documentary, power.

In his notes to the text, Thompson speaks of the importance to the company of creating certain theatrical images that helped it to convey the essential themes or myths of the Doukhobor faith. Images of fire and nakedness became the rituals of purification, and images of work and wandering became the rituals of suffering. The play opens with the ritual of the Sobrania, the semi-sacred form of Doukhobor meeting, with its singing of psalms and hymns alternating with community discussion. In rehearsals, the company had discovered the Sobrania as a source of improvisational energy for the group and the Russian words from the songs became the Russian dialogue used from time to time in the play. The "work" process of packing up their belongings—actually just platforms and benches—and journeying to new homes is a recurring action during the unfolding narratives of their persecution in Russia and later in Canada.

As the Doukhobors resettle and are again dispersed, the performance of other images of work suggests the labour expended in clearing and cultivating the land. The latter image is created by a male actor as the plough and two women as driver and horse—an image based on pictorial records showing Doukhobor women substituting themselves for horses when they had none. The journey image links with the leitmotif of pilgrimage, initiated in Scene 2, as the Doukhobors' first public act of worldly renunciation in Canada. They abandon their farms, personal possessions and clothing before going to other villages to seek converts to their new form of spirituality. Physically, this is represented by choreographed movement showing the people's assembly and quick dispersal by the Mounted Police, the latter accompanied by spoken excerpts from official Mountie reports. This episode also foreshadows the encounters to come, each of them increasing in intensity while images of nudity and fire dominate the scene. Thompson credits the work of performers Phil Savath and Larry Mollin—members of Homemade Theatre, a group trained in the Spolin method of acting—as being central to the improvisational techniques that evolved.[6]

At the beginning of the play, Doukhobors are shown burning their guns during Peter Veregin's description of their revolt against the Czar's demand for an oath of allegiance. The images of fire and nakedness evolve into greater complexity as the play progresses. Fire begins as protest. Although fire never loses that association, it also acquires the meanings of purification and religious ecstasy (the latter as "release through fire"). In contrast, nakedness begins as the sign of worldly renunciation and gradually comes to function as active protest. By the time of the nude march to Nelson in 1932, after years of fighting with authorities over matters such as the schooling of their children, the pilgrims have become militant crusaders for "a return to the simple life" (29). Then, the Doukhobor leaders are arrested and their supporters are forcibly dispersed. This episode reinforces the point that government interference over the years is the cause of the growing extremism of the Sons of Freedom.

Several times, the play emphasizes spontaneity through the improvisational games of the rehearsal process. Although the dialogue of individual scenes is mostly set, there are "game" moments of on-the-spot improvisation. For example, in the initial "Sons of Freedom" scene, the actor playing Alex McCortoff, the leader of the first parade of naked Doukhobors, must persuade members of a family to free themselves from the slavery of their possessions, including their clothes, and to set about freeing their "brothers" as well. According to the stage notes, the actor "often had to work very hard to convince them" (9). A similar effort was required later in the "Burning Houses" scene, where one man persuades another to strike a match to his house (represented by a model he brings on stage and burns).

In another scene, played for comedy, a Canadian census-taker is distracted from his assignment by the hospitality of a Doukhobor family. The father thinks it's more important to sit "at table together" than to bother with pointless statistics. Here, according to the notes, the actors contribute their own details through improvisation "to make sure that each [is] playing the scene and not the memory of the scene" (27). Another improvised comic sequence, intended to demonstrate how ill-prepared the Mounties were to handle the Doukhobor situation, establishes guidelines for changing content from performance to performance (21 ff). In contrast to the play's predominant practice of monologue and accompanying gestures, the dialogue of these scenes makes them potentially more dramatic. However, in maintaining an improvisational component, the company tried to keep the scenes as fresh and immediate as the other, more direct, forms of theatricality.

By the same token, there are also several indications in the stage directions of an adversarial role in which the audience itself is sometimes cast. While there are a number of monologues throughout the play which could be addressed to the audience, the occasions when the performance is directed specifically at the audience are more telling. These gradually underline the injustice done to those who cannot abide by the same rules required by an intolerant and exploitative Canadian society—represented by implication by the audience.

In the pilgrimage scenes of 1902, a recurring stage direction calls for the wandering Doukhobors to look "passively" at the audience at each phase of their restraint by the Mounties. This technique communicates indifference to the official fuss, which also implicates the audience as supporters (and even exploiters) of the official point of view. The most obvious example is "The Land Race" sequence of 1907, showing the Doukhobors driven from their lands in Saskatchewan for failing to meet homesteading regulations about acreage cultivation and also for refusing to swear the oath of allegiance. The confiscated 250,000 acres of "prime Doukhobor land" is offered to "greedy westerners" (represented by the men of the cast) who become ready and eager contestants in a foot race.

While this is going on, the Land Commissions officer implicates the audience as potential land-grabbers by calling line by line for the audience's repetition of the words of the qualifying oath of allegiance (15-16). Another scene identifying the audience with an anti-Doukhobor public occurs in the First World War period: here, a lady mayor and a recruiting officer speak at a patriotic meeting in the Kootenays, for which the audience is surrogate. Only when the officer insults the people of the district for being "infected with the Doukhobor pacifists" do volunteers for the army rush towards the stage through the audience (18).

Fred Davidoff's powerful monologue that ends the play—which represents the highlight of the Doukhobor conflict in Canada—is delivered directly to the audience "as he wanders about the stage." At the same time, the other Doukhobors strip in solidarity with him and the dead Paul Podmarcv of the previous scene. Davidoff's speech is remarkable not only for its content but also for providing an impassioned born-in-Canada voice that has no Russian accent. Towards the end, Davidoff also removes his clothes, speaking directly to the audience as the lights black out. A few seconds later, the lights come up to show the actors still standing naked on stage and "looking calmly at the audience" (37).

In the face of Davidoff's 28 years in prison and his assertion that "through friction I was made into a Doukhobor and in spirit to be Sons of Freedom for the rest of my life" (39), this calm becomes the ultimate moment of encounter with the audience whose forebears began it all with their broken promises to his people. On at least one occasion, a member of the audience accepted the challenge literally by joining the actors on stage and stripping "in solidarity" with the Doukhobors.[7] Thompson, however, rejected this kind of response as the aim of the play[8], unlike other encounter plays of the time.

In *Doukhobors,* several elements emerged that were to become the characteristic theatrical basis of Theatre Passe Muraille's collective creations. These included most importantly the exploration of a theme through patterns of expressive gesture—or through what Thompson later referred to as an "acting way of connecting with representational stuff."[9] Although improvisational scenes occurred infrequently onstage in subsequent plays, the principle of "playing the scene and not the memory of the scene" (27) became an important strategy for maintaining spontaneity within the rehearsal process. It often resulted in lively creative outbursts that found their way into the final play.

Another key factor was the play's informal relationship with its audience. In *Doukhobors*, this could be summed up as the surprise element. The presence of nude actors moving along platforms extending right into the audience is an obvious example of such informality. But this also emerges in the different kind of direct encounter that intermittently (and in this case rather too self-consciously) casts the audience in an unwilling adversarial role. In *Doukhobors*, Theatre Passe Muraille—from the perspective of a marginalized group—utilizes the protest mentality of the period to ruffle the complacent surface of the Canadian social order.

The group follows the same procedure in its next work, *Buffalo Jump*. The subject of the new work is another journey of protest: the 1935 boxcar trek from Vancouver to Regina to Ottawa by the forgotten men of the government work camps. This marks a second manifestation of Thompson's career-long fascination with the Canadian west. It continued intermittently through the years to his 1986 improvisational show-in-progress, *The Spirit of '85*.

The idea for *Buffalo Jump* actually originated in the west, beginning its life as a semi-documentary review, *Next Year Country*. This was commissioned from Carol Bolt by Ken and Sue Kramer at the Globe Theatre in Regina for Saskatchewan's homecoming year in 1971.[10] Bolt had researched and written a basic text for which she, in turn, welcomed improvisations by actors during the rehearsal period.[11] It was edited further by co-artistic director Sue Kramer to accommodate the Globe's small cast of six.[12] George Luscombe was the first Toronto director to express interest in further development of the script, but he failed to reach satisfactory terms with Bolt on rights to the final version. Two years later, Toronto Workshop Productions developed its own Depression play from Barry Broadfoot's book, *Ten Lost Years*.

For Theatre Passe Muraille's version of her Saskatchewan play, Bolt was willing to enter a whole new phase of development with Thompson and his actors, out of which came some of the themes but virtually none of the original text. The research and final writing were essentially hers. But the selection of material, the characterizations, and the forms of presentation were based on improvisations by the Theatre Passe Muraille collective.[13] A further source of improvisational ideas for *Buffalo Jump* came from the design commissioned by Thompson from painter John Boyle. This included cut-out enlargements of RCMP groupings, described by Thompson as the "Mountie board." Also included were the House of Commons, buffalo shapes painted red, and Boyle's portrait of country-and-western singer Wilf Carter—all of which referred ironically to the popular culture of the West.

The subject of *Next Year Country* is Saskatchewan of the 1930s. The first act is a collage of sketches, popular songs and media events evoking conditions of the times. These include the plight of the farmers, the humiliation of being on relief, and the deplorable consequences of industrial strife among the miners of Estevan. In the second act, a continuing story of one dispossessed farmer, Bill Reynolds, leads into the subject of the 1935 "on-to-Ottawa" trek as it affects Regina. Here, the strikers from the British Columbia relief camps are halted by government authorities while their leaders attempt to negotiate with R.B. Bennett in

Ottawa. The penultimate scene is an extended montage of events intercut between Regina and Ottawa, chosen to demonstrate the repressive forces that bring the trek to an abrupt and riotous end. The Regina Riot of July 1 is treated metaphorically as the "buffalo jump," whereby the workers are stampeded into fatal violence by the police. The play ends on a subdued note of irony with Reynolds and Garth, a loquacious old-timer from the Cypress Hills, sitting on a train heading back to the British Columbia camps, this time with the blessing of the CPR.

In its new version, the play is no longer a specifically Saskatchewan work. Taking its title from the metaphor established in the original, *Buffalo Jump* becomes an improvisation on the times by focussing primarily on the trek itself.[14] At the beginning, it speaks briefly of the conditions in the country leading up to the trek, including three new scenes on the prairie themes of dust, farm foreclosure and enforced departure. Yet it concentrates more on the bad conditions suffered by the men in the relief camps of the B.C. interior, run by National Defense, and the consequent strike action. It also focusses on the two months of ineffective demonstrations in Vancouver. Most extensively, this version deals with the boxcar journey of the 2,000 work-camp protesters, which ends so precipitously in a brief rendering of the Regina Riot. While the perspective is that of the strikers, the various stages of the journey of protest also focus on the widespread support won by the strikers from the ordinary citizens along the route.

In the introduction to the published work, Carol Bolt states that "myth is more appealing than fact. It postulates that heroism is possible, that people can be noble and effective and change things." To this she adds rather grandly, "I think that what we were doing in *Buffalo Jump* was making those characters tragic heroes."[15] Although both versions are "tragic" in outcome, both go some way in countering the self-pitying victim pattern in Canadian literature's usual reading of the Depression era. These versions celebrate grassroots populism in conflict with reactionary conservatism. *Buffalo Jump* does this less by documentary clarification—except where documentary still speaks most dramatically to the occasion—than by its comic interplay between improvised re-enactment of history and a lively pastiche of popular culture and agitprop parody from the period. In the words of one reviewer, "That historic journey, which was a matter of stark reality and starvation situations, has been remembered here as a piece of Canada's folk history."[16]

This was an audacious treatment for its time. Until this point, Canadian theatre had little Canadian folk history on its stages at all. In contrast, George Luscombe was putting his considerable creative energies into American themes—for example, the highly successful *Mr. Bones* (1969), a minstrel show dealing with the crisis over the abolition of slavery and the conspiracy to assassinate Abraham Lincoln. Indeed, Theatre Passe Muraille's collective was inventing their way into the idea of a Canadian folk history of dissent as they went along. They drew on historical records for specific events of the strike and trek[17], then recreated them as they saw fit in theatrical terms.

Certain historical figures appear in *Buffalo Jump*. Most prominent among these are an agitprop caricature of the unpopular prime minister of the day, R.B. Bennett, who was also represented in cut-out; and a composite character, "Red Evans," who was an agitprop idealization of the historical strike leaders "Red" Walsh and Arthur "Slim" Evans. Thompson's "west" in this play, similar to Theatre Passe Muraille's "Doukhobors" (although in a far different manner) also expresses "what we knew about them as people living in Ontario." The "west" is embodied by Wilf Carter, stampede heroics at Calgary, Brahma bull riding, and R.B. ("a lot of bull") Bennett, who actually came from Calgary. For good measure, they threw in Bible Bill Aberhart, his "Back to the Bible" radio hour, and a madly specious sermon about the Gospel according to Social Credit. Thompson uses his favourite motif of the journey, but here he reverses thematically the Doukhobors' beleaguered quest westward for the good life into an ironic retaliatory search eastward for social justice. This reversed journey invited a range of inventive theatrics. For example, there is the terror of the journey through the spiral tunnel seen from the top of a boxcar. Bible-Hour hymns become the "light" at the end of this tunnel. There is also the recorded generosity of the people of Golden to the famished and exhausted trekkers. This episode takes the form of a folksy comic operetta as in Gilbert and Sullivan.

Thompson takes this work in several directions that are different from *Doukhobors*. In the latter, much of the primary material is cast as narrative monologues, accompanied by illustrative or interpretative stage images. In *Buffalo Jump*—within individual scenes at least—there is greater integration of dialogue and its theatrical expression: for example, in the simple physicalization of a farmer's tale of struggle with the destructive wind and dust by his squirming in the coils of a tightening lariat; or in the strikers' snake dance during the Hudson Bay riot in Vancouver.

Overall, monologue is reserved for special effect while the highlights of the trekkers' story are conveyed in dialogue. Dramatized vignettes gradually establish character outlines of individual strikers, both invented and historical. While *Doukhobors* occasionally implicates the audience in the role of oppressor, *Buffalo Jump* invites its audience whenever possible to identify with the collective action of the protesters. With the cast scattered throughout the auditorium during strike meetings and confrontations, the audience is invited to dance and to share the food of the Regina picnic. When the play ends abruptly in its scaled-down version of the Regina Riot, the audience becomes the same target of crowd control by the Mounties as the strikers themselves.

The freer structure of *Buffalo Jump* is built on the technique of scenic discontinuity, which provides for multiple perspectives on the life and spirit of the popular will of the times. For example, in between two incidents at the beginning of the strike, Bennett blimpishly addresses the imperial conference on preferential tariffs. At the same time, a Wilf Carter "special" intersects a Vancouver street scene with the song "Roll on, Little Dogies" and a slow-motion calf-roping by a novice competitor intercuts two events in the Vancouver phase of the strike action. For Thompson who was inspired by John Boyle's portrait of Wilf Carter, the recurring cowboy image reflects ironically on the time "when people pretended they were cowboys, even when they were starving workers."[18]

At the point of Wilf Carter's appearance, the novice strikers are more like "little dogies" than cowboys, having just been herded into their first tentative strike march through the streets of Vancouver by their leader, Cosgrove (34-35). However, the theatrical analogue is later reversed more optimistically with the successful calf-roping by a novice cowboy (47) as a flourish to the illegal tag-day scenario. Agitprop and pop culture merge finally when the trek reaches Calgary—an Act 2 scene announced as "Dominion Day at the Calgary Stampede." In that scene, champion cowboy Evans is thrown and pursued to the rails by R.B. Bennett as an aging Brahma bull (65). This technique is compressed foreshadowing, alluding to both the Regina Riot and the Ottawa meeting with the strike leaders. However, the Prime Minister finally ceases to be a joke in the penultimate scene through the contrasting starkness of his plain style of speaking. This speech is an abbreviated transcription of Bennett's dismissive meeting with the strike leaders in Ottawa. Meanwhile, the police infiltrate the trekkers waiting in Regina. In the end, the Mountie myth—they always get their man—takes over: two uniformed actors carrying the "Mountie board" confront strikers and audience alike.

According to Bolt, the characterizations in *Buffalo Jump* "reflect the actors who originally played them and the input of those actors."[19] In so far as this applies to the characterization of the ordinary trekkers, there is a serious question in the mind of one critic about how appropriately they succeeded. In her review of the published text, Robin Endres finds the unemployed workers "depicted as unintelligent and apolitical buffoons" who "have little or no comprehension of why they should organize or of the purpose of the trek." She finds "too much simplification of political ideas," whereby Bolt and Theatre Passe Muraille have inadvertently created "a false myth—in this case, the myth of the good but hapless worker pushed around by the boss and duped by the union."[20] Although this is an unduly harsh judgement, Endres draws attention to problems in the collective approach when the improvisational energies of the actors dominate rather than serve the material. If a scene works theatrically, Thompson is the last person to insist on trimming it to the bone, even for ideological reasons.

In *Buffalo Jump*, there are a few scenes in which performance based on improvisational jamming takes over thematic content. For example, the actors transform the Vancouver tag-day sequence into exuberant slapstick involving banana skins, mistaken identity and a police chase. Earlier, they indulge in a rather shapeless elaboration about picking up girls who can mouth the appropriate politics better than the boys. The point the play wants to make, however, is that not all the strikers are necessarily political. Rather, many are restless young fellows who like cards, girls and the occasional spree. They have ordinary ambitions for work and a home. At various times, they are inane, smart-talking, wistful or belligerent about the injustice of their situation. When the strike reaches its low point and when the organization of meetings and parades becomes organization for its own sake, the strikers need to be fired by the idea of going to Ottawa before solidarity can prevail once more. That it does prevail despite the discomforts, setbacks, and rough treatment at the hands of the authorities is the point of the play. The politics of *Buffalo Jump* come from its own time more than from the 1930s. This demonstrates that repressive authority is the chief incitement to civil protest. Repression leads to "friction," to use Fred Davidoff's bitter understatement. Like *Doukhobors*, *Buffalo Jump* reflects the protest mentality in the Canada of its day.

For a production of *Buffalo Jump* five years later by Ottawa's Great Canadian Theatre Company, Carol Bolt added new material that resulted in a revised Ottawa-oriented ending. Building further on the play's folklore of dissent, she opposed its image of intractable parliamentary authority with an antagonistic will among the workers of that city. Accordingly, under the leadership of the intrepid union organizer Annie Buller, Ontario strikers and sympathizers assemble to await the western contingent. The Regina riot, rather than being a depicted event, now becomes a point of reference during a solidarity demonstration in Ottawa. When the police become active, the eastern supporters remember Regina in time to prevent the forces of law and order from inciting another such incident. In a reversed upbeat ending, the people push the police off the stage. The tone and substance of the rewriting, for an occasion geared to a particular local audience, reflected the new climate of cultural confidence in indigenous material. Thanks to the influence of Theatre Passe Muraille, that climate had been developing in the smaller Canadian theatres over the intervening years.

2. Community, Present and Past:
The Farm Show; 1837: The Farmer's Revolt; Them Donnellys

For Thompson, the creation of plays for a specific audience—and the development of theatrical strategies for engaging that audience—became an increasing concern in the collective creations following *Buffalo Jump*. There was very little precedent anywhere, least of all in Canada, for his next step during the summer of 1972. He took a group of actors to live and work for several weeks in the community of Clinton, Ontario, in order to make a play from the collective observations of that experience. The ensuing play chiefly took the form of portraiture of actual individuals in the community. The result was *The Farm Show*, which premiered in Ray Bird's barn at Clinton in August of 1972. This was Theatre Passe Muraille's first and most emulated model of the community collective creation. What was so startling at the time was Thompson's decision to create a show without any source material or preconception of the play's direction. The actors had to find their own material while working and socializing in the Clinton farm community. Then, they had to develop their play collectively as the ideas emerged.[21]

Apparently, the idea began at Brock University, where Thompson was teaching a theatre course, when someone suggested that his theatre's "leftist outlook" was bound to lead to a Soviet-style play about "some guy in love with his tractor." He took this as his *donné*. With the help of Ted Johns, then an English instructor at Brock, Thompson made arrangements to take a company of actors to Clinton, where Johns had relatives.[22] After two more community collectives—*Under the Greywacke* in Cobalt, Ontario, in the summer of 1973 and *Oil* in the following year in Petrolia—Thompson told an interviewer that the idea of going out to make theatre about a particular community came "from things we read about happening in China."[23]

The plainer truth of the matter is that the first-hand technique of collecting material for *The Farm Show* developed in some measure from Thompson's production of *Free Ride*. He directed this in between *Doukhobors* and *Buffalo Jump* in September of 1971. *Free Ride* originated as a CBC radio commission about the experience of cross-country hitch-hiking. Armed with tape-recorders, Thompson and Larry Mollin, an actor in *Doukhobors*, hitch-hiked separately to the west coast in the summer of 1971 to collect the material that became the improvisational base of both the broadcast and the play.[24] A cast of five devised and performed the final work, sometimes drawing on their own personal experiences as well as the earlier research of the two original travellers. The result was a comic and ironic piece in which one reviewer saw some "freshness of observation" and a persuasive integrity in the production despite lapses into "the symbolic implications of the road" and related clichés.[25]

In this work, Thompson had already begun to shift from his "it happened here" stance of the two plays discussed above to the more immediate interest of "this is about us."[26] In the case of *Free Ride*, the play appealed directly to a common experience of its own generation.

This does not mean that the second category necessarily had to be contemporary, as the following winter's *1837* demonstrates. Yet the subject matter of *Doukhobors*, with its admitted outsider focus, and even of *Buffalo Jump*, with its predominantly western lore, was still once removed from its actual audience, despite the counter-culture appeal of themes such as anarchy and protest.

In *The Farm Show*, Theatre Passe Muraille was trying something more difficult than in any work so far. First, they took a very local approach to audience both as the specific subject and object of performance—by seeking an audience in the very community they were depicting on stage. Second, they came in as outsiders to create local theatre where theatre itself had no regular following. The sojourn in Clinton marked the beginning of Thompson's mission in his work at Theatre Passe Muraille: to discover new audiences for theatre and to "take ordinary people and make their lives into some kind of art."[27]

Nevertheless, *The Farm Show* project was a calculated risk for its time, with a company of potentially intrusive strangers presuming to tell a community audience about its own society. It was a risk that *Doukhobors* had avoided—by addressing its advocacy ("what we knew about them as people living in Ontario") to a non-Doukhobor audience and by basing the play on secondary sources rather than on personal contacts. Through the Clinton experience, Thompson honed his skills and those of his actors in developing the social and verbal textures of character. This approach became his theatrical signature as well as his strongest influence.

In his introductory note to the published script—prepared from transcriptions by Ted Johns, who joined *The Farm Show* collective for the 1973 revival and its revisions—Thompson summarizes the company's methods:

> Most of the words used were given to us
> by the community along with their

stories. We spent a great deal of our time trying to imitate these people both in the way they move and the way they speak. We wanted to capture the fibre of what they were and this seemed the best way to do it. In any case, it taught us to watch and listen.[28]

Not only was the Clinton audience delighted, according to Johns, "in hearing their own language and observing their own culture,"[29] but so were other southwestern Ontario communities where they performed next. So were audiences elsewhere in the country when they toured the show on and off for the next four years. But tailoring the play to the original Clinton audience was the key to that extraordinary success.

Thompson's brief account of the company's mimetic methods of characterization conveys only in part the nature of *The Farm Show*—what critic Robert Nunn, in his important analysis of the play, calls its "paradoxical union of documentary veracity and extreme theatricality."[30] Although both *Doukhobors* and *The Farm Show* emerge from a basically documentary premise, the former play demonstrates the results of the company's investigation of its subject while the latter is composed of the discovery process itself. Different approaches to audience are therefore inherent in the respective plays.

In acknowledging that the Clinton audience is both subject of *The Farm Show* and spectator of its performance, Passe Muraille's encounter with this community becomes an explicit theme of the play.[31] The actors present themselves—particularly in the first act—as outsiders in the process of acquiring their credentials. In *Doukhobors*, contrastingly, the credentials for advocacy are tacitly assumed. While in the earlier play the audience is sometimes cast in an adversarial role, in *The Farm Show* the audience must be won over by less strident (confrontational) means. For a rural audience, the initial perspective of the outsider establishes a bond of authentic intention and eventual authority, while a non-farming audience is invited to participate in the same process of discovery as the actors. One of the greatest of Theatre Passe Muraille's accomplishments in *The Farm Show* was the achievement of this double audience perspective through its manner of addressing both an immediate and an extended audience (a perspective they would develop by other means in *1837*).

The structure of *The Farm Show* is episodic and anecdotal. In his introduction, Thompson likens it to "a Canadian Sunday School or Christmas Concert where one person does a recitation, another sings a song, a third acts out a skit, etc." This is what the performers do in *The Farm Show*, offering a mixture of local characters, events and songs in a variety of styles that reveal the "living community" to itself. One of Nunn's useful insights in his study of the reciprocal encounter between community and acting company refers to the mutual delight in homely creativity.[32] Theatre Passe Muraille discovered this for itself not only in the predictable customs of community celebrations—weddings, parades, fairs and the like—but also in the more mundane event of the livestock auction held on Friday nights.

Therefore, the first ensemble number of *The Farm Show* is a Huron County "auction song" celebrating a type of participatory theatre (with specific reference to names and personalities) with which all members of the audience are familiar.[33] The act also ends with an auction song—this time a comic ballad about a disenchanted farmer's wife who sold her husband at a Clinton sale "for ten bucks instantaneous" (70). In between these two songs is a whole range of concert performances in which the company shows itself establishing contact with its audience and gradually assuming that community's point of view. By the end of the first act, with its goodwill and common interests assured, the collective can indulge in this myth-making fun from an inside perspective.

Of course, in their multiple characterizations and frank theatricality of their presentational performance techniques (as opposed to a naturalistic representation), the actors are always implicitly present as performers on stage. But on occasion, they are also explicitly acknowledging themselves as outsiders who are initially unfamiliar with the way of life they are presenting and who indicate the procedures by which they have made their discoveries. Their strangeness to the work of the farm is the actual subject of two comic scenes in which the actor Miles (Potter) presents his first naive encounters with the new experience and the tenderfoot bias he brings to it. In the "Bale Scene," his gruelling efforts to help farm hands stack hay in the barn quickly rob him of any illusions of pastoral joys. Nor does he claim new insight from the experience:

> Now I ask you...why!? Why would any human being *choose*, for the better part of his life, *twice* a year, to put himself through that total and utter hell? I didn't understand it then...and I don't understand it now. (43)

The strenuous mimicry of the work in Miles' solo performance, however, belies the tenderfoot image in his real role of accomplished actor.

The company, as an investigating presence, is also evident in some of the more tentative impersonations of the first act, by which the characters speak as if in response to the actors' questions at the beginning of their Clinton stay. For example, Act 1, Scene 3—entitled "Round the Bend"—is an impressionistic and introductory overview of people in the district, some of whom will appear in more detail later in the play. Here, they are presented as going about their normal activities and pausing for brief conversations with their visitors. The latter, in turn, are mapping out the human community along the concession lines—actually painted on the floor of the stage—where they came to know the people best. The multiple voices suggest the company's first tentative glimpses of the farm people's own perspectives: the way they live, what they think of farming, and their cautious show of friendliness to the visitors.

The speakers are accompanied by the other actors performing (or acting out) the activities and objects in their scenes. Having hinted at what they can do, the performers make the next episode, "Winter Scene," into a more elaborate demonstration of their performance style. This occurs through an interpretative montage that offers the first sustained depiction of the Clinton lifestyle. The scene becomes something of a test case for Passe Muraille's documentary method, since the company was not present in Clinton during the winter. As a result of that absence, the company relied on newly found friends as the source of its impressions.

Three actors take part in this scene. One speaks and mimes an imagist "Winter Poem," covering two all-purpose crates with a large white sheet to symbolize the season. Two other actors perform a variety of male and female characters who represent family life on the farm during one snowbound day and evening: inside the house at breakfast, at chores in the barn, in town on various errands, and at a square dance at night. The progress of the day is punctuated by the voice of winter, setting the scene from indoor and outdoor perspectives. The crates function variously as house and barn. A Clinton shopping cart serves as the housewife's car when she drives her son to the hockey arena, which is indicated by a bean dryer. The farmer's snowmobile is represented by an old mailbox, another multi-purpose prop. These scenes are brief, impressionistic and rhythmically timed so that voices and movements intersect and flow in parallel directions. The objects used in the depiction—in combination with the familiar chatter of everyday routine—give witty authenticity to the make-believe of the presentation.

Thompson, self-styled as the "putter-together of structures,"[34] is shown by the text as carefully alternating themes and styles. Gradually, these slip more fully and with increasing theatrical bravura into the farm people's perspectives. Even the confident presentational style of "Winter Scene" is carefully juxtaposed with Miles' comic self-deprecation in "Bale Scene." Only at this midpoint in the act does the play risk its first sustained monologue by a Clinton character with the "Les Jarvis" scene.

The latter playfully combines its imagist language with the mime of "Winter Scene" acting as backdrop to a full-blown impersonation of a well-known local figure. Here Les (performed by David Fox)—in his own way, a performer whose peripheral stories are as lively as his central narrative—takes centre stage while two actors represent the features of the setting and the creatures who live in the speaker's bird-and-animal sanctuary. Although the actors never disappear as performers, their investigatory self-consciousness diminishes somewhat as they increasingly gain the confidence of the audience without presuming to be local authorities.

The turning point occurs when the ensemble performs "The Orange Parade," offering a contemporary perspective on the fading institution of Orangeism. In this scene, the company temporarily disappears behind the (imaginary) camera eye, as it were, to allow the community to speak for itself. This is done tactfully while the colour of the ceremony and the dignity of the anachronistic words intersect with the more casual responses of the local participants. The actors are both paraders and spectators, sharing a common awareness with the audience that the ritual celebration by Protestants of King William's famous crossing of the Boyne is mostly a thing of the past. Now, it is enjoyed chiefly by the very young and the very old. Sadly, the parade has become an irritant to the local merchants whose business it interrupts. At the same time, Passe Muraille also celebrates the theatricality of the occasion and what it says of an earlier age of faith, which lingers on as part of the fabric of a rural community.

In the next episode, "Charlie Wilson," the theatre company moves towards ritual re-enactment when an actor again introduces the scene as the company's search for a story. Here, relics and words evoke the life and character of a deceased eccentric summoned up by people who remember him: by the presence of his actual tools and letters on stage; and by an actor (David Fox) impersonating him by reading passages from those letters. Nunn sees the community and the actors as co-creators of this portrait of a lonely and afflicted man whose "outsiderhood" paradoxically "defines his relationship" to that community.[35] The scene plants the seeds of a local myth. Since the company has been privy to a number of views about Charlie's unusual personality, Passe Muraille's composite portrait creates both a new reality for the audience members who knew him as well as a moving evocation for those who did not.

By the last two scenes of Act 1, the company has established the integrity of both its intentions and its theatrical craft for a closer look at inside perspectives. The subject of "Man on a Tractor" and "Washing Woman" is farm people at work. The former is a jocular monologue enhanced by the playful theatrical ingenuity of gestural observation advocated by Thompson. The farmer chats about the intricacies of tractor driving ("you gotta be awake, you gotta be alert, you gotta be watching") and about its dangers ("I don't know anybody on this line hasn't turned his tractor...."). But the real force of his words comes with an illustrative performance: three other actors become the tractor, with the speaker "steering" from his perch on the shoulders of one of them. The sounds and movement combine with the words to form a vivid stage image, to which the audience can relate (62). That the "farmer" in this case is the frazzled actor Miles of "Bale Scene" makes its own comic point about the more assured direction in which the play now feels free to move.

The "Washing Woman" is in fact a theatricalized insider's counterpart to "Bale Scene." Marion, the harassed farmwife and egg lady, edgily describes her day from the curious vantage point inside the washing machine. As the talk speeds up, so does her gyrating motion—the washer woman has become the washing machine—until she disintegrates dramatically into a squawking chicken. Like Miles, she has lost herself in the exhaustion of her labours. In this manner, the act draws towards its close with a playful meeting of city performers and country subjects in the common humanity of temporary misery.[36] From her perch in the washing machine, however, it is Marion who leads the company through the conclusion of the scene. She highlights the theme of women's importance with her perky ballad—to square dance accompaniment—about the overworked Maisie, whose revenge on her husband is the auction block (64-68).

From here, the play builds tacitly on that bond of common human interest, moving inside this particular community for what it reveals generally about the dynamics of a modern rural community: its amalgam of tradition and change, its stability and, to a degree, the encroaching economic and social threats to that stability. If the first act strives primarily to establish a direct relationship between the company and its local audience, the second act seems aimed at the wider audience as well. This approach challenges the negative images of rural life, which predominate in Canada's conventional literary treatments of life on the farm.[37]

In the scene "Round the Bend," a young farm girl utters these common complaints and tries to escape from the so-called rural backwardness that *The Farm Show* takes pains to counter (29). The second act gives a more sustained voice to those who live the rural life on its own terms and also creates theatrical interest out of ordinary circumstances that become vivid even to those who might take for granted the life they lead.[38] Not only are individual personalities and stories enhanced by the actors' renditions, but taken together these also reveal underlying patterns that point to the essential rootedness of the life being celebrated within the seemingly incidental and anecdotal structure of the play.

In his review of the published text, Chris Johnson speaks of the artful editing that highlights "the stronger features of Clinton's speech."[39] While noting that his actors "were not just recording cameras," Thompson puts it differently:

> In the midst of talking and listening, they were already imbuing the experience with mythic dimension. They were already conscious of how the

Chapter Two: Theatre Passe Muraille 73

person they were talking to represented more than himself.[40]

The "mythic dimension," which refers to the whole social fabric of a rural community, appears more clearly in Act 2. Here, the important theme is the community in its diversity.

On the family level, the Lobbs emerge prominently as the archetypal farm family. Their community presence is both individual and representative of some of the common factors that the company sought to identify as vital grassroots material. Thus, the Lobb "dynasty"—its family tree branching "all along the Maitland and the 16th line" (74)—becomes the subject of an incremental ballad intersecting most of the scenes in the act. Some stanzas introduce particular speakers from that family (Jean, Diane and Alison) and others simply remind the audience of the generational continuity of farm community. The monologues of the act fall into two categories: speakers who are important for the subject of their stories or the tone in which they tell them (about accidents, for example); and those whose narratives are the expression of individual personality (Jean Lobb, Alison Lobb). But ultimately, all identify themselves by their interactions with the community whose values they variously represent.

The act begins with the matriarchal Jean Lobb talking about weddings: "Six girls, in *two* years, in *one* little community. Well!" (72). She speaks in graphic detail about dresses, flowers and variations in the wedding service. She has an imaginary family wedding album on her lap as a source of reference, yet her most vivid account is of her daughter's wedding dinner, for which she has no pictures. Her enthusiasm increases as she describes impersonations of the bride at various stages of her life, performed with accompanying songs by her brothers. "Well," says Jean, "we laughed till we died at the *stupidity* of it. It was simple, you know, but it was funny" (74). Passe Muraille wisely allows this village version of home-made theatricality to speak for itself rather than through accompanying performance. The incident also indicates the special appeal of the Lobbs to the theatre company, since they too have a theatrical flare in both their family rituals and their public activities. Jean Lobb's interest in the details of the wedding ceremony is familiar to any reader of write-ups in local newspapers, but her maternal pleasure in the telling makes them vivid. The additional flourish of family antics—one adult son in diapers, another in pigtails, and a third too embarrassed to sport a bikini—adds a touch of informality to a solemn occasion. The first verse of the Lobb song, which concludes her monologue, celebrates her generation of the family's genealogy.

The characteristic Canadian theme of man's interaction with nature can be found from time to time in *The Farm Show*. Yet, this theme is largely subsumed in its modern surrogate—what Johnson refers to as "the ambivalent machine," sometimes as "death's twentieth-century shape on the farm."[41] In Act 1, "Man on a Tractor" demonstrates the farmer's skilful mediation between the tractor and the land. In Act 2, the machine takes on its own manifestations of character, in both its dangerous and its useful aspects. Thus as community icon, the tractor itself acquires near-mythic proportions.

When the character Daisie talks about local accidents in a manner emphasizing human vulnerability, her stories suggest a feminine perspective on the "Man on a Tractor" scene of Act 1. They also serve as a prelude to a sombre narrative, "Accident," enacted by both man and actors-as-machine, telling of a devastating baler accident. This is followed by a brief epilogue from the wife of the victim. The woman expresses her worries about her husband's head injury, her children, and the work of the farm. When she also tells about the way neighbours have rallied to help, we get a sense of community responsibility that Theatre Passe Muraille also wants to celebrate. Paradoxically, not only people but also their tractors come to the rescue:

> The day *after* the accident, you could
> see about *twelve* tractors out in that

field, and they had the whole thing done
in a *day*. (77)

This scene is juxtaposed with "Tractor Tug," offering a contrastingly comic celebration of monster tractor power in the vocabulary of modern technology. The dramatic metaphor is the tug-of-war, an event rooted in the old country-fair tradition of oxen or plough-horse competition. This tug-of-war is announced like a wrestling match in which two performers personify opposing models of superior power and efficiency.

The unlikely shift from tractor power to spiritual power is skilfully negotiated through the mediation of another machine. This time, it's less self-assured, taking the form of a mechanically troubled double-decker bus from London. With the "Jesus Bus" scene, the play returns to the family theme in one of its several community manifestations as reflected in the second generation of Lobbs. Diane Lobb and her family are born-again Christians with an evangelizing mission. With characteristic theatrical flare, the family conducts services from its "drive-in church." The company presents Diane's story of the journey to Clinton from Halifax, where the family takes delivery of the bus, as a parable of the ailing spirit in its pilgrimage towards salvation. As described by Diane, one actor graphically performs the troubled bus in its four breakdowns on route while another interrupts the account with analogous words of Christian witness. With a final hymn and prayer, the scene concludes as a prayer meeting with the audience as congregation.

Diane's voice of calm spiritual assurance contrasts sharply with her sister-in-law Alison's chatter and bustle in the next scene. Alison Lobb carries out her kitchen chores while talking about her more conventional involvements in church (even though "You might even say I border on the agnostic") and community organizations (89). She is a thoroughly modern farmwife who likes to run things. In her secularized way, she is as vivid as Jean Lobb is in describing local activities.[42] The strength of the play derives not only from the dramatic definition and particularity of these portraits—Thompson described Janet Amos' portrayal of Jean Lobb as precise, "right down to the way she laughed"[43]—but also from their social or "mythic" typicality.

While the Lobb family celebrates the permanence of their continuing generations—verses from the "Lobb Song" punctuate all subsequent scenes but the last—the final part of the act illustrates the vulnerability of this farm community to modern cultural and financial pressures. The penultimate scene contrasts the Lobb stability with an anonymous family whose children vanish one by one from the picture frame that encloses them. Ironically, the auction motif of Act 1 is repeated as the picture of the parents is sold merely for the value of the "nice hand-crafted picture frame" (99). An explanation about why this should happen is offered in the concluding analysis by "Bruce Pallet," a character who confronts the audience with the facts of modern farming: the low price to the farmers for the food they grow, the consequent loss of profit, the foreign take-over of local food processing, and the alarming rate of disappearance of arable land.

This is the one scene in the play whose source is not in Clinton. Originally, Alison's husband Don Lobb gave a concluding monologue on agro-business,[44] but the sharper analysis was substituted in a later revision. Pallet heard a broadcast of the play on CBC Radio and invited the company to attend his Orangeville "Sunday School Class," where such issues were debated. David Fox responded by adding a new scene that provides a certain thematic balance to the "Township Council" scene preceding "Picture Frame." In the former, two actors give their comically speeded-up impression of five councillors in slow, rather bumbling deliberation on township business. It's one of the few scenes in which performance virtuosity takes precedence over content. The latter scene illustrates the small ways in which this farm community is self-governing while Pallet's monologue shows the large ways in which its destiny has been taken out of its own hands.

Interestingly, his speech is written from the farmers' point of view and addressed to the non-rural audience—the "bellyachers" who think farming "should be a public utility and that everybody should supply food for free" (100). At the same time, he firmly intends to continue in this way of life and so becomes an affirmative, if sometimes querulous, voice speaking about the hard work and his commitment to farming:

> Y'know, I just want my *kids* to make a
> *living* at it, I got *grandchildren* I want to
> make a living at it.
> So what else can I *do*? Y'know, how
> else do you *build a nation*? (102)

In its conclusion, the play returns from politics to the concert-party mode with a performance of the "Ballad of John Deere." This recitation concerns a legendary figure in the local area, from whom the tractor company takes its name. John Deere is a kind and gentle man who decides that he's drudging too hard on his farm. So, he invents the tractor. The local people soon swallow their laughter at this "spittin' and buckin'" monster when John employs his "infernal machine" heroically to rescue a poor widow's sons stranded on the river during a flash flood. Once the children are safe, he drives back into the river to rescue their kitten. Unfortunately, "white water upstream" carries him to a watery grave, but not before he has strapped the kitten to his redoubtable machine. For this brave deed, he is forever celebrated in the brand name of the tractor (104-107).

Filewod finds the geographical reference to be the only thematic link to the play. But he also suggests that, in the play's final shift to a traditional story set in a popular form, "the actors give the community its own history back to them in the form of a heroic myth." According to Filewod, this concluding gesture "embodies the idea of the play"[45] in its myth-making function. One might take this idea further by suggesting that, in relation to other songs such as the opening "Auction Song" and Act One's concluding tale of Maisie auctioning off Fat Hank, the "Ballad of John Deere" also marks in a suitably homely way the apex of the play's myth-making as a creative discovery process. The play's movement is from humorous documentary, to comic folklore, to melodramatic eponymous legend that—contrary to Filewod—does refer playfully to certain preceding themes. The song is the final sign of the company's hard-won familiarity with this community—a procedure that the audience has witnessed throughout the play.

The actors have earned their freedom to be inventive with local lore in a manner that embeds the reality of "the ambivalent machine" within the myth. This approach takes the play a step beyond documentary with its concluding spoof. In fact, the John Deere of tractor fame did not come from Clinton and the whole ballad was invented by Miles Potter.[46] Yet the Pallet monologue is still the stronger echo at the close of the play. It's the major justification for the observation by one critic searching for political meaning: that the play's "subtextual struggle placed the farmers' way of life squarely up against the forces of attrition."[47]

The Farm Show is important to Theatre Passe Muraille's repertory for trying to reach a particular audience. The play incorporates members of that audience in a recognizable way: by doing this sympathetically from an outside perspective; by revealing the actors' own experiences of discovering the community; and by gradually assuming its point of view. Another interesting dimension is *The Farm Show*'s way of reaching to an extended audience, whether rural or urban, from elsewhere. This audience relates to the image of a particular community only because the actors have rediscovered in their procedures within the play the vitality inherent in the rural way of life.

In its next work, Theatre Passe Muraille further explored its relationship to its audience. The history play *1837*, in collaboration with writer Rick Salutin, merged both the immediate and extended dimensions of audience involvement accommodated separately in *The Farm Show*. The governing factor here is a dual sense of time, described by Urjo Kareda in his review of the first version of the new play as "history with

Chapter Two: Theatre Passe Muraille 79

a double view"; in this approach, "we grasp why the events were important to them then, and why they are important to us now."[48] The play draws its audience into a sympathetic view of pioneer farmers in the 1830s. At the same time, it cultivates a present-time perspective that speaks to the audience about the colonial conditions reflected by the interpretation of our history.

When *1837* premiered in Toronto in January of 1973, it was a "Toronto-centred" treatment of the historical uprising.[49] The play marked a new phase in the theatre's continuing "Illustrated Underground History of Canada." Its historic sense of place was becoming an increasingly important way of creating "living history" for a modern audience. In his diary notes about the creation of the play, Salutin registers the company's initial excitement "at finding the history of places we've all lived around." But he also notes his opening-night annoyance when the audience laughed at a reference to "Bay and Adelaide," as if it were too "colonized" to accept the fact that important events actually happened in familiar places.[50] However, critic Herbert Whittaker's response was more in the spirit of the work when he suggested that the "true climax of the evening" would be "the audience sweeping out the doors to storm City Hall."[51]

The revised play toured the following year through the same southwestern Ontario region as *The Farm Show* had. The play's geography was expanded to give greater emphasis to the rural perspective on historical events. The first three days of the rebellion were now seen from the point of view of Colonel Van Egmond in his march from the Seaforth area to join Mackenzie at Montgomery's tavern near Toronto (Preface 201). The developing focus on the rural region was an indication of how Theatre Passe Muraille was gradually acquiring its own theatre jurisdiction in southwestern Ontario. In between the first and second versions of *1837*, retitled *1837: The Farmers' Revolt*, Theatre Passe Muraille also premiered and toured *Them Donnellys* through the area as a first step towards recovering that audience's past. Herbert Whittaker noted that the revised *1837*, which now "concentrated on the people rather than the issues," received "a standing ovation from the six tiers of engrossed spectators in Listowel's auction barn in May of 1974."[52]

Later, *1837: The Farmers' Revolt* was paired with *The Farm Show* for revival at Vancouver's Festival Habitat in May of 1976, the same year both plays were published. In an interview, Thompson highlighted the links between these two plays as far as Passe Muraille's target audiences were concerned:

> Working in a farming community like that involves us in a taking-from, but I'm trying to work from a basic taking-from that *gives*. What we're doing is really important to the areas in which we've been doing these plays. There is really a strong need for people to know who they are, to get a sense of themselves.... The farmer doesn't know that he belongs to a group that once took up arms—and until we know who we were, we won't advance. The excitement of playing to people as they discover this is incredible.[53]

The new emphasis specifically drew the attention of rural audiences to the ancestral story in their own backyard, so to speak. Yet, identification with that story was not their exclusive prerogative, since—for the purposes of the play—the farmers of 1837 are also the surrogate ancestors of the general Canadian audience. Nevertheless, the work gains in timeliness through the concreteness of its geographic specificity. For the rural audience of *The Farm Show*, it echoes back to Bruce Pallet's critique of the state of farm economics and the intrusion of foreign ownership as a threat to nationality. For the city audience, at least in Toronto, there is still the reminder that rebel leaders Lount and Matthews were hanged at the city jail and that City Hall was the location of the arms that

Mackenzie had earlier urged the hesitant Doel and Rolph to seize in the absence of the militia. This is what Salutin calls the great "what might have been" of Canadian colonial history.[54]

Salutin thought the feeling expressed in the play's first version particularly timely because it seemed to reflect a general movement in Canada at that time to overthrow colonial dependence—in theatre (Preface 186-187), in universities, in unions, and in the NDP's Waffle movement (Preface 202). In this respect, his invention in the last scene (Preface 193) is particularly appropriate in its allusion to the present. At the hanging of the convicted Matthews and Lount, the latter replies to his companion's statement, "Sam, we lost—" with "No! We haven't won yet" (264). By the time of the second version, however, he saw the hopeful signs of a year or so earlier less pronounced. As a result, he viewed the second version as "more of a theatrical and less of a political event" (Preface 202). Yet for reviewer Brian Arnott, the revised play was still political in the best sense—an example of the type of theatre that awakens "the slumbering social conscience through artistic means: art and politics being seen...to intersect at the point where men are moved to act for social change." In the case of *1837: The Farmers' Revolt*, this was "not just pointedly the reminder of a neglected past" but also "consciously full of present ironies."[55]

How the play may be seen in contemporary political terms is evident in its dual manner of establishing relationships with the audience (referred to above). *1837: The Farmers' Revolt* has a similar intention to *The Farm Show* of reaching audiences in a direct way—but this time by presenting its material as a rediscovery rather than as a single discovery. Audiences find themselves slipping into the role of a surrogate settler while remaining aware of their contemporary identities as objects of re-education. Often, this happens through direct address or satiric scenes about their own past. As Salutin points out in his preface and elsewhere, many Canadians learned their history of the events of 1837 one way while Salutin and Theatre Passe Muraille rediscovered it another way.

This creates an underlying tension in the play. Although it is not strictly speaking a documentary drama, *1837* borrows from a documentary style (and sometimes its methods) by offering a corrected view: the rebellion of 1837 is thus seen as a failed revolution. What Salutin sees as the typical view of the event by Canadian historians—"as historical farce, an unnecessary accident on the road to responsible government"—becomes for him "a serious movement for national independence."[56] Therefore, the play has a political dialectic not present in *The Farm Show*. In this version, the audience measures implicitly what it learned in school against what it experiences through Passe Muraille's audience-oriented strategies. The latter presents history as an immediate political event.

Salutin brought to Thompson the idea of doing a play about the 1837 rebellion at Theatre Passe Muraille after the production of his first work for the stage—an adaptation of William Hinton's *Fanshen* for George Luscombe at Toronto Workshop Productions in February of 1972. The experience of working on Hinton's case study of the Chinese revolutionary process led Salutin to consider the dramatic possibilities of a play about a revolution taking place long before that "right here in Ontario" (Preface 185). He saw this rebellion as part of "our missing history of resistance" in Canada. He was particularly attracted by his discovery of "widespread popular support" among the working people of the colony for leader William Lyon Mackenzie's platform of independence:

> In Ontario, they held 200 meetings in the summer and fall of that year and enlisted thousands of supporters; more than 800 were arrested in the aftermath. Two were publicly hanged. Ninety-two were shipped to a prison colony in Van Dieman's Land.... They failed, but they were no joke. Any self-respecting nation—say China or the U.S.—would glorify the crudity of that people's army,

not deride it.[57]

Thus, Salutin provides the ideological spine of the play. Colonialism is seen as an issue of class warfare and the interpretation of the 1837 uprising as an economic conflict between the proletarian (and somewhat nationalist) colonists and the imperialistic oppressors in the Family Compact.[58]

In its approach to the historical material, *1837* differs somewhat from Theatre Passe Muraille's two earlier history plays. For *Doukhobors*, the actors studied all the sources and relied on memory for choosing the material they could best relate to as performers. For *Buffalo Jump*, the playwright provided the basic research for the original script, from which the actors improvised their scenes. Although Salutin was certainly an important source of information about the 1837 rebellion, Thompson reports that "research was more individualistic" among the actors than for *Doukhobors*: "in the end, people went riding off in their own various directions and gave their own input from that."[59] Salutin's publication of his diary of the creation process of the first version of the play provides some indication of how this worked.[60] Most important to Thompson, as always, was the "really good relationship between the actor and his material."[61] In the case of *1837*, this involved a close ideological identification with the working people in Act 1. In turn, this governed what Kareda called the "more grotesque" scale on which the authority figures exist.[62]

In depicting the causes of the uprising, a chief concern from the beginning was to avoid "the way we learned it in school." To approach this from the ordinary farmer's point of view was difficult because of the lack of genuine voices of the people in the historical records. Thompson wanted to apply his principle of "texturing," which had been so important to *The Farm Show*. But this depended on the ability of the actors to build character from scanty references in books and pictures. In his diary entry of December 14, 1972, Salutin describes their attempts to place the peripheral people of history at centre stage:

> Someone who's barely mentioned in the records. Sally Jordan worked for Anne Langton, who wrote a journal. A name mentioned in Mackenzie's paper as seconding a motion at a meeting. They must build their character according to what they know of the time. (Preface 189)

He goes on to refer to what was becoming Thompson's typical approach to character through improvisation:

> We'll quiz the actors in coming days on what these characters were about at various times in 1837. Some scenes may come out of it, but more important is the *thickness*—to pour into and onto whatever and whomever we end up using. (Preface 189)[63]

Getting an authentic sense of the lives of working-class women was a particular problem because most of the extant journals are those kept by their betters (Preface 188). The Passe Muraille company's acknowledgement of this difficulty emerged in the inspired parody (initiated by Suzette Couture) of a genteel traveller and sketch writer. This spoof appeared as the overbearing character of Lady Backwash delivering a lecture on her experience to the ladies back home (and with additional absurdity when performed by a male actor). The realities of class differences appear in the final version of the play by juxtaposing this characterization with another fictitious character— Mary Macdonald, the timid mail-order bride from Scotland. In contrast to Lady Backwash, Mary has arrived at a point of no return in her travels: she feels bound to join the insurgents despite the delights of her husband's new-found affection at home.

The quality of life for the would-be settler of the times was also suggested by Paul Williams' impressionistic set. Its inter-connecting ramps with platforms at several levels and its tree-like structures evoked the realities of corduroy roads and thick forests as well as the hardships of work, distance and poor communication. Properties were appropriately sparse, consisting of only an axe, ropes, a crude table and a wooden block.[64]

Of the two "land policy" scenes, one is a dramatized sketch. Entitled "Clearing," it depicts Peter Steadman, a "squatter" settler with two years of hard labour on the land. He confronts a Magistrate Thompson, whose survey map indicates that the land in question "is part of a parcel of 1000 acres which was granted three weeks ago to Colonel Sparling of the 48th Highlanders" (207). The other scene, "The Tavern," is presentational, structured like an improvisation on the issue. It begins with Fred Bench's introduction of himself and eventually shifts into a section in which, under Fred's direction, all the characters of the scene act out the parts that tell about his bad experience at the Toronto Land Office. This technique provides for an agitprop tone by the commissioner of crown lands, who is conspiring with his friend, a private land agent pricing the land as he chooses.

The "play," which starts out as tavern clowning, becomes more sobering as the "performers" realize that Fred has lost his bid to become an independent farmer because the abuses of government patronage have suddenly increased the nominal price of land by 100 fold. Thus, the scene dramatizes both information and a critical response. It also acknowledges a dual audience: the characters who alternately witness and perform the narrative of their friend's victimization, and the larger audience in the auditorium who passes through the same recognition process as the characters. This audience is the ultimate object of the scene's partisan appeal for sympathy. It's one of several occasions in which the play engages the audience in its strategy of politicizing history.

Equally important is the ordering of this scene in anticipation of "The Family Compact"—a satiric illustration of the nepotistic list of members and holdings of the colonial bureaucracy, which provides background to the "Fred Bench" type of encounter. This scene and others in the same satiric mode draw on the stage language of popular performances—magic shows, patriotic tableaux, ventriloquism—to create authenticating metaphors. These mark an advance on *Doukhobors'* primarily affective and descriptive imagery. Although these scenes have either a thematic or chronological context within the first act, their impact is similar to that of political cabaret or revue.

In his account of the rehearsal process, Salutin indicates how each scene developed its final form: through the collective's characteristic trial-and-error method rather than out of any clear sense of direction. The scene that is most like a documentary is "The Family Compact," based on Mackenzie's satiric piece from *The Advocate*, in which he lists and cross-references 30 names by number (Preface 188). In the first version, this eventually became an expressive epic listing—in Robert Wallace's words, "that long list of names growing like a snake as five or six actors progressed through the set like children playing leapfrog."[65]

However, in the revised version, the information is embedded in the structure of a magic show performed for the audience. Mackenzie plays the role of a conjuror who, with the help of his assistant, transforms three volunteers into the entire Family Compact. This device puts Mackenzie—as the source of the original satire—into a metaphoric relation to the facts he is disclosing. He is the performer who uncovers (from under his assistant's cape) the most remarkable conjuring trick of all—the nepotistic contrivance by which "this band of criminals" transforms itself "into the ruling class of this province" (215). The performance metaphor of conjuring both documents and editorializes, although in a manner different from "The Tavern" scene. This time, an extended conceit takes the audience through the whole investigatory process from beginning to satiric conclusion.

A reverse procedure occurs in the condensed conceit of "The Head." This scene begins with the assembling of the satiric image from which an authenticating context subsequently emerges. The episode follows the Lady Backwash parody of the privileged dilettante seeking local colour and looks briefly at the political power of privilege. It accomplishes this through a burlesque portrait that puns—as Mackenzie was fond of doing in *The Advocate*—on the name of Sir Francis Bond Head, Lieutenant-Governor of Upper Canada. To the accompaniment of descriptive narrative, four actors solemnly assemble themselves into a tableau formation of a head. It then speaks in the actual words of Bond Head at a pre-election gathering in 1836 (224). The image was created initially by Janet Amos in an improvisational session using historical pictures. Later, Neil Vipond found the Lieutenant-Governor's actual speech (Preface 190). The words uttered by the talking head—spoken by an actor who plays one of the eyes—are blatantly authoritarian and imperialistic. The episode is an example of the documentation mockingly authenticating the burlesque portrait.

Theatre Passe Muraille tried "to really identify with the main struggles and passions at the time" (Preface 189-190). In keeping with the spirit of this kind of performance metaphor, Salutin himself found the basis for another theatrical image in an 1830s' handbill for a travelling ventriloquist (Preface 190). This became the source of "The Dummy" as a metaphor for colonial dependence. To give it specific point, Salutin wrote a ventriloquism sketch that eventually became an introductory skit to Mackenzie's Reform rally after the election. As performed by two farmers to the onstage audience of Reform supporters, the ventriloquism act becomes a metaphor for the contemporary process of political change instigated by Mackenzie.

One farmer plays John Bull, the imperial ventriloquist, while the other plays Peter Stump, the Canadian axeman puppet. Thanks to Mackenzie, Stump slowly begins to speak his own voice. Salutin called it "Agitprop of '37" (Preface 199). The scene is directed first to the gathering of farmers who are now primed for Mackenzie's speech. The latter is a sardonic review of his Reform movement's past defeats in the Assembly, concluding with the call to revolutionary action. Second, the scene addresses the actual audience in the auditorium, who is persuaded by the aptness of the modern theatre-of-protest idiom. Once more, what began as a satirical conceit gives dramatic context to both historical information—Mackenzie's treatment by the Assembly after the 1836 election—and the progress of the action.

Similar to "The Family Compact," "The Canadian Farmer's Travels in the U.S.A." scene (which leads up to "The Dummy") has an authentic source in Robert Davis's 1836 book of that title. For Salutin, this was a happy find that helped to sustain his thesis about a proletarian groundswell for rebellion. Davis took a trip to the United States out of disgust with the election of 1836. He admired everything he saw and returned resolved on improvement at home (Preface 188-189). "The key is to satirize the farmer's enthusiasm for all things American," Salutin records: "To put *through our eyes* [my emphasis] what we saw through his" (Preface 192). In its historical context, the scene briefly exposes the Canadian apathy of the time in contrast to American enterprise, thereby making Davis's point. But Passe Muraille's point is the modern one to which *its* audience—to whom Davis informally introduces himself at the beginning—can respond without historical instruction.

The scene becomes a broadly comic flashback of his trip and is a typical Thompson improvisation (like some of the *Doukhobors* scenes). The detail of the scene is ever changing, allowing for the onstage fun of surprising the actor playing Davis into a spontaneous response to something unexpected. With the actors playing both people and objects, anachronisms abound, thereby reducing the historical distance further. A *jeu d'esprit* in the stage directions suggests that the performers are thoroughly comfortable with their mocking view of the American way of life. The latter is crammed with liberties (except for slaves): free enterprise, free education, free elections, free land—"We'll just sweep those Indians off of it...."—and free assimilation—"Bring your whole country"—(231). In its freewheeling treatment of a free-wheeling nation, the scene discovers real danger: that the Upper Canada of that day is a possible target for American annexation. Therefore, the scene is more persuasive as a contemporary comic satire than as an argument for revolution in 1837. It's also a humourous reminder that there is more than one face to imperialism, even in this present day. The modernity of the play is never clearer than at this point.

Thus, the first act reaches its climax with the politics of resistance. Its concluding scene, "Lount's Forge," addresses the audience with a reprise of complaints against oppression and hints at action to come. The second act, however, investigates the politics of failure. In a more linear and conventional chronicle, it argues that—with the exception of the valiant Waterloo veteran, Colonel Van Egmond—"the bourgeois leadership" lets the revolutionary side down (in Salutin's words "Then as now"—Preface 192). Although the fictional characters of the first act reappear as participants in the rebellion during a series of short scenes, the act refers more concentratedly to historical personages. Mackenzie is shown in conflict with Toronto's cautious middle-class reformers: Rolph, Parsons and Doel as well as the celebrated William "Tiger" Dunlop of the Huron Tract. The latter is suspicious of Mackenzie's brand of treasonous radicalism. That makes Dunlop into a villain in the play, although he is remembered historically as a strong critic of the Canada Company's neglect of settlers' rights.

In structure, the major scenes of Act 2 combine documentary and dramatic elements. Satiric sketch (for example, "The Family Compact" and "The Head") is replaced largely by polemical elaboration to emphasize what Salutin saw as "the guts of our politics—what we make of this event and why we are returning to it now" (Preface 198). The dramatic exchanges between leaders or hoped-for leaders—in scenes such as "Doel's Brewery" and "Tiger Dunlop"—are introduced by a present tense narration. This is filled with historical fact and is addressed to the audience in its capacity as contemporary spectators.

In the former scene—written by Salutin from actor improvisations (Preface 191)—Mackenzie speaks to the audience, outlining the crucial history of the occasion before arguing for urgency with the other characters. According to him, there is an unguarded store of arms at City Hall. If the rebels act now instead of waiting for rural support, they have an excellent chance of seizing power. This is Salutin's great "might have been" of Canadian history. In the latter scene, which Thompson has always described as a skilful example of actors' "writing on their feet," Dunlop identifies himself briefly in the third person before disparaging the radical proposals of Mackenzie and Van Egmond.

In the process of devising a structure for the complicated events of the four-day revolt in Toronto, Salutin initially created a composite account based on several sources. Then he distributed it in numbered sections among the actors. "Each one," he records in his journal, "has to say his section as they come up in sequence, though everyone acts out the events" (Preface 195). This established the basic pattern for a cinematic depiction—variously combining narration and enactment—of the wide scattering of action. The revision, with its emphasis on the farmers' rallying in the countryside, presents the first three days from Van Egmond's perspective as he journeys from his home near Seaforth to meet with the Toronto forces on December 7. This gives a double focus and helps correct the *"longeurs"* Mary Jane Miller noted in the first version.[66] The progress of his journey from town to town, which he narrates as it happens, is interrupted by messages, rumours and accounts of the insurrection begun in Toronto three days ahead of schedule (thanks to the countermanding orders of Dr. Rolph). These events are variously reported, enacted, or presented as first-hand accounts. As the old soldier nears his goal, the tempo increases dramatically. Despite the discouraging odds, he manages to persuade fleeing rebels to rejoin Mackenzie and Lount at Montgomery's Tavern.

Each phase in the action of "The Battle," which directly follows

Van Egmond's arrival, is clarified through a running account by a rebel soldier who functions like the on-the-spot narrator of a documentary film. The "camera eye" cuts briefly to the failed attempt of Peter Matthews' diversionary action at the Don Valley Bridge, Bond Head's mustering of his army in downtown Toronto, the meeting of the two opposing forces at Montgomery's Tavern, and the defeat of 200 poorly armed farmers at the hands of 600 trained militia.

This defeat is signified by an actor standing on a table under which two others are crushed. The as-it-happens account of the scene concludes with the actor playing Mackenzie giving a third-person resume of Mackenzie's escape, Van Egmond's capture, and Mackenzie's establishment of a provisional government on Navy Island. At the end, the actor shifts back into character briefly to speak his defiance at the pursuing government forces. This method of stepping in and out of character and the use of on-the-spot narration are not only convenient presentational devices but also a means of maintaining direct contact with the audience. In essence, "then" becomes "now" in the present tense of a documentary style of performance that shifts between narrating and enacting events.

Political and polemical elements blend adroitly in the two gestural scenes at the end of the play in which stage metaphor is particularly strong. Their stark focus is on the consequences of "the unreliability and timidity of bourgeois leadership in a struggle for Canadian independence" (Preface 192). The more theatrical of the two scenes began in rehearsal with a captivity exercise in which Thompson looped a rope over the heads of the actors and invited them to react to their return to Toronto as prisoners (Preface 195). Later, it occurred to Salutin that this was an opportunity to use the lists of names of actual people charged with sedition, which he had gathered. Thus in "The Rope," the shackled prisoners wind twice about the ramps, speaking their names and the circumstances of their capture, then uttering their defiance or their greetings to the imagined crowd around them. By extension, the audience is invited once more to identify with the plight of the people.

Politically and polemically, the final scene called "The Hanging" encapsulates the whole *raison d'être* of the 1837 enterprise. For Thompson, it meant the necessity of coming to terms with the historical defeat—"part of learning what it is to be a Canadian."[67] For Salutin, the contemporary implications of "why we are returning to it now" (Preface 198) are found in Lount's refusal to accept defeat as final. With Salutin's last line for Lount, "We haven't won yet," and the quick pull of the noose, rhetoric and physical gesture cross the barriers of time in a persuasive ironic combination. This derives in part from Salutin's determination to "wring something positive" out of the admittedly "negative" colonial past of a still "colonial" country and to make a contemporary political point in light of Canada's current nationalist climate (Preface 193).

Lount's preceding public address to his defeated comrades in arms makes the contemporary point about history, which the whole play has been addressing. He assures his compatriots that the farmer, Matthews, and the blacksmith, Lount himself, will never become national symbols. Lount was right, of course, but not for the reason he gives: that, in "their love of liberty," the working people of Upper Canada will soon rise again and therefore will have no need of martyrs. They have not become symbols, the play implies, because the writing of history in this country is so colonized that the nature and justification for their dissent as well as the real cause of their failure are virtually unknown.

Salutin's ideology and the increasingly metaphoric theatricality of Theatre Passe Muraille combine in *1837: The Farmers' Revolt* to give the past, in Thompson's phrase, "current language."[68] In this play, the political act of discovering Canadian history comes through its treatment of history as an immediate political event. Passe Muraille's audience strategies are more complex here than they were in *Doukhobors* and *Buffalo Jump*. This may be seen in the play's more specific examination of the grounds for advocacy under Salutin's guidance. It also may be seen in the shift from a reliance on insistent image in the earlier work (e.g., fire, cowboy) to the use of theatrical metaphor in the exploration of that advocacy in *1837: The Farmers' Revolt*. Stage metaphor is simultaneously a witty way of drawing the audience into the performance process of the play and of engaging them in its issues.

For Salutin's future work, his association with Theatre Passe Muraille was seminal. In the collective work of *1837: The Farmers' Revolt*, he became aware of the tremendous potential for "creative breakthrough" in improvisational playmaking. Again, theatrical metaphor was to become the vehicle for his political and polemical concerns in *Les Canadiens*, as will be discussed later.

The developing historical focus in southwestern Ontario of Theatre Passe Muraille's work at this time led to the creation of *Them Donnellys*. This was a collective play initiated as a touring vehicle rather than a Toronto production during the interval between the two versions of *1837*. Its performance history, even more than that of the revised *1837*, reflects Thompson's continuing attachment to the regional audience that attended *The Farm Show*. Premiering in the Victoria Hall of Petrolia, Ontario on November 19, 1973, and performing elsewhere in the area (including three days beginning November 30, 1973 at Stratford's Festival Theatre), the play was not shown in Toronto until nearly a year later.

Thompson's regional interests were also stimulated by a plan undertaken by Petrolia citizens in the spring of 1973. They set out to restore and put to proper use the old opera house on the second floor of their historic civic complex, eventually to be renamed Victoria Playhouse Petrolia. In the early phases of this restoration project, the theatre committee sought advice about the possibilities of establishing "a large-scale summer festival," possibly approaching the dimensions of the Shaw and Stratford Festivals. Thompson, among the many people invited to visit the site and offer their views, advised that the restored theatre should "function for the people who built it"[69] and therefore should operate as a regional rather than national theatre. He made his point in practical terms by opening Theatre Passe Muraille's *Them Donnellys* in the still unrenovated hall and by selling out all tickets to local audiences for three performances.

The following May, Thompson was invited to return with an acting collective to research and create *Oil*, a play about the life and times of Petrolia itself. The play premiered at the theatre on June 24, 1974, and after three weeks was followed by a run of the new rurally oriented *1837: The Farmers' Revolt*. The next November, the company returned with their revised *Them Donnellys*, subsequent to its Toronto premiere.[70] The work later acquired a new life as a regional play in a further development entitled *The Death of the Donnellys*. The script was revised by actor Ted Johns (of the original collective) for production at Huron County's Blyth Festival and was directed by Thompson in 1979. Since its founding by Keith Roulston in 1975, the Blyth Festival was in many ways expanding Theatre Passe Muraille's principle of local plays for local audiences through commissioned and occasionally collective work.[71]

Thompson's conception of the Donnelly story was of "a series of brilliant anecdotes" gleaned from his reading in years past of two books: Thomas Kelley's sensationalized account *The Black Donnellys* (1954) and Orlo Miller's more thoughtful and dispassionate *The Donnellys Must Die* (1959). But unlike James Reaney, whose *Sticks & Stones* opened in Toronto five days after the Petrolia premiere of *Them Donnellys*, Thompson was not committed to an elaborate vindication of the Donnellys as a much maligned family. He was interested in "their mixture of evil and good" and their status as local legend.[72] Thus, *Them Donnellys* developed as a popular entertainment that featured feuding, violence and murder—the obverse of community in *The Farm Show*. The play had a calculated appeal to audiences living in the actual localities where Donnelly folklore still flourished.

This is acknowledged in general terms by the emphasis in *Them*

Donnellys on the most familiar highlights of the story. It is specifically acknowledged in the prologue of the play, in which Jim Donnelly's lethal quarrel with Pat Farrell over land is presented in two versions: the "actual fight" and the "mythic fight." The latter, in a brief burlesque of Kelley's approach, is presented as oral tradition—a grandfather's tall tale about times when "men were much bigger than they are today."[73]

For this project, Thompson gathered twelve actors as well as a fiddler (Jimmy Adams from Listowel) and a writer (Frank McEnaney). The collective approach was a new and apparently more difficult experience for McEnaney than it had been for Salutin.[74] As with *1837*, the different members of the collective also researched parts of the material and made individual contributions to the play. *Doukhobors'* actors Phil Savath and Larry Mollin (from the improvisational group Homemade Theatre) were instrumental in the powerful staging of the stagecoach war, the fire sequences in Act 2, and the murders in Act 3. Characteristically, *Them Donnellys* began from feelings and images rather than from specific political ideas. In this respect, the play is closer to *Doukhobors* than *1837*. For *Doukhobors*, the alternative life-style was a personal connection that some company members could discover in the historical material. For *Them Donnellys*, according to Thompson, the personal link was in "the theme of a bunch of energetic young boys growing up in a small town."[75]

In coming to understand the Donnelly boys and their friends in this way, the actors were able to suggest the connections between the high-spirited hell-raising of idle youngsters and their subsequent brutalities. Unlike the Reaney version, theirs is not a complex reinvention of the tradition whereby the Donnellys become the mythic representations of a higher life. These Donnellys are as realistically flawed as their neighbours. Instead of taking sides, Passe Muraille's play shows violence breeding violence from all sides. When Flannigan burns the Donnelly's stables, Bob Donnelly retaliates by cutting out the tongues of Flannigan's horses. Only by the third act does malign motive against the Donnellys begin to emerge in a definite way.

In outline, *Them Donnellys* is a rowdy folk romance of pioneer life. In this play, local stories are shaped into archetypal conflicts of love and loss, pride and ambition, anger and vengeance. The action is presented through discontinuous episodes rather than integrated linear sequences. Act 1 emphasizes the rowdy mischief of the Donnelly boys and their friends—events that are stimulated by the boys' aim to rescue Maggie Thompson from her recalcitrant father. Act 2 exposes the transformation of cocky behaviour into destructive commercial rivalry. Finally, Act 3 show the fatal acts of community revenge. Almost every scene is choreographed as a physical confrontation. In the first act, such conflicts are relatively minor in consequence and comic in tone. But they become increasingly serious when the stagecoach rivalry turns into a feud by fire, the maiming of horses, then a tangle of malicious litigation. These conflicts are horrifying in their endorsing of violence by the end.

Like the farmers of *1837*, the characters possess vivid moments rather than developed individuality. For example, Mr. Donnelly challenges his son Tom with a belt after the report of a theft from the Granton post office. Then, Constable Jim Carroll tortures someone into falsifying evidence. Or Grouchie Ryder, a burning two-by-four in his hand, bitterly describes the conflagration of his barn. The Donnelly brothers are virtually interchangeable—except for "Cripple" Will, who represents the best and worst of this proud and vindictive family. However, the play makes its strongest impact through its collective confrontational actions rather than through intimate involvement with particular characters.

With the regional audience in mind, Theatre Passe Muraille brings a strong element of rural popular culture to the images and events of the play. Country fiddle music, song and dance combine into a vivid collage of pioneer activities such as barn-raising bee, wedding dance, chivaree and stagecoach travel. "Clydesdales, the backbone of Ontario rural life, gave me a time-flashback to the 1880s," Thompson told

Whittaker.[76] In this spirit, the miming of horses by the actors, the versatile use of an actual farm wagon as an extension of the stage, as well as other objects—including a cutter and sawhorses used as a "fence"—provide authentic images of the period.

This direct appeal to the audience through the creative use of authentic farm objects is reminiscent of *The Farm Show*. In that play, simple properties included familiar items from Clinton which were given whatever playful mimetic function the scene required. Along the same general principle, the farm wagon of *Them Donnellys* is a property with many functions. However, the difference is that it also provides a mobile playing space on a normal scale. After its initial function as wagon (storing the three ladders from which the actors build the "barn" in the opening raising bee and fight), it signifies "prison" for Mr. Donnelly and "store" for the pilfering Donnelly boys. On several occasions, it also represents a "stable" where, for example, Flannigan discovers his mutilated horses. Sometimes, it is moved about to suggest "journey": Mrs. Donnelly runs on the spot in the wagon (while moved by another actor) to signify her racing across the fields to warn Will about the gang searching for Thompson's cow. Last of all, the wagon becomes Will's house—an extension of the main stage on which the charred bodies of his murdered family still lie.

Building the set onstage as a prologue to the play is Theatre Passe Muraille's new technique for engaging the audience. Similar to the informal opening of *The Farm Show*, the actors enter early, walking and chatting among the audience. Then on signal, while the house lights are still up, they begin the "barn-raising" with lots of noise, drinking and fiddle music. Three ladders are raised gradually and tied with rope to represent the walls and roof of the barn. At the same time, a small fight gradually develops into a big one between Jim Donnelly senior and Patrick Farrell. Thus, the play begins.

The completed structure made from ladders serves varying functions during the play—particularly the Thompson house where the chivaree takes place. Here, "inside" and "outside" are important features of the scene. Inside, the bride and groom are preparing for bed while outside, the "Roman Line" characters are sneaking around with their pots, pans and sticks. Later, when the unwanted Donnelly boys appear, Bob climbs onto the ladder "roof" while Will stirs up excitement downstage with his violin. From both inside and out, people peer through the "windows" between the ladder rungs. But mostly, the ladders are places for climbing. For example, one of the ladders becomes the mast of Will's imaginary ship during the courting scene with Maggie Thompson. In this as well as other ways, the theatricality of *Them Donnellys* differs from that of *Sticks & Stones*. In the latter play, the physical use of ladders as stage properties is elaborated into metaphoric suggestions of struggle and entrapment.

In comparing *Sticks & Stones* to *Them Donnellys*, Brian Arnott said "the Passe Muraille actors furnished delight and amazement by creating with fewest props a living picture of the people and the times no scene designer could hope to equal." In the Reaney production, on the other hand, he opined that "the Donnelly story was successfully obliterated by never-ceasing exercises in orchestrated prop shifting."[77] When the second act of *Them Donnellys* calls for stagecoaches, once more the actors build onstage. They create two coaches from stools and benches (reminiscent of constructing the train in *Buffalo Jump*) while both Flannigan and Will Donnelly harness actors to perform the horses. Movement is indicated by the "horses" pacing on the spot and tossing their heads with the strain of excessive speed. The motion of "wheels" is simulated by Will's and Flannigan's twirling two long sticks, which clash three times to indicate when the coaches are bumping. Of course, the violent physicality of the "Stagecoach War" is its most important element. The violence reaches its peak when the coaches collide at the water pump and topple over. Then, passengers are scattered and the panicked Flannigan horses leap off the stage, dragging the driver on his belly up the centre aisle and back.

Chapter Two: Theatre Passe Muraille 99

The enactment of horses, both here and subsequently, is perhaps the most powerful feature of the scene and is a good illustration of the physicality of Thompson's theatrical method. In *Doukhobors*, he was building on the physicality of the Doukhobor spiritual experience through the capacity of the actors to project the energy of naked sweating bodies on stage. Also, one of the memorable scenes in that play depicts women actually functioning as horses hitched to the plough. In *Them Donnellys*, the performers are building from that same kind of physicality in order to enact the horses themselves. Horses are important to the play not only as "living" images in "time-flashback to the 1880s" but also as expressions of the full impact of human violence. This is especially so in their agonized screaming and leaping when the horses are mutilated later in the act.[78]

The other powerful stage reality of the act is fire, choreographed as a duel between Will and Flannigan. They have sticks in hand similar to the stagecoach "wheels," but this time the ends are bound in kerosene-dipped burlap for quick ignition. The confrontation between the two men alternates between action and freeze as the consequences of the "duel" are briefly enacted "with much yelling and confusion" by other performers (Act 2, 13).[79] The actual murder of the Donnelly family in Act 3 is a starkly ritualized variation on the violence hitherto depicted—a combination of movement and freeze for the assault on each victim. The action is conducted by Carroll, who signals each murderous attack by striking the floor with his stick. Each victim dies "as though...being beaten to death" while the burning of the victims is indicated by the glow of red light in which the bodies "shiver and jerk" to the accompaniment of sharp fiddle sounds (Act 3, 20).

Critical response to the original touring version of the play pronounced certain parts better than the whole. One reviewer said that the future of the play "will depend on some sharp editing," but individual scenes were strong, such as James Donnelly's return from jail and the stagecoach war.[80] For the revised production at the Trinity Church space, which opened on October 16, 1974, there was a concerted effort to restructure the basic material into tighter scenes, with some changes in a rather cluttered third act. Most significant was the further articulation of the folk element, including the occasional flirtation with gothic supernaturalism borrowed from Kelley. This was achieved mostly by the inclusion of music written and performed by Phil Schreiber and featuring country singer Shannon King as the "Singer." The lyrics, variously written by the second collective, provide a more structured context for the old-time country atmosphere evoked by the fiddle music and step dancing of the original. In the introduction to the characters, for example, where originally the actors broke informally from their dance to name themselves and to announce their roles, they now sing and dance to a ballad (performing solo or in pairs for each verse) that introduces each in character.

The subsequent songs, like the scenes they elaborate, usually point to the highlights of the tale: Jim Donnelly, singing his story from the Kingston jail, intersects a scene showing his family's difficulties at home; a ballad by the Singer (in the persona of Maggie pleading with Will for rescue) frames the courting scene; the stagecoach incidents and their fiery consequences are punctuated with stanzas of a driving song with the ominous refrain "We're riding fast as glory / On a hell-bound rig" (Act 2, 5, 8). Death as personified in the character of Jim Carroll is the subject of the ballad stanzas tracking his vicious activity against the Donnellys throughout Act 3. Initially, he is glimpsed as a white-faced death's head, axe in hand, in Jenny Donnelly's premonitional hallucination at the beginning of the act. Later, as the song begins, he is revealed in his natural dimension by the simple process of slowly wiping the white from his face.

A song that plays ironically on the supernatural element is Will's half-sung and half-spoken threat to the self-appointed vigilantes who intrude on his land in search of William Thompson's lost cow. The scene derives from the traditional hearsay that Will literally played the intruders off his land with the power of his violin. His mocking song draws on a motif already established in Father Connolly's fanatical sermon in which he asserts that "The devil has shown his clubfoot in Biddulph" (Act 3, 4) and must be destroyed. Taunting them sinisterly with the names they have given him, Will grabs his mother and spins her into a wild demonic dance that sends the others backing off in fear.

This is the third time in the play in which Will is shown to have a bizarre influence on the behaviour of others. In Act 1, he uses the destructive incitement of his violin in revenge against the Thompsons by stirring up his friend and later enemy, John Kennedy, into a frenzy of chivaree house-smashing. At Tom Ryder's wedding, in the aftermath of the fire feud, he initiates the row with the constable, who is trying to arrest his brother Jim, by bursting in "doing an Indian dance, making war whoops and spinning like a dervish" (Act 2, 16). Not surprisingly, Will is the Donnelly whom the vigilantes want to kill most. But given the devil's luck, they get John instead.

The strong images of inflamed parish priest, diabolic Will, and death-bringer Carroll infuse the previously discursive third act with a new power. These scenes progressively highlight the inexorable pattern of the community force against the Donnellys. After the murders, the play concludes on a quiet elegiac note with a folk-song survey of the Lucan graveyard where, years later, all the participants lie. Tonally, this is an improvement on the original ending, which offered a guidebook commentary from the modern graveyard custodian about its exact location off Highway 4 from London and the subsequent fate of the original gravestone. The change is another reinforcement of the stronger folkloric emphasis in the Donnelly storytelling.

Ted Johns' later revisions for the play, *The Death of the Donnellys* in 1979, reversed the evolution from a written script (Carol Bolt's *Next Year Country*) to a new collective performance piece (*Buffalo Jump*) to a degree. As an actor, Johns was part of the collective process for both versions of *Them Donnellys*. But the play that evolved further under his hand is in some respects a more literary treatment, even though he followed the same general line of action and incorporated most of Passe Muraille's presentational techniques.[81] The link with the popular Donnelly tradition still remains in the "realistic" and "mythic" fight scenes (with deference to the chief sources, "Uncle Orlo" is telling his nephew the version he heard from "Grampa Kelly") and in the use of songs throughout. Nevertheless, the rewriting shifts the play away from gothic folk romance to tragicomic folk realism.

In most cases, the imagistic force of the characters in *Them Donnellys* translates into more rounded personalities with clearer relationships and motives. Thus retained are original scenes that best serve the naturalistic context of the revised work either as expositional or documentary shorthand. For example, take the early sequences leading to Mr. Donnelly's arrival home from jail, the belting scene, and the original "Talking Blues" (after the Ryder wedding at the end of Act 2) which provides a compressed version of the many abrasive legal entanglements that now prevail in Biddulph Township. Elsewhere, particularly in Acts 1 and 3, anecdotal events are reworked into more extended units of cause-and-effect action that incorporates certain motifs from discarded scenes. For example, the hostility of Maggie's father to Will occurs in the much revised chivaree scene, and John Kennedy's hatred of his old friend Will over his marriage to Nora emerges in a new expositional opening to Act 3. Only Act 2, with its presentational approach to feud and fire, is virtually unchanged.

The strong comic tone is retained in Johns' more crafted depictions, which recall Thompson's description of "a bunch of energetic young boys growing up in a small town." The comic tone is also enhanced by developing William Porte as an elderly dupe. But there are notable changes in the relationship between Maggie and Will, now elaborated over two scenes and reaching its climax at the chivaree. Led on by the hooliganism of Kennedy, Will offends Maggie in a brash comedy of errors, which spoils their plan to elope. Her rejection of Will leads to his drunken assault on Kennedy, making the latter so blinded by pain that he breaks up what is left of the newlywed's household. The impulsive dream of family glory, which Will had hoped to share with Maggie, is his new stagecoach line. This is a detail that bridges Acts 1 and 2. Given the turn of events at the chivaree, it prepares for Will's aggressive behaviour—as always with his family's support—against his business competition.

Will's later behaviour with the constable at the Ryder wedding has a nasty as well as a mocking edge, with his ironic invitation to dance merely an excuse to knee the hapless officer in the groin. In his mature years, however, Will's better side stands out in his confrontation with the mob in search of Thompson's cow. Rather than taking up the role of "devil"—as the new priest, Father Connelly,[82] has reportedly cast him—he makes initial overtures of peace. Only when these are rejected—and all but the ominous Carroll have backed off—does he speak his defiance using his violin. One of the strongest indications of transformation from folk romance to folk realism in *The Death of the Donnellys* is in these modifications of Will's character. His demonic element has been scaled down to naturalistic proportions.

The extensive rewriting in Act 3 shows the playwright giving greater weight to the moral ironies of the story. This involves a more schematic expansion of the terse and highly charged action scenes preceding the murders in *Them Donnellys*. There is also a literary attention to language as well as to dramatic structure. An entirely new opening scene of exposition, in which already familiar characters debate the appointment of a new constable, introduces the two crucial motifs: the zealous campaign of Father Connelly in his reported sermonizing against "backsliders and deprecators" (61); and the recent appearance in the district of the ruthless Jim Carroll, who reputedly operates on the principle that "if you can't bend the law to fit the case, you bend the case to fit the law" (62).

The impact of Father Connelly's fiery language—unlike in *Them*

Donnellys, he never appears in person; yet his rhetoric alone is enough to stir people—and of Jim Carroll's corrupt efficiency dominates the act. This scene and what follows also establish those people who are naively persuaded by the renewed vigour of the Church and the law, those who exploit it, and those who are its victims (namely the Donnellys). The emphasis is on specific suspicions (Grouchie Ryder's) and personal resentments (Kennedy's). There is also a sympathetic articulation of the Donnellys' personal responses to the intensifying situation—especially by Julia, Jim senior and Will.

The playwright's decision to keep Father Connelly off the stage suggests the writer's greater interest in the effect of the priest's language on particular people than in his physical presence as an ominous community force. This role is now reserved exclusively for the figure of Jim Carroll. The unfortunate influences of the priest's zealotry are filtered through his parishioners. First among them are Kennedy (73) and the increasing hostility of neighbour and former friend, Grouchie Ryder. In this version, his change of heart is already foreshadowed in the first act. For Julia Donnelly, Father Connelly's zeal is an alarming form of religious hypocrisy, which she reports to Will when she comes to warn him of the advancing mob:

> He told *me* he would forgive us *all*. He called *you* a devil and a cripple! He told *them* that Satan's angel stamped you the night that you were born. And *then* he said, "Cut the evil from this parish and heaven's angels will descend and bring a whole new world!" (71)

The depiction of Carroll is still close to the folk figure of Death in *Them Donnellys*. His motiveless malignity comes only once into the naturalistic foreground through his choice of Pat Ryder—ironically the one who helped appoint him—as the victim of physical coercion for a perjury conspiracy against Tom Donnelly. This example of bending the case to fit the law provides Carroll with the pretence of legal entrance into the Donnelly farmhouse on the fatal night. Carroll is still the stage manager of the violence that has been simmering among the others for years. But he is a silent presence in the crowded confrontation at Will's. At the end of the scene, he momentarily comes into focus as the sole object of Will and Julia's defiant dance. This scene is appropriately framed by stanzas of the death song, which intersect Carroll's activities in *Them Donnellys*.

In Act 3, Johns makes the point that, despite the faults on all sides, fundamentally decent people are now being viciously persecuted by those who claim legal or ecclesiastical sanctions. The fears of Julia Donnelly dominate two scenes. Even those of her newly arrived niece Bridget, a more extended character in this version, are not misplaced. Ironically, Jim senior is too sensible to fear "just a gang of men" who think they have "a dandy new idea that it's gonna change the world" (69). Passe Muraille's massacre scene now finds an emotional context in the basic humanity of the victims and becomes more than the ritualized climax to a series of violent events.

The scene also underlines the way people lose their human identity in crass acts of zealotry. At first, the only identifiable figure is the already dehumanized Carroll. But at the end, the anonymity of the actual killers—whose motivations have been previously traced—is lifted starkly. As before, the death of John at Will's farm is a naturalistic coda to these events. However, instead of the elegiac ballad that concludes *Them Donnellys*, what we have in *The Death of the Donnellys* is a speech in blank verse by Will. He already anticipates the legends and controversies that will soon arise from "this butchery" and bitterly notes the "measure of how far we are from heaven. / How close we are to hell" (85). This moral flourish is his comment about Father Connelly's misguided aspiration for "a whole new world" (71) while five bodies lie before him as an ironic reminder of sanctioned brutality.

In his author's note preceding the published text, Johns identifies the play as neither history nor documentary but "as a study in law." In a terse allusion to the three-act progression, he cites the laws of family, of society, and of God—all of which can be seen as both justly and unjustly punitive in the play. Whereas the collective version concentrates on the performance of the story in broad sweeps, the written version shifts to interpretation. The folkloric resonance of the characters in *Them Donnellys* is thereby replaced by rather obvious ironies of cause and effect.

To a petulant Maggie Thompson, the Donnelly dreams turn "black" because (in her view) Will is demonstrably unreliable and insulting (34), not because she is the lovelorn victim of an intransigent father. "On a bad day" (74), the Donnellys have been as nasty as the neighbours who now harass them for William Thompson's cow. So, his offer of peace is resisted. Nor are the Donnellys destructively charismatic any longer. But more mundanely, they are the eventual and, of course, undeserving victims of a moral outrage that violates "the law" at all levels. Of the several possible routes to the formal dramatization of the Donnelly material—of which Reaney's poetic epic structure is the richest as well as the most convoluted—the Johns development in *The Death of the Donnellys* is a narrowing rather than an expanding of the potential scope of the original play. It largely absorbs *Them Donnellys* through a process of conventionalization.

3. Showing West: *The West Show; Far As the Eye Can See*

Theatre Passe Muraille's most far-reaching regional impact was initiated in Saskatoon during the summer of 1975 with *The West Show*. This project, financed by a generous Canada Council grant, marked a return to rural interests after the success of *I Love You, Baby Blue*, an investigation into blue-movie sex, performed to sold-out houses in Toronto during the previous winter. In exchange for rehearsal space in Saskatoon, they also established a fruitful relationship with Andras Tahn's young 25th Street House Theatre. Thompson directed the latter's first collective show, *Prairie Landscape or...If You're So Good, Why Are You in Saskatoon?* This association was seminal to that theatre's direction for several years to come and led to its best-known collective play, the nationally toured *Paper Wheat*.

During the previous winter, *Almighty Voice*—a Theatre Passe Muraille seed show on a prairie theme, directed by Clarke Rogers—had already been developed and had toured through the prairie region. A work inspired in part by Rudy Wiebe's short story "Where is the Voice Coming From?", *Almighty Voice* established the first phase of a creative association between Theatre Passe Muraille and the western Canadian novelist. This association continued in the "Sam Reimer" sequence of *The West Show*, leading in turn to the full-scale collaboration of *Far As the Eye Can See* in 1977.

In essence, *The West Show* is an amalgam of Theatre Passe Muraille's established and new procedures.[83] Originally, Thompson reports, they had intended to develop an entirely modern piece, but the history kept creeping in. So the combination of past and present in the eight sections of the play invites comparison with both *The Farm Show* and *1837*. Like *The Farm Show*, the new work is a collection of self-contained units. Critic Robert Nunn describes this play as "self-reflexive" in that *The West Show* "includes the process of creating the show as part of the show."[84] In rhetorical terms, this refers to the frequent use of direct address at the beginning and sometimes at the conclusion of an otherwise dramatized sequence (rather than the characteristic monologues of *The Farm Show*). The opening narration may either describe the origins of a story (i.e., Sections 3 and 5), initiate the transformation of actor to character (Section 2) or, as in *The Farm Show*, acknowledge the company as outside visitors (Section 5).

However, there is a substantial difference between the two works in their expressed and implicit relations to audiences. In the first place, the "West" is not an intimately observed single community where everyone knows his or her neighbour. *The West Show* addresses the people of Saskatchewan at large. For this play, as Thompson told an interviewer, "we were more interested in stories than portraits. We wanted to convey the mythic sense of the West through personal experiences as they were actually lived."[85] Passe Muraille's characterization of those personal experiences, with a notable exception in "Janet Reitz" (Section 5), is improvisational invention freely drawn from factual sources. Some of these came from actors' readings and some from their travels, separately and together, investigating and living in various communities around the province.[86]

In contrast to what Thompson was designating as "myth" in *The Farm Show* (material grounded in factual particularities that reflect social typicality, e.g., "Jean Lobb"), Passe Muraille's mythic West emerges from perceptions of certain patterns in the society they were exploring. The common factor throughout *The West Show* is the relationship of the people to the land; the common theme, similar in a general way to *1837*, is "the struggle of the dispossessed for greater power."[87] Like *1837*, this work presents its popular history from the point of view of the ordinary people who made it. It's another example of Thompson's interest in "making history current language."

In his introductory account of the published version of the play, Thompson writes of his impressions of Saskatchewan people locking themselves "into their own cultural coulees, their *islets du bois*" (18). Actor and script editor Ted Johns speaks of the composition of Saskatchewan society as "islands of people on a prairie sea."[88] These verbal metaphors derive from the typical prairie landscapes of vast fields dotted irregularly with bush or poplar bluffs. They also refer in part to the company's discovery of the diverse and isolated ethnic groups that compose Saskatchewan society: Métis, Mennonite, Scandinavian, Indian, etc.

In counter thrust to patterns of insularity and individuality, Passe Muraille also discovered the Saskatchewan of collective and co-operative action within, and sometimes beyond, the individual groups. The tension between individualism and collectivity in the play becomes the governing "myth" of Saskatchewan in the work as a whole. *The West Show* thus anticipates the more precise versions of Saskatchewan co-operative movements offered later in collective creations by 25th Street Theatre and the Globe Theatre in Regina.

Theatre Passe Muraille's discoveries are expressed through a new gestural dimension to *The West Show*'s reference to itself as performance. This involves the introduction of a flexible set that can be re-assembled for each scene as an "accomplice" in the task of engaging audiences in the play-creating process. It comprises two components: a portable raked stage depicting an aerial view of a Saskatchewan farm in winter (which breaks into five jigsaw-puzzle pieces designed and painted by ceramic sculptor Joe Fafard of Pense, Saskatchewan); and a three-quarter-scale Red River cart (an advance on *Them Donnellys*' wagon) that usefully disassembles into rack, wheels and axle. (Both components were executed by resident designer Bob Pearson.) The onstage manipulation of these elements in suggestive variations provides a visual comment on the individual scenes as well as offering an overall unity to the play.

The play's dominant images are of wholeness and fragmentation. In individual scenes, the harmonious whole can be suggested by Fafard's complete painting while the disruption of normality is indicated by the set's fracturing into various configurations. The design also allows for symbolic transformations into whatever setting or property related to the land which a scene requires. For example, up-ended pieces become Tom Sukanen's spectacular prairie boat or a segment on its side serves as a tractor in the farmers' demonstration against Trudeau. The assembled Red River cart is the authentic Métis vehicle pulled, like Mother Courage, by Madame Tourond as she escapes with her family and possessions from the fiasco at Fort Garry to a new life at Fish Creek. Its wheels and axle become the enemy's cannon in the Rebellion of 1885, symbolically splitting apart the "land" with its force.

An examination of the stage directions as well as extant pictures and drawings[89] indicates the more studied approach in this play to the use of set and properties in comparison to the random transformations of *The Farm Show*, where a collection of objects serves whatever function the moment requires. In *The West Show*, it becomes important to notice how the components of the Red River cart are used. They are most prominent, of course, in the historical piece "Madame Tourond." In seven brief scenes, this sequence presents the two rebellions, 1869 and 1885, predominantly from the point of view of an historically obscure matriarch whose destiny was affected by those struggles.

At the beginning, the overturned rack becomes the bier of the heroine's husband, who has been brutally murdered at Fort Garry. Soon after, it is a symbolic trap for the fleeing Louis Riel. Later, after its use as a transport—the one expression of what the play's transcriber Ted Johns describes as "the Métis nation, healthy and on the move"[90]—it is disassembled. The components become a "wall/seat with a buffalo robe spread over it," with a wheel of the upright axle forming the "cooking area" of the Fish Creek encampment (28). In the scene following, Dumont spins that wheel with his rifle butt to punctuate his accounts of the subsequent history of his people up to 1884 (29). The disassembling of the cart gradually becomes associated with the disintegration of the Métis people, climaxed by the cannon metaphor referred to above.

In another kind of scene, the modern use of the cart components underlines moments in the farmers' struggle towards collective action and at the same time echoes the images of hope and oppression that haunt the historical Métis story. In the "Louise Lucas" section, the rack, draped with bunting, becomes the podium from which Louise, "Mother of the CCF," makes her first tentative experiments in public speaking. Without bunting, the rack represents the prison of domestic drudgery for one of her farm-wife converts to community action (73). In "The Tractor Demonstration," one wheel becomes the rising sun of "the lovely July day" of 1969 when the farmers decide to protest Federal agricultural policy. The other wheel becomes the gigantic platter of refreshments prepared by their supportive wives (79, 83). The overall effect links new activists with old, the brave efforts of the early Métis with those of the populist movements of more recent times.

The expressive use of the stage as land is perhaps most effective in the "Janet Reitz" and "Sam Reimer" sections of the play. In the latter, the playing area for the solitary individualist—whom the voice of God calls to proclaim peace in Vietnam—is a single piece of landscape "isolated at the centre of the stage" (39). The other segments are used in a background arrangement to emphasize how Sam stands apart from his complacent Mennonite community. At the end of the sequence, discouraged by the scepticism of pastor, wife, psychiatrist and other figures in the recalcitrant world of the possible, Sam reassembles his farm (the five stage pieces) in preparation to die from his own guilt and discouragement.

For the investigatory journalism of the northern Indian and Métis communities in the La Ronge area, three of the stage pieces are in vertical positions, "twisted about to form an abstract design" that suggests by its impersonality the alienation of the native people under white administration (52). Another piece represents the indoor furnishings at district court, later in the house of Métis social worker Janet Reitz, and also at the land office of the Department of Northern Saskatchewan. These scenes all emphasize the efforts and failures of native people either to thrive under the white system or to function independently of its bureaucratic paternalism (52, 57, 60).

When the last piece of stage is raised into vertical position, it becomes the cabin on Janet's trapline (63). She has retreated to a place she loves because her endeavours to develop native self-reliance at home and at work are confounded by the apathy of the native people and by the bureaucratic indifference of the Department of Northern Saskatchewan. She has difficulty keeping her own children at school while the Métis Society loses to commercial development its bid on the land where it planned an independent housing project. Finally, she is fired from her job at the welfare office because she insists that recipients are in greater need of a clean water supply than monetary handouts.

Needless to say, there are no components of the Red River cart in this sequence, although its heroine is implicitly the true descendant of the indomitable Madame Tourond. The episode could make an uncomfortable comment on the disappearance of Louise Lucas's ideals into the modern bureaucracy of the provincial NDP, except that "Janet Reitz" precedes that sequence rather than taking its chronological place at the end of the play. Thus, there is no pointed emphasis here on the contradictions between past ideals and present realities.

This suggests that, in contrast to *1837*, *The West Show* is largely a treatment of the positive responses to oppressive circumstances rather than a confrontational political overview of their causes and consequences. Don Kerr notes that, even within the individual sequences, except for "Janet Reitz," the opposition is barely imagined. For the Riel Rebellion, the emphasis is on the personally lived efforts of the ordinary people as represented first by Madame Tourond and later by Gabriel Dumont, the favourite son of recent historians (e.g., George Woodcock). In the handling of the modern populist movements, Don Kerr notes, the politics are "put in the context of somebody's kitchen, somebody's farmyard" but without focus on "the powers that have tried to destroy us."

> What is Louise Lucas fighting? The banks are mentioned once. And the farmers in 1969? Trudeau is a tiny comic shrug. There is no CPR, or Grain Exchange, or Free Market, and nobody even gets squeezed by that vaudeville team, Cost and Price.[91]

Although there are proportionally more defeats than victories in the play, Passe Muraille manages to side-step the traps of negative history, which are unavoidable in *1837*. This is neither because history has been kinder to the native people of Saskatchewan than to the defeated settlers of 1837; nor because the farmers of the present, depicted in the closing lines of "Tractor Demonstration," are collectively secure after their activism of 1969. Rather it is because the emphasis is on the *romance* of Saskatchewan—on those who alone or together believe that the battle for the good life is worth fighting.

The play opens with the parable of the eccentric Tom Sukanen, who has all the prairie virtues of initiative, self-reliance and vision, but to his cost refuses to accept help. In the last scene, everyone works together in the collective action of protest, although the play closes with a few cautionary lines of postscript. It is now 1975 when times are good for some, but the problem is still "sunset city for a lot of farmers" (86). The question is left open as to whether the co-operative spirit of the past will hold fast in the collective memory before conditions become universally tough once again.

Section 6 of *The West Show* begins with an actor's chat with "Myrtle." She's a person who likes to talk politics, particularly about how little help governments (either Conservative or Liberal) gave to farmers in the bad years. "So they had to unite! And they did! And they discussed issues and they got some action!" For her, the great panacea is the founding of "a co-operative party—the CCF!" (65). The changes she refers to are those that occurred with the creation of grain pools, co-operative stores and health insurance (the first mentioned soon to become the subject of 25th Street Theatre's *Paper Wheat*).

As a result of Theatre Passe Muraille's influence by example, other theatre companies sought out their own stories and performed them for the people most directly affected by those stories. However, while *Paper Wheat* is the true descendant of *The West Show*, Theatre Passe Muraille always looked for new challenges in its own work. The visit to Saskatchewan provided new friends, new material and, with Joe Fafard's set, a fresh way of exploring performance metaphors, which advanced well beyond the visual image-making of John Boyle's cut-outs in *Buffalo Jump*. However, *The West Show* remained structurally a variation of the play of juxtaposed scenes and characterizations, even though the work displayed a more sustained use of narrative in some individual sequences. Theatre Passe Muraille's association with novelist Rudy Wiebe led to further thematic and formal developments on another western subject a year or so later with the collaborative creation of *Far as the Eye Can See*, premiered in Edmonton.

In certain respects, both socially and politically, Saskatchewan and Alberta are strong contrasts. Instead of Myrtle's egalitarian myth of collectivity, represented politically by the farmers' "co-operative party—the CCF," Alberta's political myth is one of monolithic capitalistic paternalism. Initiated in bad times by the eccentricities of Bible Bill Aberhart's Social Credit party (briefly parodied in *Buffalo Jump*), the myth was updated in the early 1970s by Peter Lougheed's corporate conservatism. This invites a different approach to the Alberta story, distinct from the composite depiction of the Saskatchewan of *The West Show*.

Structurally, *Far As the Eye Can See* offers a multiple focus on a single issue: the struggle of a group of farmers (in the Dodds/Round Hill area near Edmonton) against a thermal power-plant project that requires the purchase and strip-mining of their farms. In *The West Show*, the "enemy" is often an outside force (eastern Canada in the cases of the Riel rebellions and the farmers' tractor demonstration of 1969). In *Far As the Eye Can See*, the enemy comes from within the society itself and is represented by a provincial government in alliance with a big business enterprise, Calgary Power. At stake is the traditional and currently prosperous way of life of some 80 farm families in an area comprising approximately 50 miles of prime arable land. The issue is complicated locally by the existence of a small-town population that needs the business and the work that the new project will bring. The larger question concerns the future need for power that affects the high-density population living nearby in the city.

The real-life story (which reached its ambiguous conclusion in the summer of 1976 with the indefinite postponement of strip mining in the area) was suggested to Thompson by Wiebe as early as the spring of that year. They had been planning to collaborate on a new project ever since the novelist's enthusiastic response to Theatre Passe Muraille's improvisations from his fiction for *The West Show*. In a later recollection about Theatre Passe Muraille's improvisations at that time from his novel *Peace Shall Destroy Many*, he wrote "in my imagination exploded a whole new way of seeing what I had written 16 years before."[92]

In the fall of 1976, Thompson and Wiebe together did some preliminary exploration of the story on-site. They talked to Calgary Power officials as well as farming people who had been actively involved in the local agricultural-protection society and whose celebratory annual meeting they attended that November. Certain ideas for the play began to emerge, including Wiebe's suggestion for a mythical dimension rooted in the three figures of "The Regal Dead." This image developed into an extended fabular device by which the events of the present are debated in comic counterpoint by key characters from Alberta's past. The two researchers also got a sense of the farm people they wanted to portray—in particular the model for Betty Mitchell, the active farm wife in the local movement.

In some important respects, the association with Rudy Wiebe resulted in the best working relationship that Theatre Passe Muraille ever experienced with a writer. From the company's point of view, Wiebe showed his appreciation of the actors' verbal skills, quelling the writer's natural impulse to write the dialogue himself. Generalizing later from this particular collaboration, Thompson observed that "it really requires a substantial amount of confidence on the writer's part to realize that, when David Fox and Ted Johns are jamming onstage, there is magic dialogue being written." Then, the writer has only to "grab hold of that and somehow finish it off."[93]

From Wiebe's point of view, it was also a fruitful experience because he was doubly engaged in the advisory capacity of dramaturge and of eventual playwright. After participating in four weeks of preliminary jamming (beginning in mid-February of 1977) using the most experienced "writers on their feet" at Thompson's disposal,[94] Wiebe took home more than 300 pages of notes. From these, he wrote a first draft of the play just in time for the full-cast rehearsal period of three more weeks. Further development and rewriting took place until the opening at Theatre 3, Edmonton on April 12.

Thompson's decision to incorporate the work of a writer more closely within the collective process arose from the need for stronger narrative structures for the more complex stories that now challenged him in collective creation. In the winter of 1976, he had been confronting this requirement the hard way in the problematic development of *The Horsburgh Scandal*. A play with a multiple focus on a single character, this is another of Theatre Passe Muraille's underground histories of southwestern Ontario. In its struggle towards a more sustained dramatic narrative, this work anticipates *Far As the Eye Can See*. Yet overall, *The Horsburgh Scandal* still hovers between Passe Muraille's characteristic juxtaposing of theatricalized and scenically self-contained events (as in *Them Donnellys*) and a degree of forced narrative continuity and character building.

Ironically, that may be attributed in part to Thompson's characteristic refusal up to this point to let the writer on the project actually write. In this case, the writer was playwright Betty Jane Wylie. For some years, she had been gathering material for a play about the late Rev. Russell Horsburgh, the United Church minister from Chatham, Ontario. In a sensational trial in 1964, he was found guilty (wrongly, as it turned out) of contributing to the juvenile delinquency of adolescent parishioners for whom he was establishing radical outreach programmes. Wylie approached Thompson because her research, including tapes of interviews with the principals, had yielded so multi-faceted a person that, she recorded, "I thought I needed a collection of minds to approach the man."[95] From her point of view, Passe Muraille's playmaking process was far from a meeting of minds for the insightful probing she initially anticipated. What was emerging, or seemed to be emerging, in the rehearsal process as she records it was more like a theatrical exploration of social surfaces rather than depths. Yet the point of this was not at all clear to her for some time.

Nor did she see her function clearly as "writer" on the project, finding difficulty adjusting to Thompson's precept that, for most of the rehearsal period, the writer as well as the director must serve the performers rather than any script. Like Salutin at the beginning of *1837*, she went home at night wondering why they needed a writer, although this concern lasted for her almost to the end. "Paper was denied me," she recalls. "Dialogue was a no-no. Information was suspect."[96] Three days into rehearsal, the 15 scenes she bravely handed to Thompson were brushed aside. Ten days into rehearsal, she offered to go away for three days and bring back a script. "It's not our way,"[97] Thompson replied. At one point, she thought that maybe her task would be to select and compile some of the better improvisations, but that does not appear to have happened either.[98] Ten days before the end, she offered the collective a deliberately simplistic three-act outline "with a beginning, a middle and an end; with a protagonist, an antagonist, a pivotal character and an obligatory scene—all the things you take in Playwriting 1."[99] (She herself had been writing plays since 1962.) This made everyone feel better for the moment, but it turned into a temporary measure only.

Eventually, the playmakers fell back in some measure on a "playwriting" technique of the sort she outlined, resulting in an expedient shift from the social depiction of communal events to cause-and-effect naturalism. For example, a hard-headed mother and her "incorrigible" daughter play out several soap opera scenes of personal conflict and malice. In the ensuing mechanics of crime and detection, these scenes explicitly target the scapegoat hero. While obviously a means for moving the action forward, here the crude psychology of individuals conflicts with the play's major focus on the complicity of the community as a whole. In contrast, the character of Horsburgh himself is sustained primarily in the social dimension of a man ahead of his time[100] rather than through psychological probes.

Wylie was less impressed than Wiebe by the actors' verbal facility. (Although Fox, Johns, Peterson and Terry Tweed were in the cast, so were a number of actors inexperienced in the process.) In her concern for language, Wylie would preserve the good lines no matter where they came from (sometimes from the actors and sometimes from the real-life people of her researches) and later would remind the actors if they lost them. On one occasion when two actresses asked her to write "some witty lines," Thompson excised them because they sounded "like a play." Occasionally, she would suggest lines surreptitiously when talking about the play during coffee breaks. "I wish I'd said that, an actor says ruefully. You can!, I say, and he does." At one point, she took three of the actors to her church's annual dinner, resulting in an improvisation the next day (a tiny fragment of which remained in the eventual play). This incident led her to criticize the "terrible inaccuracy" of improvisation and to wonder if "emotional truth make[s] up for this?"[101]

Nevertheless, the strongest features of the play in performance, especially in Act 1, were the theatricalized depictions of the restless teenage crowd in action. Another strength was the comic range of quick transformations by the actors from swinging teens to perplexed parents and self-righteous old fogies. In essence, this is vintage Theatre Passe Muraille in transition and in need of a writer both admitted and committed to a total collaboration. In any case, Rudy Wiebe would accept no less.

The differences in the Wiebe experience are instructive by comparison. He joined *Far As the Eye Can See* as a novelist interested in a new writing experience, whereas Wylie came to *Horsburgh* as a playwright with a playwright's expectations. Perhaps because he was an enthusiastic novice, Wiebe also had more confidence in the potential of the actors for handling the subject matter. But most important, he had also secured the more advantageous ground rules from the company. While she played "court stenographer," recording everything occurring in rehearsal because she did not know what else to do, he did the same—but with an agreement with Thompson that, when the improvisational process came to an end, he would be writing the play. Therefore, unlike her, he had no worry about trying to write something then and there. At the first rehearsal, he presented a rough outline and within two days the actors were fluently jamming characters and scenes and offering ideas of their own (although not necessarily material that was finally used). If he also felt, as he puts it in his introduction, "assaulted" and "derided" on a regular basis,

> there was always the adrenalin of a marvellous discovery, or the gradual growing to necessity of a character's or a scene's demands, to pull you along and make you forget everything in a moment's magic.[102]

Over the weeks, Wiebe kept notes of the best work, typed them up each night and, along with Thompson, offered suggestions and alternatives for the characterisations of the historical figures—in particular, Crowfoot and Princess Louise; Ted Johns did his own research on William Aberhart. Like Wylie, Wiebe actually wrote only one scene of his own. This was Crowfoot's signing of the treaty (Act 3, scene 1), structured theatrically as an enactment similar to "The Tavern" scene in *1837*. Wylie eventually wrote "Everymin," the parody of a morality play which ends Act 1 of *Horsburgh*; it's an episode in which she finally satisfied some of her anxieties about the quality of language. Unlike Wiebe, unfortunately, she was not given the opportunity to go away and structure the play. However, without Wiebe's guidance in *Far As the Eye Can See*, the five developing story lines could never have been sustained so ambitiously.

According to Passe Muraille's usual way, the success of the creative process depended on how much personal reference and fluency the actors could bring to the material they were developing. Two members of the initial jamming sessions, Connie Kaldor and Layne Coleman, came from the prairies. Kaldor developed roles such as Louise Lucas and the Bessborough Hotel in *The West Show* while Coleman, among his other roles, created the bewildered country fellow who comes to the big city in *If You're So Good, Why Are You in Saskatoon?* While David Fox and Janet Amos could draw on their experience in *The West Show* and *The Farm Show*, they also worked from a local base during the Edmonton phase of the rehearsal process. Amos met the model for her character at the Dodds/Round Hill Agricultural Protective Society while Wiebe introduced David Fox to an old Polish farmer living near Strawberry Creek. The latter's accent and gestures helped the actor acquire specificity in his role as Anton Kalicz.

When Alberta actor Dennis Robinson—a key collective performer in Theatre Network's *Two Miles Off: Elnora Sunrise with a Twist of Lemon* during the previous season—joined the company in Edmonton, he was further able to develop the contrasting roles of Joe Nussbaumer, the hot-headed would-be activist, and Orest Kusnick, the wry owner of the local cafe. With the exception of Eric Peterson, who was assigned to develop further the role of John Siemens (the idealistic Mennonite engineer for Calgary Power, who seems to echo something of Wiebe as well), the remaining members of the cast were hired as performers in roles that the collective had already established.

While there is some multiple characterization, the doubling in this play occurs more as a matter of expedience than according to Theatre Passe Muraille's usual custom of emphasizing performance. On this occasion, the theatricality comes largely from Wiebe's mythic dimension, embodied in the historical fantasy of "The Regal Dead." This concerns three lively ghosts from Alberta's past: Chief Crowfoot, William Aberhart and Princess Louise Caroline Alberta (after whom the province was named). That these characters should collectively be designated "regal" makes its own witty Albertan point. That's especially true when the then current premier of the province—very much alive—joins this incongruous combination at the end of the play as the *deus ex machina*. In an ambiguous way, he saves the day for the farmers.

Far As the Eye Can See differs from both *The West Show* and *1837: The Farmers' Revolt* in its treatment of history as fable. *The West Show* juxtaposes independent scenes of past and present while *1837: The Farmers' Revolt*, although set in the past, mythologizes that past in light of the present. In a reverse procedure, *Far As the Eye Can See* interprets present events in light of the past. Perhaps only Albertans can fully appreciate the satiric connections the play makes between the era of William Aberhart and the Conservative regime of Peter Lougheed. The former initiated 40 long years of Social Credit government while the latter campaigned and won power in 1971 on a platform of change—according to one political critic, "not of policies, but of style."[103]

In its contemporary action, the play also offers a more comprehensive and sustained example of the causes and effects of collective action than did the earlier plays. The scene of the strategy debate in the Mitchell living room in *Far As the Eye Can See* is developed much more fully than, for example, the "Tractor Demonstration" scene in *The West Show*, to which it alludes. The characters are fictional and, at this level of action, the style is mimetic rather than presentational, allowing also for considerable embroidery of the Protective Society's procedures for saving their land from strip mining. This translates into family conflict in the case of Anton Kalicz, his urbanized son Wadu (Walter), and his ex-hippy granddaughter, Caroline. It also develops into a problematic love affair between Caroline and the young Calgary Power engineer, John Siemens.

In a lesser degree of emphasis, the story lines also focus on differences of opinion between Betty Mitchell and her quizzical husband Roger, and between Betty and representative Round Hill townspeople. Each of the Regal Dead is allowed to intervene once in these complications—that is, "to shoot one arrow" (108) at the contemporary character of choice. Over the course of the play, the Regal Dead also develop a certain collective dynamic as a quibbling trio with concrete character identities in their own right. This provides a largely comic level of debate to the play, their points of conflict with each other illuminating the naturalistic conflicts they are witnessing and attempting to influence.

The thematic function of the Regal Dead is to broaden the specific case by mythologizing the changing relationships of succeeding generations to the land. Aberhart speaks succinctly of this to Crowfoot, almost as if in fulfillment of divine will: "These Albertans, in 1977, will develop the treasures *under* the earth, as my generation reaped them *from* the earth, as you people gathered them *upon* the earth" (131, emphasis in original). That the latest phase of history need not be an "inevitability" is the political point of a play whose essential subject is conservation, both of land and a way of life that's still possible.

Nevertheless, the relevance of the Indian position to the present—as represented by the great Blackfoot chief who "gave this earth away" (130) and received a lifetime pass on the CPR for his cooperation—at first seems little more than an historical gesture. Certainly, Crowfoot's act of intervention in the contemporary scene is the most tenuous dramatically. The link to Caroline is through geographical place. He approaches her as she is busily shedding her faddish radicalism and rediscovering her childhood playground on her grandfather's farm. This is the place by the Battle River where Crowfoot's people once engaged in conflict with their traditional enemies and later died by the scores in battles with the white man's diseases. His intervention, the first of the play, merely warns her that to remain at her grandfather's place will bring her emotional pain. But the narrative context for this—her star-crossed love affair with John—is not specifically established yet.

As the play progresses, however, Crowfoot functions effectively in the role of cynic on the subject of the white man's seemingly endless propensity for destruction and self-destruction (110). In one of his lighter moments, of which he has several, he laughs uproariously at the thought of anyone, least of all a woman, thinking she can get the better of the CPR (116). His is the irony of hindsight, reaching its peak at a dramatically crucial point in the present-time action—just after Aberhart has somewhat dishonourably inveigled old Anton to sell his land. To counter the Princess's outrage at the sell-out, Aberhart, now angry at her superior manner, challenges Crowfoot to "tell the Princess Louise Caroline Alberta how you sold out" (148). In the re-enactment of the signing of Treaty No. 6, Crowfoot shows how, exactly 100 years before, he was caught in the dilemma of either submission or starvation of his people. If he expects the worst now, it is because he knows all about relegation to a blanket-size patch of land—as Anton will discover if he sells.

Over the course of the play, there is an ironic blurring of distinctions in the terms applied to land negotiation—such as "giving away," "selling out," and "expropriation." Crowfoot's "sell-out" is a matter of point of view; in Betty Mitchell's parlance of the present time, treaty signing looks remarkably like an early model for "expropriation" (cf. 152).

Princess Louise Caroline Alberta is a light-hearted reminder of Alberta's colonial past. Like Lady Backwash of *1837: The Farmers' Revolt*, she is the perennial 19th-century lady traveller—in this case, to a part of the country that in real life she never actually saw. She is a member of the not-uncommon class of imperialist who, like her "Great White Mother," wields charismatic power from afar. In contrast to Lady Backwash, however, the Princess is less a caricature than an escaped heroine from drawing room comedy. Her chief characteristic is her altruistic romantic sensibility. Sketch-pad in hand, she gushes about the beauty of nature and hates the thought of Alberta turning into another slag heap like Wales.

Instead of an imperialistic heavy-weight, she is chiefly a comic foil to the loquacious William Aberhart, her self-congratulatory tour-guide of scenes of his former triumphs. Her link to the present is fanciful, but as an individual personality she is on the "right" side, finding Aberhart's pompous sermonizing tedious and his intervention in Anton's affairs disgraceful. Thus, the Princess develops into the appropriate person to sustain the increasingly disheartened Betty Mitchell in her fight to save the land. Her little *exemplum* about the challenge and discouragement of learning a difficult piece of music, which she demonstrates charmingly on the piano, has no direct bearing on the issue. However, it shows an engaging quick-wittedness, designed as much to put the materialistic Aberhart in his place as it is to encourage Betty to maintain the fight to prevent "the only thing left with my name" from becoming "a running sore of a strip mine!" (155)

More directly crucial to the strip-mining issue itself, and the best-rooted in particular history, is Aberhart's influence on Anton. The stubborn old widower is under pressure from two directions: his granddaughter's impetuous desire to go back to the land, and his son's eye for a good profit. There is also the third matter of his own age and loneliness (he talks a lot to his deceased wife, Anna), unassuaged by Caroline's offer to carry on the family tradition. In the characterization of Aberhart, the Theatre Passe Muraille collective, with special credit to Ted Johns, managed to create a genuinely comic and folkloric hero/politician out of the ideological, bible-thumping, apocalyptic tradition of historical memory. William almost always speaks in the prescient manner of the political orator (based on Johns' study of extant recordings).

Old Anton, the one-time immigrant miner, cannot forget the stirring radio voice that once gave him "the sign" to put the Hillcrest Mine disaster behind him (an important topic in Wiebe's fiction), to acquire his own land, and to keep it "free from the mortgages and chattels and encumbrances of 50 bigshots that live in the east!" (134) The new sign, Aberhart spuriously argues, is the coal a few feet under his hard-won land. The Aberhart characterization is appropriately double-edged. On the one hand, it reminds the audience of Depression poverty, when Aberhart's evangelical philosophy of progress seemed crucial to the well-being of the province. On the other hand, it parodies the manipulative nature of the political demagoguery he came to represent.

The better spokesman for progress in the context of the present is the unexpectedly humane young engineer, John Siemens, with his private poetic vision of contemporary industrial prosperity and the necessary power to make it possible (138-139). Through his advocacy, the issue itself becomes double-edged. The rocky and rather overly extended love affair between Caroline and John is an attempt to personalize the complexity of a genuine conflict between concerns for conservation and the broader principles of social and economic vision. But, if Aberhart is any example, how principled are politicians when concerns of public well-being are left in their hands? At the end, the farmers and their prime lands are spared through the cartoonish intervention of Aberhart's "chip off the old block," Premier Peter Lougheed, who descends like an icon in a large shiny unused coal scoop to save the day—for the time being. In the words of the stage directions: "Nothing human has been resolved by this mechanical statement" (171)—neither the farmers' sense of security, not the general need for power and employment, nor (least of all) the love affair of John and Caroline.

Yet without the efforts of the Protection Society to get an informed opinion on the current prognosis for eventual reclamation, the government would not have intervened, even for the time being. It is well enough to note, with William Thorsell, the anomaly of an audience won over (emotionally at least) to the side of the "comfortable individual capitalist defending his private interest against the wealthy corporate capitalist speaking for the public good."[104] But however characteristically Albertan these politics may be, the emphasis of the play is elsewhere. It's the idea that a small group of citizens could take on the impersonal, virtually one-party monolith and actually make itself heard. Edmonton audiences applauded this with standing ovations. That a Toronto reviewer should see the ending as dribbling "into a giggle" with the arrival of Lougheed in his coal scoop from on high[105] misses the point, which the local audience grasped instantly. In the choice of a theatrical rather than a polemical ending, the play gives its original audiences a rare opportunity for spontaneous laughter at the expense of their own politician, even as it cautions vigilance for the next round.

The localism implied here—what Thompson in an earlier context called "particularism" (as opposed to "regionalism")[106]—is, of course, a key factor in Theatre Passe Muraille's collective creations of the 1970s. Paradoxically, whatever extended audience appeal the plays have enjoyed comes first of all from the company's recognition, through both content and performance style, of its first audience. The main distinctions to be drawn between Theatre Passe Muraille's collective creations of the period and conventionally developed plays are more than multiple authorship and presentational structures. Primarily, they lie in the foregrounding of the actors as performers who are establishing direct lines of communication with an identified audience that had little experience of a genuinely indigenous Canadian theatre.

Passe Muraille's collectives became increasingly adept in their audience strategies from *The Farm Show* onward. In that play and in *The West Show*, audiences are invited to share a sense of the actors' discovery of the material through their theatrical transformation of that material. In *1837: The Farmers' Revolt*, the actors encounter the audience dialectically with their discoveries. The earlier methods of literally invading the audience, in *Doukhobors* as adversaries and in *Buffalo Jump* as friends, were simpler and more obvious. In *Them Donnellys*, in contrast to *The Death of the Donnellys* in its narrative dimension, the collective process of creative storytelling is shared openly through the transformational elements in acting and scene depiction.

Structurally speaking, *Far As the Eye Can See* steps back from its audience, the presentational performance style translating into what Alan Filewod describes as the "rhetorical conceit" of the Regal Dead.[107] This introduces the new element of "fantasy" into Thompson's work. Fantasy was manifested further in Theatre Passe Muraille's interpretation of Robert Kroetsch's *The Studhorse Man* (1981), in the commissioning of Michael Ondaatje's stage version of his novel, *Coming Through Slaughter* (1980), and more important to this present study, in Thompson's work with Maria Campbell and Linda Griffiths on *Jessica* (1982). As an audience strategy in *Far As the Eye Can See*, the impact of the Regal Dead on its local, essentially urban, audience is strong (as indicated above) because of its irreverent overview of the politics of place, then and now. Theatre Passe Muraille is the first to give Aberhart a theatrical life of any consequence, demystifying a local hero as it were.[108]

During his years at Theatre Passe Muraille, every collective creation was a new project for Thompson and in some way a new challenge. Neither he nor the actors who worked with him most frequently wanted simply to repeat themselves. Although there are some recurring techniques in the plays chosen for discussion here, the context and scenic purpose shift. There is the tavern re-enactment scene in *1837: The Farmers' Revolt*, for example, and the treaty-signing re-enactment in *Far As the Eye Can See*; the machine mime in *The Farm Show* and *The West Show* and, of course, transformational acting at all levels of mimicry, from portraiture to animate and inanimate objects. But gifted improvisers such as David Fox, Janet Amos, Anne Anglin, Eric Peterson and Ted Johns could not remain satisfied with the simple structure of juxtaposed scenes of *The Farm Show*. That's why, for example, they were interested in the more formalized experiment with set and properties of *The West Show*.

Though still a collage of discontinuous episodes, the latter play

128 *Playwrights of Collective Creation*

also marks a shift within its individual sections from the portraiture in the community collectives of the period to the dramatization of story scenarios. This calls for closer attention to succinct and sustained character-building. Such a progression can be observed in the work of some of the individual performers in these plays. Take, for example, Janet Amos' improvisational growth from Jean Lobb to Madame Tourond to Betty Mitchell; or David Fox's from Les Jarvis to Tom Sukanen to Anton Kalicz. However, at the time of *Them Donnellys*—in effect, a chronologically ordered collage—character is primarily defined scenically through physical image or gesture: for example, in Will's violent spinning "like a dervish" at the Ryder wedding, or the wrathful Grouchie, burning stick in hand, simultaneously describing and responding to the destruction of his barn.

The two strong improvisers of character roles, who emerged from the Theatre Passe Muraille experience as one-man performers in separately developed works, are Eric Peterson and Ted Johns. Peterson's chameleon-like performance skills first gained attention when he joined the second collective for *1837: The Farmers' Revolt* and, under Thompson's directorial guidance, further developed the character of Mackenzie.[109] His subsequent roles encompassed a rich variety: for example, Grouchie Ryder in *Them Donnellys*, Sam Reimer in *The West Show*, the Rev. Jimmy Hamilton in *The Horsburgh Scandal*, and *John Hornby* in Passe Muraille's collective of that title (directed in 1976 by David Fox). All of these helped prepare him for his best-known collaboration with John Gray—*Billy Bishop Goes to War*. Although Ted Johns has written straight dramatic comedy—for example, *Garrison's Garage* for the Blyth Festival in 1984—he has also specialized in one-man plays that he performs. These include the ever popular *Naked on the North Shore* and *The School Show* (1978), which was also performed at Blyth. The latter is a virtuoso piece with seven characters in full scenic development.

In the trial-and-error improvisational procedures of collective playmaking, the creative energy emerges largely from what Linda Griffiths called the "bouncing off" process[110] that occurs among actors as well as between actors and director or writer. Often, the most fruitful catalysts at Theatre Passe Muraille were the spontaneous physical impulses. For example, Rudy Wiebe tells of an early rehearsal in Paul Thompson's house of the arm-wrestling scene between old Anton and his son. During this scene, Connie Kaldor suddenly ran into the kitchen and returned as Caroline, jug of water in hand, which she then threw over Wadu to ensure that her grandfather wins (91, 121). Yet spontaneity can also fade away in the continuing work despite starting out as a good idea. An example is the Davis scene of *1837* (with all of its final improvisational elements). According to Salutin's account, this was continually stressful for actor Miles Potter. But the scene finally worked when, on impulse, Thompson turned it over to Janet Amos (198). Then there are the many efforts and attempts that never found their way into the play at all, as Don Kerr describes after his three-day attendance at rehearsals for *The West Show*.[111]

In the plays analyzed, a general pattern of growth towards more complex structures is observed. But one has to be cautious about seeing this as a conscious development towards the collective creation of a literary text, since theatre—not a text for theatre—is the aim. The formal strength and originality of the collective creations of Thompson and Theatre Passe Muraille in the 1970s—as theatre pieces and incidentally as texts—lie primarily in their inventive explorations of performance. This is particularly true where an expressive physical image or metaphor reflects both the source and the performance core of the scene. This happens in scenes such as "The Head" and "The Dummy" in *1837: The Farmers' Revolt*, "Picture Frame" and "Jean Lobb" (imaginary photograph album in hand) in *The Farm Show*, to name only a few. Predictably, the collective shows are often least durable when they aspire to conventional representationalism in a sustained way: for example, the love life of Caroline Kalicz or the discord between mother and daughter in *The Horsburgh Scandal*. However, one of the great virtues of these plays—as recently noted by Ronald Bryden—is their infusion of sheer entertainment value into the national and regional themes of modern Canadian drama.[112]

The remainder of this study comprises an investigation of the direct and indirect influences of Theatre Passe Muraille on three participants in the company who developed as individual playwrights: writer Rick Salutin, composer John Gray, and actor Linda Griffiths. In his association with *1837*, Rick Salutin found a continuing vehicle in the theatre for what he considered important Canadian social, political and cultural themes. As well, he has left his mark as a dramaturge, working with two Newfoundland companies in developing their own collective plays. John Gray, beginning with his collaboration with Eric Peterson, has become a noted composer of musical plays. Linda Griffiths, whose collective work began at 25th Street Theatre and continued under Thompson's tutelage at Theatre Passe Muraille, is perhaps the one performer/playwright who has adhered most closely to the collective playmaking process in her plays. Thompson worked closely with her on the two projects he actually suggested: *Maggie & Pierre* (1979) and *Jessica* (1982). The latter is a play that began as a collective creation. A study of Griffiths' work, therefore, continues in some measure the study of Thompson's.

Fiona McMurran and John Jarvis in a scene from Theatre Passe Muraille's revival of *Les Canadiens* (1978), directed by Miles Potter. Photo: Theatre Passe Muraille.

Chapter Three
Rick Salutin: Playwright of Occasion

As a writer in the theatre of the 1970s and early 1980s, journalist, editor and union organizer, Rick Salutin, might be described as a playwright of occasion, especially if one applies the phrase in the broadest possible terms. Salutin himself recently identified "occasional theatre" as that which is concerned with "what's going on here and now," as distinct from mainstream theatre's preoccupation with "the eternal verities." The first is topical, directly addressing a particular audience that does not usually go to the theatre about issues involving their own lives or commitments. The other serves a bourgeois audience whose tastes in theatre, he thinks, eschew "a real confrontation with the present; because there is so little in it for them."

The context of these remarks is a 1987 commentary on a number of "occasional" performances about current issues in which he had lately participated either as writer or audience—occasions such as a strike benefit for Eaton's employees or the "Against Free Trade Review."[1] In alluding to the "occasion" of a particular audience for which such theatre is performed, he rather wistfully recalled Paul Thompson's first important step with *The Farm Show*, now more than 15 years past. In that collective creation, Thompson established "intense relations between actors and audience" and so defined the political quality of that play even "though it has no explicit politics at all."[2] He also recalled the spontaneous political impact of *1837*. The latter play, as previously discussed, demonstrates how Salutin and Theatre Passe Muraille were able to turn historical events into a living occasion for audiences by elaborating on popular entertainment techniques for making past events timely.

The playwright's remarks, outlined here, evoke the timely and interactive elements that, in his view, have now been marginalized to "occasional theatre." But he neglects to mention that, in earlier days, they were also marginalized by and large to the "alternative theatre" in which he was an active force and which represented a different effort for a time towards the creation of a different kind of Canadian mainstream. This suggests that, to some degree, Salutin has always been a playwright of occasion in one or more of the implications of the term—either in helping to turn a theatrical event into a political occasion for its audience (as in *1837: The Farmers' Revolt*) or in responding through his later plays to topical events.

In tracing the development of his thinking about *Les Canadiens*, for example, Salutin reveals how important the occasion of the election victory of the *Parti Québecois* on November 15, 1976 became in the final shaping of that play.[3] In a general way, his 1981 *Nathan Cohen: A Review* also has a context in that same occasion, to the degree that both the new play and the second act of *Les Canadiens* explore matters concerning the uncertainties and confusions of English-Canadian cultural identity raised at the time by the power shifts within Quebec. His later full-length work, *S: Portrait of a Spy*, an adaptation in collaboration with Ian Adams of the latter's controversial novel, still had a certain topical relevance in 1984. After years of investigation into RCMP wrong-doing, the federal government instigated its new civilian secret service (CSIS).

Finally, Salutin is also a playwright of occasion in one further sense: his work for the stage has often been a response to invitations to participate in projects initiated by certain theatre companies—that is, before the so-called bourgeois evasions he sees in recent Canadian theatre took precedence over timely social drama.

After *1837: The Farmers' Revolt*, Salutin continued to work from time to time on collective projects. *The Adventures of an Immigrant* with Thompson and Theatre Passe Muraille in 1974 was an improvisation on varieties of Toronto's immigrant experience. The production was taken to various ethnic halls and performed on one occasion in a Toronto streetcar.[4] The following year, Salutin joined Chris Brookes and the Mummers Troupe in St. John's to participate in the collective creation of *IWA: The Newfoundland Loggers' Strike of 1959*. This company made its first appearance in Toronto in June 1975 with *Buchans: A Company Town*. Only a few weeks previously, Salutin had donated the prize money from the second-place Chalmers Award won by *1837: The Farmers' Revolt* to the Mummers Troupe. As a result of his association with *IWA*, Donna Butt later sought his participation as collaborating writer for Rising Tide Theatre's *Joey* in 1981.

Salutin also wrote four scripted plays in the intervening years. The first was a 17th-century incident in Turkey, *The False Messiah*, premiered in March 1975 and subsequently revised. At the time, reviewer Urjo Kareda suggested "the actors were making it up as they went along."[5] The other scripts, all on important Canadian themes, are the subject of discussion here: the highly successful *Les Canadiens* in 1977—a commission from Centaur Theatre at the suggestion of director Guy Sprung for "a show about the French and English in Montreal using the Montreal Canadiens as a metaphor;"[6] the independently initiated work, *Nathan Cohen: A Review*, directed by Paul Thompson at Theatre Passe Muraille at the beginning of 1981; and the *S: Portrait of a Spy* collaboration with Adams, premiered in 1984 at The Great Canadian Theatre Company in Ottawa under the direction of Patrick McDonald.

For Salutin, both playwriting and theatre in performance are social experiences. He has always been involved in some sort of collaborative relationship during the playmaking or playwriting process, as the case may be. For *1837: The Farmers' Revolt* and similarly for *IWA*, he was a member of a collective. In the former, he made key contributions in theme, research, some on-site writing, and the final preparation of the text for publication. For *IWA*, certain elements that concerned him at the time in the structuring and dramatization processes of collective documentary are evident in the play. For *Joey*, he was "writing consultant," described on the typescript of the play as collaborator with the acting collective.[7]

For *Les Canadiens*, there was a key collaboration between Salutin and the Canadiens' goalie of the time, acknowledged in the playful authorial designation in the published text as "assist: Ken Dryden" and in the introductory commentary by both Salutin and Dryden. Although Salutin was responsible for writing the play, Dryden was either the source or the catalyst for much of the contemporary material that went into the first version. He provided the playwright with valuable insights and personal contacts during Salutin's research as well as the ideas for certain scenes (Introduction 16-19). While *Les Canadiens* at the Centaur was not a collective creation in the same sense as *1837: The Farmers' Revolt*, director Guy Sprung and his actors made substantial contributions during the rehearsal process from which the first version of the play evolved.[8] Salutin had originally written *Nathan Cohen: A Review* as a monodrama. But on the advice of its director Paul Thompson, he changed it into a multi-character play for four actors. For *S: Portrait of a Spy*, co-authors Salutin and Ian Adams divided the writing tasks.

Similar to the collective creations I have already discussed in this study, my emphasis here is on the product of creative effort rather than on the exact origin of detail—that is, beyond the point of public statement by those engaged in the process. Fortunately, Salutin himself has made a number of important remarks and critical points in his essays and interviews, which can often be applied to the work in which he has been engaged. Admittedly, the nature of much of his collaborative work creates certain difficulties in formulating an overview of his personal achievement.

However, Salutin's individuality as a playwright is most clearly identifiable in two general ways: through his polemic on nationalistic and political themes, and through the metaphoric theatrical style with which he strives to temper his polemic dialectically. The latter is the style he came to understand primarily through his experience with Theatre Passe Muraille on *1837: The Farmers' Revolt*. While the balance between these elements is not always achieved, the recognition of the need for balance reflects (in his three most important plays) a quality of social passion and insight rare among Canadian dramatists of the contemporary period. His participation in the two Newfoundland collective projects, although secondary to his own growth as a playwright, provides a useful perspective on the strengths and limitations of the collective process. Just as useful are his general, if controversial, comments on the documentary postulations that he sees informing that playmaking mode.

1. *Les Canadiens*

The first version of *Les Canadiens* premiered on February 10, 1977. The play combines the elements of occasion which identify Salutin's work: the occasion of a particular audience—the minority English-speaking audience of Montreal, and the repeated occasion of a popular event—here a hockey game. The latter provides an extended sports metaphor that renders the historical events politically relevant to the Quebec election. It's hockey as history and history as hockey. Some months later, *Les Canadiens* was revised extensively for the anglophone audience of Toronto—and by extension the rest of Canada. In this version, Salutin relates the implications of the separatist election victory to the contemporary uncertainties and confusions of English-Canadian political and cultural identity.

In his introduction to the published (revised) version, Salutin recounts how *Les Canadiens* was inspired initially by sports writer Red Fisher's remark that "ever since the Plains of Abraham, the French people have been number two—but on the ice, they're number one" (12). This led the playwright to combine Quebec's hockey story (as represented by the history of its most famous team) with his perception of the *Québecois* as a subjugated people. His thesis is that popular identification with *les Canadiens* kept the subliminal nationalist spirit alive. Although the play seems to be about a hockey team, *Les Canadiens* is also about the "occupation" of Quebec since 1759, the historical resentments against oppression and exploitation (especially in wartime), and the culmination of the Quiet Revolution in the *Parti Québecois* election victory of November 15, 1976. Now, dissent need be sublimated no longer in hockey by its fans—although, paradoxically, this was never the case for the team itself.

In a thematically and structurally sustained way, *Les Canadiens* marks an advance on the popular performance techniques employed to political purpose in *1837*. Whereas the latter, particularly in Act 1, draws randomly on popular entertainment devices of several kinds (ventriloquism, magic show, satiric mime, etc.), *Les Canadiens* relies entirely on the one expanding stage metaphor of the highly theatrical game of hockey. As Mary Jane Miller points out, this game is "drawn from our own popular culture," not borrowed from another. Virtually the whole play is set in or about the arena—even the scene about the battle of the Plains of Abraham near the beginning of the play. The opening hockey foray transforms quickly into times past with the game clock pausing at 17:59. In a novel revival of Living Newspaper technique, the message board reads, "The Conquerors and the Conquered."

The episodes of the first act, described in the introduction as "the myth of *les Canadiens*" (21), end climactically with Montreal's hockey riot of 1955. This was a protest against NHL president Clarence Campbell's decision to suspend Maurice "Rocket" Richard for fighting on the ice. The famous uproar is seen here as the heralding of the so-called Quiet Revolution, indicated as such by the fast forwarding of the game clock and message board through subsequent disturbances of the 1960s. A peak event is the October Crisis of 1970 and the proclamation of the War Measures Act. The play's second act, covering election day, concludes with "the demythologization of *les Canadiens* and their replacement by the reality of 'just a hockey team' " (21). The hockey myth explodes on that evening with the team's astonished realization that, for the first time, their fans are indifferent to the game and are totally absorbed in the election results flashing on the message board. Political action has at last replaced the surrogate tradition of hockey as Quebec's true nationalist enterprise.

The model of collective creation of the Passe Muraille type is evident not only in the playwright's reliance on the discovery and use (with the help of Ken Dryden) of the "found" material of interviews and first-hand observation but also in aiming to address a specific audience in particular ways. In the first production, the Montreal audiences of the city's anglophone minority were invited to a satirical encounter with the prejudices of their own tradition through the appeal of a play about their home-town hockey team. However at the Centaur, according to one reviewer, the play was largely successful "as a sentimental tribute to hockey's most illustrious team." The success was a response to the way Guy Sprung's production brought the familiar atmosphere of the Forum to the stage:

> The foot-stomping and hand-clapping began even before the gum-chewing actors, suited up in the red jerseys and hockey gear, glided onto the stage. When the familiar organ strains of the national anthem began, several people stood up as if they were at the Montreal Forum and one woman was heard to say, "This is the part of the game I resent the most."[9]

Those who noticed that it was more than just a play about hockey pointed to Salutin's limited Torontonian understanding of Quebec's English community, which was "caricatured as totally elite," as a definite weakness in the work.[10]

For Salutin, the play's pro-French-Canadian nationalism was its more important element at the time. But he put the matter differently in his account of the subsequent rewriting undertaken in the following year for George Luscombe's Toronto Workshop Productions, on which the published play is based (Introduction 22). He decided that his perspective in the first version "was not directly useful" to English audiences in Quebec, given the pressure of "their particular problem, which is becoming a minority" (22). He therefore determined to cast a wider net, to explain Quebec to the rest of English-speaking Canada (at least as represented by Toronto). In this revision was the ambitious hope that the play would provide "an opportunity...to re-think what kind of country *we* want—with or without Quebec—and in the urgency of crisis to re-shape what is obsolete or undesirable" (23). Therefore in its revised form, the play may be seen as a serious attempt at political encounter with the English-Canadian community of Canada at large.

His success at this is strongest in Act 1, which is a satirical investigation of nearly 200 years of history. The material is presented in a variation of the documentary style that Salutin disliked in principle yet acknowledges he is using here (22). In keeping with the hockey setting, the game clock and message board establish the chronology of each scene. The messages, which usually read like contemporary headlines, often provide ironic comment on the foreground action and sometimes provide information about the current state of the country (see 76). This device also reinforces certain minor themes—for example, economic class struggle. Similar to documentary drama and the collective creation that derives from it, the act is structured episodically, each scene shaped to make its own specific point by combining the history of Quebec with that of its hockey team. The historical characters, including players and owners, are identified by name and the actors perform their multiple roles in accord with the public personalities whom history (and legend) remembers. The game itself is portrayed on stage in a stylized way, with actors on roller skates demonstrating the familiar playing style of *les Canadiens*.

From this semi-documentary approach, Salutin's mythic interpretation takes over in inventive ways. What is offered as fact paradoxically becomes an expression of the political myth concerning the fanatical dedication of *les Canadiens* to winning the game; likewise the fans, for whom the team has become a symbolic release for suppressed nationalist feelings. Although the tone is essentially comic, the historical scenes about the hockey club are slightly fictionalized to conform to the pattern of struggle between conquered and conquerors, oppressed and oppressors. This method counterpoints the *Québecois* myth of hockey with English-Canadian myths of conquest. Here, Salutin draws on collective creation's fondness for the irreverence of popular theatre techniques.[11] Two of English Canada's national heroes, Wolfe and Macdonald, are burlesqued while Orangeman bigotry is also targeted. Wolfe, in imperious condescension to the Canadian "peasant," hears out his Gray's "Elegy" and gracefully assents to painter Benjamin West's death-scene pose (31-32). Macdonald builds his nation through "foreign" railway deals and national unity through a hanging (39, 45).

The counterpointing myth of French defeat and English oppression is established by the recurring figures of the Woman and her Son. At the beginning, she is the wife of the habitant farmer who shoots Wolfe. Wounded himself, the farmer dies in a mischievous parody of Wolfe's poetic leanings by reciting the lines written on the Forum's dressing-room wall from McCrae's "In Flanders Fields": "To you from failing hands we throw the torch." As the farmer tosses his rifle to his son, it magically transforms into a hockey stick (36). For a long time afterwards, the Woman as mother continues to nag the boy to mind the farm, go to church, and go to school rather than spending his life at the hockey rink. She is a survivor, not a dreamer. Meanwhile, he not only invents the game of ice hockey but also transforms into a succession of early NHL stars. This is signified by the ritual passing of the hockey stick.

According to Mary Jane Miller's careful comparison of the two versions of *Les Canadiens*, the Woman figure is considerably strengthened in the published work, eventually becoming "the play's chief metaphor for the growth of political awareness in Quebec."[12] But first, she turns into a poor urban mother whose small son is glued to hockey broadcasts on the radio when he should be sleeping. Although she is always resentful of the English oppressor at whatever historical moment her scenes are occurring, she is slow to accept the symbolic place of hockey in their lives. Finally, not only does her resistance disappear but she also becomes an ardent fan, spitting out her resentments at games with the best of them (i.e., anglophones) and bursting into triumphant song over the splendour of the Rocket's scoring record.

In his revisions of the second act, Salutin shifts ostensibly from the "documentary" elements established for myth-making purposes in Act 1 to what he identifies in his introduction as "a more traditionally 'dramatic' mode: unity around a central character and his 'problem.' " While the original Act 2 emphasized the specifics of the contemporary team familiar to the Montreal audience, Salutin now stressed what he calls "a more sculpted, fictionalized approach" (Intro 22). He uses this primarily as a polemical strategy for his encounter with English-speaking audiences over contemporary issues. Despite its fictionalization, this act is in some respects more of a conventional documentary than Act 1.

The most conspicuous revision occurs in the transformation of the real-life goalie Ken Dryden of the Centaur play into the fictional forward Dave Kirk. He provides a rather self-conscious voice for English-Canadian puzzlement and insecurity in the face of the new *Québecois* activism. Those members of the contemporary hockey club impersonated in the Centaur version become anonymous players in the revision.[13] Dryden's pre-game "goalie's nightmare" of being abandoned on the ice

Chapter Three: Rick Salutin   143

by his team becomes a kind of English-Canadian identity crisis as Kirk, the star forward, anxiously finds himself playing goal instead.[14]

The second act also provides for the re-entry of the Woman in several contemporary roles that provide a dramatic contrast to her suppressed resentments of Act 1. The Woman becomes an irate French teacher who is less than committed to the linguistic ineptitude of the class until she discovers belatedly that they belong to *les Canadiens*. In Kirk's nightmare, she changes successively into a familiar television personality, a *chanteuse*, and finally a man-eating version of the television chef, Madame Benoit. If witty caricature is the expression of cultural self-confidence, the nightmare women function aptly as symbols of the new spirit of aggressive Quebec womanhood in the 1970s. Near the end, when she appears once more in the same persona as in Act 1, she explains to the bewildered Kirk that at last "we stood up" after years of letting the team do it for them (173). The occasion of the election both informs and influences the myth while the anglophone and francophone roles of Act 1 have been reversed.

Nevertheless, in its somewhat belaboured effort to reach this point, the act falls into certain traps of what Salutin, in another context, has described negatively as the tape-recorder method of the documentary style.[15] For example, the opening scene is a rambling interview-style monologue by the retired Jean Beliveau, now working for Forum management. As if to authenticate the myth in Act 1 of every poor boy's dream, he first reminisces about his early successes in hockey, then chats about his community service, and finally shifts to recalling what it was like to play centre. There is a low-key documentary self-consciousness in the amiable chats that follow between a fictional Dave Kirk and guards, management, old-timers and other players. Essentially, it's a typical game day in the contemporary life of the team, with only a hint of tension in the mildly unsettling speculations about the impending election.

Intermittently, the pace quickens and the tone shifts to recall the collision course already threatening toward the end of Act 1. We see this threat, for example, in the broad comedy of the language lesson and again in the nightmare sequence, where the undefended goalie Kirk is under assault during a surrealistic reversal of the old myth of winners and losers. In the characterization of Kirk himself, however, the informational discussion mode of much of the act's dialogue offers too inviting an entry into didacticism.

Even though hockey still carries the play, the argument is reduced to a pious bleat of bewildered good intentions in its representation of the English-Canadian response to Quebec's resurgence. Two kinds of somewhat related points are attempted: the team's known federalist sympathies (Introduction 19) and the English-Canadian identity crisis as Salutin views it in the play. As represented by Kirk, anglophone Canada is anxious to please. In this hockey club, he tells the French teacher, the French and English players have always got along for the sake of the team, but now they realize it wasn't fair that the language was always English (129). In the threatening nightmare, he gains a moment of respite with his defensive insistence that "we do have our own voice and we use it just as well as you" (145). He is absurdly rewarded for this by the sound of Sylvia Tyson singing "Four Strong Winds," to which he makes the improbably feeble response:

> There it is. That's our voice. Close to nature. Quiet, but really caring. Sort of innocent, but really sincere. I knew we had it.... For a minute I almost believed we didn't have our own voice. It's so soft and hard to hear. (147)

Thankfully, the cultural cliché about Tyson is drowned out by a rousing *Québecois* nationalist song from Pauline Julien. In ideological assertion, Kirk is embarrassingly outclassed. The old sustaining myths of conquest have evaporated with little wit to replace them on that side of the debate in Act 2. Salutin is more effective in expressing aggressive rather than defensive positions.

Like Kirk, the team is also embarrassingly outclassed in the waking nightmare of the game. Indulging too easily in the polemics that the figure of hockey as politics invites, Salutin has the players stop the game at one point to make a unanimous pitch for federalism, summing up all the clichés of the Canadian nationalist argument, both the vaguely idealistic and the specifically economic (168). Most of these have already been mentioned throughout the act in various exchanges among the team members. That the team is the one living example "of French and English working together" is a tentative point in the pre-game discussion (154) and is offered again almost as tentatively in the last scene. Kirk encounters some kids playing a street hockey game of *les Canadiens* versus the Russians and, of course, winning on the international front. While Quebec no longer needs "more than just a hockey team," there is the hint of Canada's need of a sustaining myth (*les Canadiens*?) until the entire country also achieves the political maturity for which Quebec has become a model.[16]

The play works best, both politically and aesthetically, when its ideological clash of opposites is relatively free of dramatized didacticism. The strong populist images of oppressor and oppressed in the mythic Act 1 are not matched in the English-Canadian generalities of Act 2. Even in the climactic turning point of the hockey game on November 15, 1976, the diffuse polemics tend to diminish the dramatic impact. Salutin's point may be that telling caricature can only arise from a condition of cultural self-confidence, which is no longer present outside the *Québecois* jurisdiction; but in Act 2 of *Les Canadiens*, he is sometimes heavy-handed in showing it.

2. Nathan Cohen: A Review

Salutin's next individually written play—*Nathan Cohen: A Review*—premiered in January 1981. In it, Salutin found more specific ground for his exploration of the uncertainties and confusions of English-Canadian cultural identity by focusing on the growth of Canadian theatre as reflected in the criticism of the former drama critic of *The Toronto Star*, who died prematurely in 1971. For Salutin, the play marked a different dramaturgical direction by concentrating on a single historical character rather than on a cross-section of society as his vehicle of social enquiry. As in the characterization of Mackenzie in *1837*, he was also attempting historical rehabilitation—in this case, to explode the myth of "Nathan the Terrible."

Salutin admired Cohen because "he took culture absolutely seriously—as seriously as politics and railroads." Salutin was convinced that the critic "was very hard on Canadian playwrights because he believed they were absolutely essential to Canadian culture."[17] This admiration was not the popular view of Cohen during his lifetime. Many believed that he actually hated theatre and merely delighted in making personal attacks. His utter self-confidence in himself as Canada's most important drama critic was greeted with suspicion, and he was the subject of caricatures by Pierre Berton and Mordecai Richler.[18] Wayne Edmonstone's literary biography—*Nathan Cohen: The Making of a Critic* (1977)—was the first systematic effort to refute the opinion that Cohen "impeded the country's cultural development—or worse...chose to ignore its potential." For Edmonstone and for Salutin after him, such a view "wilfully disregards the reasoning behind Cohen's theatrical criticism, and ignores his early and almost fanatical dedication to the development of a distinctive Canadian culture."[19]

Salutin had begun with the idea of a one-man show. But discussions with Paul Thompson (who had already pushed the monodrama to new limits in the recent *Maggie & Pierre* with Linda Griffiths) led to a more varied approach when Thompson suggested adding other characters.[20] Thompson told an interviewer that the intention was not to present "a formal biography" but to "attempt to understand what has been happening in Canadian theatre over the years, as viewed through the eyes of one of the most outrageous characters in Canadian theatre history."[21] To effect this, three all-purpose actors—in addition to the main character—play multiple characters in the established manner of Passe Muraille's collective creations, including one performer as the younger Cohen of the first act.

Since the central conflict is between the critic's developing vision of an indigenous theatre and what actually unfolds on Canada's many stages, theatrical performance itself is the major structuring device of these episodes. The protagonist's ongoing debate with the theatre and its audiences develops as the controlling stage metaphor. This is cogent to Salutin's view of his protagonist's ironic dilemma in his later career. In effect, Cohen is represented as a star performer and is depicted as such in the second act of the play. As noted by Rosemary Sullivan, he becomes "the only discerning audience for his own act."[22]

The play is a "review" in the sense of a partisan retrospective survey, not a critique of the same order that Cohen himself practised, although the play lay itself open to snide speculations by some reviewers about how Cohen himself might have reviewed this work. It begins with the older Cohen's early arrival at a theatre in his capacity as a reviewer.[23] His legendary public persona is reproduced: the tall stout figure, flamboyantly draped in a black coat, cape-style, and sporting his self-admitted affectation, a cane. As he awaits the performance (in an upstage position facing "us," the actual audience of the play), he ruminates in a witty dramatic monologue about his procedures as a critic. Then he rummages through his pockets to find bits of earlier critical pronouncements (satirically geared to the many productions of *The Man of La Mancha* at the O'Keefe Centre in the 1960s) and finds himself settling back into the memories of his career unfolding on the stage before him.

At first, it is as if Cohen were watching "some 1940s-type naturalism" (47) in the actual play he has come to see and he occasionally comments accordingly. But as he starts to respond directly to the setting of his former days as English-language writer for the Yiddish Communist newspaper, the *Wochenblatt*, he begins to address the character of his younger self with helpful advice about the wording of his first theatre review. The unembarrassed identification of the older Cohen with the younger establishes an encouraging rather than critical tone, even though the memory device also sets up the potential for self-criticism.[24]

At this point, Salutin seems prepared to adopt either of two dramatic modes: Passe Muraille's characteristic theatricalizing of documentary material or the freer invention of a mimetic comedy of ideas. The latter is anticipated in the presentation of the young Cohen's debate with his ideologically oriented old editor, whose Jewish biases against "Canadian" culture are not far removed from those of most people of his day. The "1940s-type naturalism" is soon interrupted, however, by a Chagall-like folk scene. During the young man's tentative speculations—based on his own Cape Breton experience about the possibility of multicultural artistic expressions in Canada—the older Cohen temporarily switches his onstage memory from the newspaper scene to a comic anecdote about his Gaelic-speaking father, the only Jew in a Scottish community. As the act continues, the theatrical—as opposed to the mimetic—choice predominates.

Salutin uses other styles of popular entertainment, roughly appropriate to the period under scrutiny, to cover highlights from Cohen's reviewing days at the *Wochenblatt* and elsewhere. The revue format—the popular form of theatrical expression in Canada during the 1950s and ironically a genre Cohen found tiresome—provides snippets from some published reviews of the period, bound together in a song-and-dance routine. These include "Nathan's on the prowl," with the older Cohen as "audience" occasionally quoting himself from the floor. The best of these moments is the performance of a mini-sketch in which Hart House actors playing a scene from *Romeo and Juliet* are visibly shaken by the onstage remarks of the new young critic (64). An iconoclastic radio broadcast is also performed amusingly. In this, Cohen proclaims the need, with eager prompting from the older self, for indigenous Canadian playwrights instead of "claptrap from England and jazzed-up journalism from the States" (68). While the pastiche structure gives a theatrical immediacy to Cohen's apprenticeship years, the precise direction of Salutin's interest in Cohen's criticism is not particularly focused. In addition, the play's manner is sometimes an outright distraction from the substance—for example, in a Jehovah-like outburst of pontifical self-parody from the older Cohen at the end of the radio scene (69).

Not until nearly the conclusion of the act, in the first dramatic confrontation between the critic and a theatre practitioner, do we recognize what now appears to be Salutin's strongest emerging theme: Cohen's populist respect for audiences. Although this is only hinted at earlier, Cohen's essential irony will hinge on this theme. The scene, specified as a naturalistic episode of relaxed conversation at cocktail hour, is actually a dramatized debate between Cohen and Mavor Moore, based on an exchange of ideas published in 1950.[25] The critic defends the audience against the playwright/director's complaint about the chronic philistinism of the Canadian public, for whom culture means a "profile of a hockey player in *The Star Weekly*" (72).

In questioning the contemporary quality of actors, directors and designers, Cohen asserts the Canadian theatre's own responsibility to show "why" it should be preferred by the audience to what Moore describes as "third-rate Americans at the Royal Alex" (71). This recalls the radio broadcaster's expressed conviction for the need of Canadian plays to reflect the life and "native voices" (68) of that Canadian audience; or the impromptu aside when Cohen praises the theatre of Clifford Odets for its language: "The real speech of ordinary people—improved. The sights and sounds of everyday life, pushed beyond what they merely are, to what they can be. And should be" (69). This statement is not unlike Salutin's own argument against the "documentary style" of a later day.

In providing for a two-actor characterization in the first act, the memory device combines with the pastiche structure to establish ground rules for the performance metaphor developed specifically in Act 2. The first act identifies the older Cohen, although physically on the sidelines, as the central figure of the play while his younger self, as a product of memory, has yet to attain the authority of an autonomous centre-stage presence. Change is signalled symbolically at the end of the act when, in response to the impasse of the debate with Moore, the older Cohen declares "now is the time to mount the stage." This he does, proclaiming "the time of the critic." Consequently, he decides to monitor the fledgling theatre, to watchdog the crucial question "what kind of a theatre," and to guide the standards by which it must be judged (72-73).

In Act 2, Cohen "performs" his critical roles in a series of self-contained, largely comic confrontations with *his* audiences—artists and theatre-goers—who often respond unhappily to his pronouncements. For the most part, this is the more integrated view of Thompson's "outrageous" figure in action—the critic who is viewed popularly as an object of vituperation rather than the source of fruitful ideas. The act progresses from a lampoonish version of the last days of elitism in the Dominion Drama Festival, interrupted comically by Cohen's "plebian" Jewish declaration for new multicultural voices (76), to the play's closing encounter between the "star" critic and a young writer/director of an alternate theatre (whose play he had come to see and belatedly discovers that it has been postponed for a week).

At the last, only on this still unproven ground is Cohen appreciated as the one person who will take the young writer and his theatre seriously. Although this is a dramatically tentative moment, perhaps deliberately so, it points implicitly at the importance of the Cohen legacy to the indigenous theatre movements that were just beginning at the time of his death. To Don, the young writer, Cohen is not a "star" but a "hero." This is Salutin's way of hinting that Cohen's struggle to cultivate a serious audience for his pronouncements and judgements may not have been entirely in vain. But, like the ending of

Les Canadiens, he leaves the matter open for his own audience to ponder.

In between these two scenes are a number of more emphatic moments that convey the frustrations of a principled critic whose social sympathies and ideals are the backbone of his cultural vision of Canada's near future. In light of this, Cohen was often hard on modern American dramatists such as Eugene O'Neill and Arthur Miller, whose work was frequently seen and indiscriminantly admired on the Canadian stage, in either amateur or professional productions. One scene is a clever dramatization of a CBC talk from 1951 about what Cohen viewed as the distressing state of American drama—as illustrated by *Death of a Salesman*. A rendering of Linda Loman's defense of her husband at his graveside becomes an onstage debate between the text and the critic. In response to key speeches, he charges Willy with self-pity and resignation, then accuses American drama generally with failing to value struggle (79-81). A playful composite scene notes Cohen's comic struggle to resist the charms of the American musical by interspersing a medley of songs from several of them (including *Guys and Dolls* with its "Good Old Reliable Nathan") with sardonic pronouncements about "commodity" theatre and the sell-out to "speculators and draftsmen and critics" (83). He tries to demonstrate that Broadway should not be the model for the new Canadian theatre.

In the penultimate scene, Cohen interviews the latter-day Clifford Odets—once his ideal of a working-class voice, now sadly a poolside sell-out to Hollywood's movie industry. With cynical recognition, Odets observes that since the 1930s American theatre no longer has an engaged audience, but only critics who dictate what people see. Ironically for Cohen, but in a different manner, there are elements here that point to Canada as well. The promise of the Stratford Festival quickly dissipates for him into an empty theatrical flourish with no respect for language or meaning—another kind of "theatre as a commodity" (89). Similarly its audiences, ironically his own readers, are too easily impressed either by the cultural status of the event or by Shakespeare. This is nicely, if faintly condescendingly, revealed in a sketch about a Toronto family on a day-trip to Stratford. The mother is impressed by what Cohen condemns as all the wrong reasons; meanwhile, the father is more interested in the hockey news (an echo of Moore's point)—an honest reaction at least—but even he yields to the prestige of "one of the finest theatres on the continent" (88).

Thus, Cohen's committed effort to cultivating a thinking audience has failed by and large. He in turn becomes a target, though an imperturbable one, for the onslaught of narrow nationalist—Think Canadian!—sentiments that were found sometimes in the rising indigenous theatre of the 1960s (92-93). As adversary, he is dubiously celebrated as a "national institution," as a "star" spectacle. Like the Stratford Festival, he is attended but not understood. In a cheap shot by an irate actress from the cast of *Hair*, she complains that this could happen only in a country where "instead of culture we get somebody who talks about culture" (96).

Talk is not only a necessity but also a problem in this play. The scenes consisting of public talks or essays edited into dialogue represent the public rhetoric of the Cohen voice (the Cohen/Moore debate is the best example). Yet in the better moments, Salutin transforms this documentary material into an autonomous dramatic reality through pure invention (the DDF lampoon or the burlesque of the conventional family's visit to Stratford). While there are several clever theatrical devices for establishing the reality of the protagonist at the theatre, on radio or on television, they work best when they present him actively in an adversarial situation—for example, in his critique of *Death of a Salesman*, conducted as a coherent argument with the characters.

On occasion, however, either in dramatized scenes or in off-stage comments as in Act 1, there are patches of pontification which recall the initial conception as a one-man show. Examples include the stentorian apostrophe to an enlarged photograph of the Stratford Festival stage (89) and the immoderate denunciations of American theatre as in the scene referred to above (78). The theatricality, apt in many ways, allows for little tonal shading; and the "outrageous" manner, which is sometimes merely pompous didacticism, diverts attention from the serious substance of Salutin's defence of his "hero."

The decision to write about Cohen as a performer in a play of many styles succeeds as an often entertaining documentation of the considerable energies the critic devoted to the theatre in all its variety. It also provides an overview of the divided sense of purpose between excellence and less worthy aspirations in the Canadian theatre of Cohen's day. In a general way, that still speaks to us today on issues such as commodity theatre, neocolonial respect for foreign products, and narrow nationalistic bias. Nevertheless, it is disappointing that Salutin (like Edmonstone) avoids almost entirely the latter days of his protagonist's critical encounter with the rising alternative-theatre movements. Perhaps the playwright treads lightly for reasons of tact, but his choice to return to Odets for his penultimate scene interrupts the Canadian focus—hitherto the spine of the play—at a crucial point. The digression hints of Cohen's now-old-fashioned hopes, for which Odets and The Group Theatre of the 1930s are still his model. Yet if so, this is an unexplored irony. (Perhaps Salutin does not want to entertain the possibility that his hero might have failed his audience of readers instead of the other way around.) Thus, the reasonable expectation of some specific reference in the play to the new theatre of the post-centennial era, about which Cohen held controversial views, is also disappointed.

The more serious difficulties of this play, however, lie in the inevitable limitations of its structure as a vehicle of dramatically sustained exploration of Cohen's ideas about the theatre. It is tempting to suppose that Thompson and Salutin are in some measure at cross-purposes, that Theatre Passe Muraille's presentational style is both a service and disservice to the subject. From the director's point of view, the play is a "show," a playful theatrical pastiche of modern Toronto's theatre history with an emphasis on the "outrageousness" of the character who is reviewing it. For such a pastiche, collective creation's characteristically discontinuous structure and stylistic variety are more or less adequate. But from the playwright's point of view, this is the story of a critic who, in Salutin's words, "took culture absolutely seriously." More and more, the play becomes concerned about the collision of ideas between an impassioned proselytizer and his audience.

However, the play's episodic theatricality inhibits an integrated overview of the protagonist's philosophy of the theatre, although the dramatized scenes of debate go some way in countering that defect. Ultimately, *Nathan Cohen: A Review* leaves the full implications of its best insights unrealized. The extended theatrical conceit of the critic as *unwitting* star performer who becomes his own best audience is an intelligent amalgam of the elements of "show" and "idea." But this does not quell our innate suspicions of the "outrageous" media personality of the play who, almost from the beginning, seems to thrive on his own unwavering convictions. And the last scene, with the novice theatre director pronouncing him a "hero" rather than a "star," begs more than answers the question about the real nature of Cohen's influence, even on the simple level of judgements of good and bad.

The biographical basis of the play lends authority to Salutin's pro-Cohen position. But it does not challenge the common charges against the critic: that he wantonly destroyed careers, failed to understand the Stratford stage, aspired to the mandarin status of a New York critic and, worst of all, was contemptuous of the audience. The play functions only as a partisan counter-assertion to these charges. Docudrama has "its drawbacks," Salutin told an interviewer before the opening of his next play, "because your focus is split between the documentary background and establishing the characters."[26] Even as a generalization, the comment has an application to *Nathan Cohen: A Review*: the format does not provide for a critical probe that might also admit to the possibility of conflict or self-questioning in the protagonist himself, not to speak of the possible blind spots in his powers of discernment. For this dimension, if he had cared to pursue it, Salutin might have had to push further in the direction of "a more traditionally 'dramatic' mode: unity around a central character and his 'problem'." But as he acknowledged in reference to *Les Canadiens* (Introduction 22), this lends itself more to fiction than to documentary.

3. *S: Portrait of a Spy*

In collaborating with Ian Adams in 1984 on the dramatization of *S: Portrait of a Spy*, Salutin removes himself twice over from the usual factual basis of his plays. In the process, he moves more directly towards the mimetic drama of character and ideas that emerged only in certain scenes of *Nathan Cohen*. Adams' novel in itself offers a "fictional context" to the documentation he gathered as a journalist about the RCMP Securities Service. "My intention," he states in the introduction to a later edition,

> was to write about the RCMP Security Services and to present the information that I had gathered within a fictional context, so that I could share with readers my perceptions of the role that this secret government plays within our society.[27]

Its characters are fictional composites, not *roman à clef* depictions—although, at the time of its first publication in 1977, one character was sensationally taken to be so.[28] The play takes further steps towards fictionalization to function, in Salutin's words, "as primarily a psychological thriller."[29] Its major focus is the conflict between DV, a "prairie cop" dedicated to the defence of his democratic heritage, and S, a British-born "superspy." The latter is the civilian superintendent of counter-espionage (the Russian desk), who is discovered by his subordinate to be involved in the intricate game of survival as a triple agent.

Salutin's deliberate choice to write in a dramaturgical style different from his more usual structures is evident in the formal contrasts between the play[30] and the investigatory and documentary style of the novel. Salutin eliminates the journalist/narrator of the novel so that the action unfolds entirely in a dramatic present rather than through the partial retrospection of the novel's *in medias res* time scheme. Instead of the novel's investigative and often second-hand reports of characters and events, the play dramatizes events in present time, paradoxically allowing greater license than does the novel for psychological probing of the antagonists. The play also has a more explicit political statement, running as support to the main action, on the role of security services (both in Canada and at large) in controlling radical impulses for change at every level of society. As in the novel, there is still a strong indication of the power of the "secret" government over the elected one, of the often bumbling ineptness of the latter (notably represented in the character of SG, the solicitor general, who technically holds jurisdiction over RCMP Security), and of the ironies of CIA infiltration on all sides.

The general aim of the adaptation is ambitious both structurally and stylistically: transforming the novel's rather flat documentary reportage into dramatized encounter. This attempts to provide a coherent line of dramatic development, to give a personal dimension to the antagonists, and at the same time to provide an encapsulation of the public worlds in which they move. For the latter, the style of scene shifts from a dramatic mode of personal exchange to a documentary mode of public encounter. And of course, Salutin means to write satire. While the play does not succeed in all ways, it does try to highlight its political points with caricature and the occasional appropriation of presentational devices.

Salutin told an interviewer that Adams would write out the agreed scenes in prose and then he would turn them into dialogue.[31] However, this gives an oversimplified impression of the actual use the play makes

Chapter Three: Rick Salutin 157

of the stage, despite its predominance of two-person encounters (for which such a writing procedure might seem suited well enough). Basically, the work is naturalistic but adapts a dramatic shorthand for its rapid shifts in time and place. For these quick changes, the model of collective creation's fluidity of scene organization is useful.

For example, to present the Ottawa worlds in which the antagonists circulate both publicly and privately, there is a montage of scenes early in the play, which follow S anecdotally on his "trapline" of professional contacts in several high places. These brief glimpses are intercut with a sustained scene on another part of the stage, showing DV in argument with his wife as they dine in a Chinese restaurant. This montage of scenes is both illustrative and expositional in its introduction to S. It also initiates a motif of personal conflict between DV and his wife Pat who resents competing with her husband's work, specifically with his preoccupation with his boss's possible disloyalty (14-31).

Throughout the play, the collective's recurring use of monologue is variously employed. In the aforementioned montage, it functions as exposition— initially as the means of introducing the EA (executive assistant to the solicitor general). EA is a brash and knowing young man who has many sharp and uncomplimentary remarks about his superiors as well as a cynical interest in speculating on the source of power in this nebulous world of political and bureaucratic opportunism. Sometimes EA addresses the audience directly and at other times speaks to an implied conversationalist in a social gathering. This technique is a carry-over from the novel, in which the same material is addressed directly to the author/narrator. Later in an important scene in Act 2—a Washington party at the Watergate Hotel marking the turning point of S's fortunes with the RCMP—EA functions as narrating commentator. His caustic observations set the scene and frame the action for SG's public humiliation at the hands of the CIA on the matter of S's apparent involvement with the KGB as a double agent (17-24). Monologue is used less successfully, however, when it is a mere convenience for self-expression. DV's extended drunken rhetoric to himself about the "monster" he is determined to face is a self-conscious and rather clumsy means of emphasizing his hardening resolve to trap S (37-39).

The direct encounters between S and DV in the first act clearly establish the conflict of the play. From these, a specific line of action is built whereby DV undertakes secret procedures for confirming his suspicions against S. Thus on the level of intrigue and suspense, the act operates quite effectively within the spy/thriller tradition. The wider political and jurisdictional implications of DV's concerns as they reflect on S's possible duplicity are variously conveyed—for example, in the "trapline" montage referred to above. Stylistically, however, certain points are also emphasized editorially through the intermittent use of broadly satiric theatrical devices that are tonally reminiscent of passages in *1837* and *Les Canadiens*.

For example, in the concluding scene of the act—an RCMP hearing in which DV expects to demonstrate his case against S—the high-ranking officer who presides does so in the guise of a horse's "head" that stupidly nods but never speaks. The "dream-like and murky" atmosphere that this scene (47) is intended to convey (despite the naturalistic exchange between the two antagonists) is also an echo of the nightmarish prologue of the play. There, the scene is dominated by a colour-film projection of the RCMP musical ride at Expo 67 in which the picture and sound grow increasingly distorted (4). Although not as extreme stylistically, the Watergate party in Act 2 is presented as sinister comic relief in its farcical depiction of a fatuously inept SG in the hands of caricatured CIA types.

The attempt at psychological inwardness with respect to the two main characters, however, is contrived and formulaic. One is reminded that, as a playwright, Salutin has not really attempted this depth of characterization on stage before. Although Adam's author/narrator ruminates in the novel on the possibilities of penetrating the interior life of S, the investigatory structure of that work essentially prevents this

Chapter Three: Rick Salutin   159

from happening there.

The play takes greater dramatic license, largely through the antagonists' rather predictable relationships with women. Requisite spy/thriller sex scenes try to bring the novel's intimations of S's sensual side to dramatic life. Apart from introducing the thrills of danger and of potential betrayal, the purpose is to indicate something of S's quality of mind, whereby sexuality is titillatingly translated into cerebration. Thus his articles of faith, contrasting with those of his East-German love, Krista Gollner, emerge in allusive coital spy-talk in Act 1 (which seems deliberately to obfuscate the nature of the relationship itself and certainly the precise allegiances of each). S, the hollow man, is committed to his own considerable personal power as a survivalist (intimating that experience has taught him "there's nothing else" worth considering in the espionage game, 34). In turn, she is committed to principles of power that transcend individual vulnerability. (Her murder in Act 2 obscurely demonstrates a willingness to die for an idea.)

At best, this scene and a later one in a similar vein—a chat during a meeting on a bicycle path rather than in bed—lay the groundwork for the ultimately disillusioning impact of S on DV's own faith in the system he serves and for which he has also put his rather stodgy marriage at risk. This marriage is tiresomely under his wife's scrutiny throughout much of the play. But since the tightest dramatic element of the work is in the shifting cat-and-mouse relationship between these two men, the women in their lives serve largely to emphasize aspects of character which prepare for later turns their relationship finally takes.

In Act 2, however, the playwrights virtually abandon the relatively clear sequence of cause and effect (even with its digressive strategies of broader political and deeper psychological intent) that emerges in Act 1. The result is a disconnected series of scenes that precede the climactic verbal undermining by S of DV's dearest convictions. Ultimately in conflict are DV's dogged loyalties to the values he still believes his agency serves and S's superior recognition that the secret-service game worldwide is both a diversion from and an instrument of oppression. According to his philosophy, therefore, "it doesn't matter who is on which side, who does what to whom" (Act 2, 31). At the end, S produces his final ace for survival (despite some pain in the recognition of his own emptiness in contrast to Krista, for whose death he is probably responsible); and a disillusioned DV, even his marriage over, resigns to coach amateur hockey.

The problems of focus in Act 2 show the writers in difficulty chiefly over the effort to integrate plot requirements with the political aim to castigate a whole system of undercover oppression. Here, the latter intention is more intrusive, and the spy/thriller encounter between mouse-turned-cat and vice versa reaches its peak only with logistical difficulty. The opening scene is a digressive piece of thinly disguised domestic agitprop in which DV, demoted to his native Saskatchewan, nastily infiltrates a group of Indian activists out of his own frustrations (but in the brutal style "typical" of the RCMP). His sudden recall to Ottawa is pointedly at the behest of the CIA, not the RCMP (Act 2, 6). This is one of several occasions in which the emphasis on the CIA's real control is hammered home.

While the plot thickens with S's revelation to Krista that he is under investigation, her possible role in this is unclear. Her sudden murder, which follows very soon, is equally mystifying. Anticlimactic bedroom talk (presumably serving as exposition) between DV and his wife Pat awkwardly deflects a major moment of dramatic expectation: suddenly S has retired quietly from the Security Service. The satiric Washington scene—which, in terms of plot, prepares for his enforced return for further investigation—is a clumsy distraction both structurally and tonally at an already confusing point in the play.

Only in the penultimate confrontation between S and DV, while S is escorted from Australia back to Ottawa, is the balance restored belatedly between idea and execution. This occurs in a taut "Socratic" dialogue, in which the superspy leads his captor through a maze of disillusioning recognitions about the realities of his misplaced faith in service to "the country, the things we believe in" (Act 2, 30). That the superspy himself, as he plays his last successful card, is ultimately disillusioned about the value of the survival game gives a concluding edge to the formula of the psychological thriller (Act 2, 40). In comparison, DV's final moment (in the epilogue) as a hockey coach who makes his team play their "own game" rather than watch the Canadians and Russians on TV (because it is easy to be spectators in this country) is rather too pat an echo of *Les Canadiens*.

The play is an uneasy alliance of the demands of both spy/thriller and political polemic, although occasionally it has strong moments of interior conflict and self-doubt deriving from both. But on a political theme, the theatricalism of the open stage—with its direct acknowledgement of the audience—has served Salutin in the past better than this. Here, montage, narrative frame and caricature break through the mimetic mode of spy/thriller to an extent, but they seldom get beyond satiric embellishment. Unlike *1837: The Farmers' Revolt* (or *Les Canadiens* in part), *S: Portrait of a Spy* is not a political play that draws the audience into an investigation of the issues. Rather, it is only a play that dramatizes a particular viewpoint about politics.

Thematically, *S: Portrait of a Spy* resembles Salutin's other plays in its identification and exposure of a popular myth. The latter is not simply the myth of the RCMP, who stand for the "true north strong and free." In fact, the RCMP have been exposed before (in *Buffalo Jump*, for example). More importantly, "the mythology of espionage" acts as an instrument for repressing impulses for social change. If the insight fails to emerge as compellingly as he might have hoped in his collaboration with Ian Adams, the intention is interesting for what it states generally about Salutin's commitment as a playwright. "The strength of any mythology lies in the fact that it doesn't appear as such," he told an interviewer when discussing the play a year after its production. "By writing about it, you try to make people aware that it is a mythology—only one possible response to a given reality."[32]

In Salutin's plays, the Canadian reality lies in its colonial subservience to the many faces of imperialism and its attendant mythologies: in history and in the reading of history; in the sublimation of *Québecois* political and cultural identity in a hockey team; in the hostility by theatrical producers to Nathan Cohen's critical struggle for an indigenous theatre; and in the duplicity and credulity of the Canadian "horsemen" on the international, not to speak of the domestic, scene. As a playwright, Salutin denies that he is political in the doctrinaire sense of being a partisan socialist:

> What you try to do is reveal the ways in which reality works. By revealing what is normally hidden, you provide audiences with a better understanding of how the world works, so they become better equipped to make decisions in that society.[33]

As for Salutin's growth as a playwright, we may observe a stylistic ambivalence between presentational and mimetic modes of dramatic representation in his efforts to examine and communicate "the workings of reality" to his audience. As early as 1977, he expressed discontents with Canadian "documentary style" (on related cultural and artistic grounds) which seem to inform his own preoccupations, at that time and later, as a playwright working on social subjects. Noting then that we need to be brought closer to our Canadian experience rather than be distanced from it, he was already objecting to the Brechtian element in documentary which "pulls back from the event to take an observer's stance."[34] In collective creation (as will be discussed further below), he observed that this often meant narrating events "in retrospect" rather than " 'playing' the drama of a situation in the present."[35] In his speculation that "a kind of anti-alienation effect may be on the agenda for Canadian culture at this point,"[36] we might see evidence of this agenda throughout the evolution of his own dramaturgy.

S: Portrait of a Spy illustrates his most determined effort towards a sustained dramatic realism (although it is not entirely without its elements of presentational theatre). The second act of *Les Canadiens* also shows him already moving in that direction through the focus on the fictional Kirk with his representative "identity" problem. Yet its best expression is in the satiric theatre of the nightmare game that keeps the hockey metaphor intact. The growth of *Nathan Cohen* from the original idea of a monodrama shows Salutin attempting to open up his material dramatically, although not realistically, in the performance structure that also provides for all of the additional speakers in the play. They combine documentary with mimetic function. The performance metaphor relating to Cohen's role as a critic, however, does not lead to an exploration of the character nor the conflicts of the man behind the role. The restrictions on personal material imposed by Cohen's widow may be the cause of these limitations. Thus in the play to follow, Salutin works with Adams through a popular literary sub-genre rather than a theatrical mode in order to attempt this exploration in a more conventional format.

The example of *S: Portrait of a Spy* demonstrates, however, the problematic nature of Salutin's move to embrace dramatic realism as the means to involve the Canadian audience in, not to distance it from, its own experience. In each of the three plays under discussion, there is some point at which talk (in either monologue or dialogue) becomes didactic statement rather than dramatically realized conflict. This didacticism is most conspicuous when Salutin is fictionalizing his characters. He is apt to make them say what he wants to say rather than exploring the reality of their natures. With Dave Kirk, this is a relatively minor point in the context of *Les Canadiens* as a whole, where the expanded metaphor of hockey-as-history is the informing idea and structure of the play. In *S: Portrait of a Spy*, where there is no sustaining theatrical metaphor (only the brief satiric joke of the horse's "head"), the characterization of DV is burdened with the weight of the play's informing political idea. Salutin's best work occurs when theatrical metaphor—either extended as in *Les Canadiens* or condensed as in *1837: The Farmers's Revolt* (i.e., "The Dummy")—integrates ideas and expression.

4. Salutin in Newfoundland

From time to time, when Salutin has commented informally on collective creation in interviews, he has spoken essentially from the writer's perspective rather than the collective's. He praises the actors' commitment to the material they have researched themselves and the audience immediacy that comes from actors' speaking in their own words. But he also notes the problem of achieving "a coherent point of view" and "a distinctive style."[37] Eventually, he complained about the formal predictability of collective creations and their lack of intricacy, resulting from few "serious attempts to develop the form."[38] His collective experience in Newfoundland on two widely separate occasions, where his main function was dramaturgical, gave him the opportunity to explore in the case of *IWA* (1975) and to test in the case of *Joey* (1981) some of his own concerns with the form.

On the evidence of the transcript of *IWA* (particularly in comparison to the Mummers' earlier *Buchans: A Company Town*) and of Salutin's two later magazine pieces on documentary style (written a few months apart and, perhaps significantly, in between the first and second versions of *Les Canadiens*[39]), he was already attempting on that first Newfoundland project to influence the advance of collective creation towards a more dramatic structure. This was consistent with his later castigation of what he generally considered the inadequacy of the Canadian "mindset that concentrates on what *really* happened as opposed to dramatization, fictionalization and the like."[40] Here, he was criticizing the documentary style as he saw it operating in other art forms as well as collective creations. But he was pointing specifically to the collective's recurring technique of direct address to the audience through monologue—particularly narrative retrospective in the voice of the research subject. This technique is one of the "stylistic choices" that distances an event, evading what is "most essential about that situation."[41] He was citing the tape-recorder approach to collective documentary playmaking "flourishing at the moment in Newfoundland, Ontario, Saskatchewan and Alberta." The result, he thought, was an emphasis on the "real" only "in the trivial sense of something which actually existed or exists."[42] Thus in *IWA*, certain kinds of information and responses to events are handled through fictionalized characters and dramatic episodes, rather than through narrative units as used in *Buchans*. This approach was enough to make Alan Filewod observe that "Rick Salutin's contribution as a writer appears to eclipse Brookes's typical structure."[43]

By the time of *Joey*, the case becomes interesting because Donna Butt wanted to take the process a step beyond *IWA* with Salutin actually writing the play from the material created in the rehearsal period. (An interpretation of "the way reality works" rather than the "real" was by now at issue.) As a performer and director in collectives for much of her theatrical career,[44] Butt had come to the conclusion that collective playmaking, almost the only source of new work in Newfoundland, had exhausted its potential for variation: "we were victims of our own success. Audiences came to love and demand the collective with its humour and familiarity—with the occasional serious scene thrown in." However, her suggestion for an authored play proved unworkable because Salutin felt deeply disadvantaged by not being from Newfoundland. The play that evolved finally from the extensive research already done by the company, with Salutin as "working consultant" on the dramatic structuring, was not the kind of play Butt had hoped for.[45] As far as Salutin was concerned, collective creation had also exhausted its interest for him.[46] This suggests that he had now tested the capacity of collective playmaking to develop as a form.

The work of the Mummers Troupe was compatible with that of Theatre Passe Muraille, although by no means identical in purpose. Like Theatre Passe Muraille, the Mummers created community plays from the experience of living among their subjects (their first occasion, *Gros Mourn*, premiered a year after Theatre Passe Muraille went to Clinton). However, under Chris Brookes's direction, the Mummers also used theatre as a tool of political and social "animation"—as in the Third-World sense of popular theatre. While in general they shared Passe Muraille's cultural concerns of indigenous theatre and drama, theirs was a Newfoundlanders' rather than Canadian nationalism. As a militant socialist, Brookes interpreted cultural needs in the political terms of a popular people's theatre.[47] At particular issue in the 1970s was Brookes's perception of an older Newfoundland being swamped by post-confederation social and economic malaise—what journalist Sandra Gwyn described in 1976 as the foreclosure of "the Newfoundland way of life." The Smallwood "resettlement programme" of the late 1960s was a prime example of this. Gwyn quotes Brookes's remark about the mission of his theatre: "We have to show people themselves before they forget who they are."[48]

Both *Gros Mourn* and *Buchans: A Company Town* are what Alan Filewod describes as interventional theatre. The former play was devised as a somewhat belated challenge to federal expropriation of small communities on the west coast to create a national park (Gros Morne). The latter play depicts the life and history of a community threatened by the depletion of its mining resources. Both were created to address the needs of a specific audience. Although also performed elsewhere, both plays retained the authenticity of their initial aim. *Gros Mourn* combines documentary presentation with the agitprop techniques of popular theatre. *Buchans*, in its variety of narrative strategies of direct address, conveys an authentic documentary reflection of the actors' first-hand contact with the community who supplied their primary audience. This occurred in a manner analogous but by no means identical to that of *The Farm*

Chapter Three: Rick Salutin 167

Show.[49] Contrary to Salutin's view, this technique is designed to establish a special intimacy rather than distance between audience and performance.

The Mummers' interest in labour history, which was stimulated by their researches for *Buchans*, made the infamous logging strike of 1959 a natural choice for the subject of their new play. Besides, in a period of post-confederation disillusionment, the strike offered them an opportunity to demythologize the only living Father of Confederation, Joey Smallwood. His role in the creation of modern Newfoundland was ripe for scrutiny. The civil strife arising from the events of 1959 was in some sense Newfoundland's version of 1837. Although not literally a political independence movement, this trouble was a volatile workers' issue exacerbated by the interference of the Smallwood government in the fundamental rights of union men to chose their own bargaining agent.

In his controversial intervention during a radio broadcast of February 12, on the 48th day of the strike, Premier Smallwood proclaimed the activity of the International Woodworkers of America (which had organized only recently for decent working conditions among the loggers of Newfoundland) "not a strike" but a "civil war."[50] Within a few more days, Smallwood had decertified the outsider IWA union organized by British Columbian Landon Ladd and replaced it with a union of his own. The result was bloodshed between angry loggers and the police in the town of Badger. From the left-wing perspective of Brookes and the Mummers Troupe, the IWA strike suggested the paradox of a beleaguered class victimized by economic and political forces masked as Newfoundland patriotism.

With his similar view of history as class struggle, Salutin was a suitable candidate to collaborate with the Mummers Troupe. Besides, the services of an experienced collective writer seemed to be called for at this point in the Mummers' own development. If there was a difficulty in the collective creation of *Buchans*, it was in the struggle to discover and develop a coherent structure for the play—given the collective's need to accommodate everyone's ideas of what should be included and the inherent problems of integrating the individual contributions. As an entirely historical play with many settings rather than a community collective, *IWA* made different demands on the company in terms of its manner of research (gathered more by individuals than by the collective[51]) and play development.

The whole company[52] assembled to make the play in September of 1975. Included in that process was a few days' visit to the logging communities. Although Salutin was credited on the programme as the playwright "who guided and shaped the rehearsal work towards its final form," his later recollection (when he was comparing his work on this play to that on *Joey*) suggested that much was actually initiated in rehearsals: "we discovered concerns and created scenes as we went along. New research would be done and new writing demands made on the company."[53] According to Brookes, Salutin's participation was to "mould the rehearsal improvisations, nudging the actors towards themes he wanted to explore."[54]

In contrast to the investigatory documentary structure of *Buchans*, built mostly on monologues and retrospection, *IWA* is structured partially as dramatic fiction. Thus, the former play's emphasis on the original voices of the company's research process is replaced in the latter in two ways. Broadly comic characterizations dramatize the vicissitudes of typical logging-camp life and politicize the loggers in the first act while a narrative line establishes the role of women in the second. The main focus of the second act is on the fictionalized character of Mary, created and performed by Donna Butt and based on her first-hand research gathered at Badger.[55] Mary is an older housewife who overcomes her conventional sense of propriety to become militant on the picket line after her husband Gerald is arrested. Through her experiences there and in successive events, a personal drama of "conflict" and "choice" is developed. This is what Salutin advocated in his essays as the preferable dramatic style of "'playing' the drama of a situation in the present" rather than "describing it in retrospect."[56] By the end of the play, when defeat is assured by the action of the Smallwood government and by the violence it provoked, Mary's spirit of resolve in the last scene for "da next time" carries the political weight of the work.

Documentary presentational theatre in *IWA* is reserved mostly for politically charged public events that clarify the historical "minority report" (so designated on the programme). It also provides the context for the fictionalized dramatic dimension of the play. Here, Brookes's inclination for satiric theatrical gesture, prominent in *Gros Mourn* though more restrained in *Buchans*, reasserts itself in the emphatic political bias of the work. The radio culture of the period is a primary vehicle. Thus with more documentary ingenuity than metaphoric point (and used more appropriately in this regard by Salutin in his own play to follow), the union negotiations are structured as a "Hockey Night in Canada" broadcast of a losing game between the rookie union and the Anglo-Newfoundland Development (AND) Company. The details of this game are reported in the voice of "Foster Hewitt" (with post-game foolishness by "young Howie Meeker"). More relevant to the logger culture is "Woodland Echoes," the radio show sponsored by Bowater (Paper Company), with which the play opens. This is a programme of songs, personal messages and announcements quickly mapping the life and terrain of the forest industry in a catchy send-up manner. Later, the scene parodies itself in order to satirize the fear of the reported interest by the Soviet Union in Newfoundland's labour struggle.

Smallwood's radio speech and his subsequent actions are the satiric focus of the second act. They are directly preceded by a montage of voices giving brief indication of the influences—mostly financial—on his decision. The speech itself is a masterpiece of found drama, easily edited to give the most offending highlights. At the same time, it retains its most characteristic rhetorical feature—an unconscionably long, ambiguous and paternalistic preamble seemingly calculated to appeal to the better judgement of all good Newfoundlanders (even as Smallwood is poised to strike at the heart of the IWA movement). The broadcast is presented simply but effectively with Smallwood onstage and listeners of contrasting persuasions responding passionately as he speaks to the radio audience. The decertification of the IWA on March 9 in the House of Assembly is presented as a circus act with Smallwood, hoop in hand, ordering the attorney general and the leader of the opposition to jump.

During that ugly and fatal day of the riot in Badger (which follows the premier's action), Constable Moss is accidentally killed. For their presentation, the Mummers borrow from the *Buchans* technique of retrospection with a montage of first-hand glimpses of events as reported a day later. This is Brookes's style prevailing over Salutin's. The retrospective narration serves not only to defuse the still-controversial subject of how the riot started but also to give focus to an authentic-seeming people's perspective on the event. This was hysterically inflated by Smallwood himself when he created a martyr out of the unfortunate constable. Thus, instead of the funeral of Moss, the funeral of the IWA is the subject of the penultimate scene of the play. It begins with a long expressive monologue by Mary describing the hatred and violence that have now come to Newfoundland as well as her experience of these events in Badger. Smallwood, with power saw in hand and accompanied by ringing phrases from both his radio speech and an address to the House of Assembly on March 11, rips to shreds a paper funeral cortege of unwinding newsprint that reads "R.I.P., IWA."

As a drama, *IWA* makes use of fictional dramatization of representative experiences in combination with a theatrical approach to public events. In doing so, this play marks both a stylistic overture towards a somewhat more complex dramaturgy in the Mummers' collective-theatre technique and a reassertion of their strengths as political satirists, which first emerged in *Gros Mourn*. But in the last analysis, the result is an uneasy alliance of Salutin's advocacy of mimetic dramatization and Brookes' talent for theatrical political satire and improvisational buffoonery. Although first-hand interview material was collected for *IWA* as well as *Buchans*, the experiences and controversies that the latter play explores were obviously seen by the theatre company as sufficiently removed in time to allow for the less localized and more "creative" treatment of the workers, which the partially mimetic approach encouraged.

While the fictional passages—at least in the second act—give a personal emotional resonance to the documentary units, the play ultimately suffers from problems in pacing and tone. For whatever this might signify about the contributions of the actors, director or writer, there is a disproportionate amount of foolery (sometimes to the point of idiocy) from the naturalistically sketched male characters of the loggers (whether performed by male or female actors). This may be the Mummers' way of demonstrating that the logging community is not intrinsically militant, but rather that it consists of a naive, basically mild and conservative people who have been awakened by the organizers at last to the injustice of their situation. Yet the effect is to let the women, particularly Mary, carry the day.

At its best, this play—like *1837: The Farmers's Revolt*—is engaged in the irreverent exposure of a political myth, although the methods of the two plays differ. The earlier play establishes Mackenzie as a genuine voice of the people, not as the erratic rabble-rouser that history remembers. In contrast, *IWA* exposes Joey, the ostensible "man of the people," as a vainglorious autocrat, the tool of economic interests who felt personally threatened by the power of IWA organizer Landon Ladd. For the dramatization of this political point, the irreverent gestures of a theatrical approach to public events—an important aspect of documentary style ignored by Salutin in his later critiques—were an essential political strategy. This occurred most particularly where these scenes functioned as authenticated agitprop—a tacit corrective, perhaps, to Smallwood's own 1973 memoirs.[57]

As a play, *Joey* provides a good example of how limited is collective creation's aspiration towards structural and psychological intricacy—unless a writer is prepared to take over from the initial development process as Linda Griffiths was later to do with *Jessica*. Given Salutin's opportunity—if he had felt free to take it—of broadening *IWA*'s direct attack on Smallwood's demagoguery concerning government interference in the loggers' issue, he showed remarkable restraint in the matter of the politics of the new play. Certainly, the IWA issue shows up in *Joey* as a blot on Smallwood's political career; one character is even represented as eager to bring up the issue early in the play. Yet on the whole, the treatment of the central figure—in the opinion of Newfoundland playwright and reviewer Al Pittman—"leans a little more kindly towards J.R. Smallwood than history ever will."[58] Reviewer Gina Mallet was more blunt in her remark that "Smallwood is watered down into a lovable eccentric." She regretted that the IWA strike was not exploited dramatically as the play's climax, with "the hero toppled when he abandons what is demonstrably his own union stand."[59]

The play, in effect, is a compromise: an attempt to balance the comic energy of the now characteristic Newfoundland folk humour (pervasive in *IWA*, and the most constant and skilful element to emerge from Newfoundland actors over the years of collective playmaking) with the more difficult enterprise of creating a stage portrait of a still living and controversial political figure. In a pre-production interview, Donna Butt described *Joey* as "an epic piece of drama" that not only highlights "so many vital incidents in his career" but also uses a "double focus" to include the people affected by his political actions. "You can't present Joey," she noted, "without the people he served—the people in the outports who simply worshipped him and many of the people who eventually turned against him." She went on to state the company's more complex intention: "Our biggest challenge has been to find and portray Joey's inner self, to share his reflective moments." Here she makes particular reference to Joey's "special relationship" with his friends in the Confederation campaign and later with cabinet minister Greg Powers, who withdrew his support at the time of the IWA strike.[60]

Among the reviewers, only Pittman noted the dramatic sensitivity of the moment when Joey seeks unsuccessfully to beguile Powers back. But the effort to dramatize the man behind the bow tie and the self-important manner is, inevitably perhaps, tentative. The more accessible idiosyncrasies of Joey's public personality prevail, and the episodes through which the play highlights his career are a relatively brief and impressionistic treatment of events familiar to a Newfoundland audience. The characterization, therefore, is essentially a semi-caricatured line drawing, through which that audience brings its own memories and opinions into play; it is not the in-depth, potentially tragic reading that a writer might offer on the subject of the province's controversial founding father. While the company's decision to develop a double focus on Joey and the people whose lives he changed was fitting, it precluded in this play a closer, more stringent examination of the man himself.

The work falls tidily into two chronological parts within a framing device. In the latter, the Joey of today has his own brief opportunities by way of introduction and conclusion to the play. In the first act, his bond with the people is clearly established. He is the undoubted folk hero of Confederation, a self-styled socialist with an abiding commitment to relieving the poverty of the outports with Canadian social services. In the second act, he becomes the self-righteous politician, still convinced he is champion of the people but increasingly ego-bound and autocratic in his energetic, almost single-handed pursuit of decolonization and modernization. Now he is shown increasingly removed from his populist base, although he is as well-intentioned as ever towards the electorate, which he now alludes to as "my people." In the IWA crisis, he feels personally threatened by the "eyes shining for Landon Ladd, the way they shine for me" (89). In the near-fatal struggle between the premier and the new generation of Liberal politicians led in the late-1960s by John Crosbie, Joey's dedication to change begins to ring a little hollow even to himself. But the *dramatic* reality of much of this is only partially successful in the parallel comic/ironic scenes of the outports in which representative Newfoundland types reflect the actual impact of change.

In the first act, the outport scenes tabulate the issues Joey is broaching in his Confederation campaign. At the same time, they identify the nature of the opposition to his solutions. A proud Newfoundlander such as the fisherman Eli of Round Harbour says he would "just as soon go right to the bottom as become a foreigner in me own country." To which his wife Mary wryly responds, "But Eli, if you goes and drowns yourself, I won't have any pride to cook for supper" (48). Although often pithy, the outport scenes—especially in the second act—are too frequent and too extended on the nonsense level. That's why they can't provide a consistent and explicit dramatic focus on Joey's demagoguery as it affects the people he claimed to want to serve most. Instead, the collective indulges in the comedy of "before and after" Confederation life-styles and expectations, the thick-headedness of mainlander perceptions of the new "frontier," and the farcical intransigence of local insularity.

Occasionally, however, the changing way of life that Joey was eager to initiate catches up with him—in particular, the scenes dealing with the resettlement of outport people who cannot believe (although they must) that Joey would thus betray them. That he himself has lost touch in his role as man-of-the-people is ironically indicated in one of his rare moments of troubled rationalization—a brief monologue addressed to his absent friend Greg, which begins with the querulous "Why would anyone want to go on living there?" Such a moment becomes an implicit comment on the paternalistic political style of Joey who, like his former loyal admirers, is becoming an anachronism in the increasingly pluralistic society he himself initiated. In essence, the play is a nostalgic recollection—the people's story focusing on the absurdities and contradictions of social progress, and the hero's on the vainglorious scramble for a place in history.

In contrast to *IWA*, *Joey* is a reinforcement of commonly

Chapter Three: Rick Salutin   175

perceived notions of the past, not an argument for dissent. In this respect a play about politics rather than a political play, it is the product of a kinder theatrical era than that initiated by Chris Brookes nearly 10 years earlier. Its nostalgic "animated album" approach to the life and times of Joey Smallwood (to use Pittman's phrase) is a reminder, by way of contrast, that collective creation in the 1970s often functioned most effectively because the playmakers were not actually "writers" crafting scenes in the literary sense; they were talented improvisers who could encapsulate meaning in theatrical strokes that were often as much gesture as talk, or a witty combination of both.

For example, in *IWA*, Joey laying the union to rest with a power saw in hand makes a more striking point about his political methods than do his plaintive rationalizations in *Joey* about hating violence and resenting Landon Ladd. *IWA* also has a certain sardonic authority in its accompanying satiric paraphrases of the premier's actual public utterances, which is lacking in his fictionalized private talk in *Joey*. Similarly, *IWA*'s theatrical metaphor of Smallwood as ringmaster of the House of Assembly during the decertification of the union gives more edge to the illustration of one-man rule than the elaborately farcical ineptitude of *Joey*'s first yes-man cabinet, although neither goes very far toward illuminating the underlying problems. The theatricality of *Joey* is mostly of the comic-skit variety (dating back to *IWA*) with a large measure of inverted Newfie jokes, cross-talk and exaggerated behaviour from the outporters. Added to these examples is some fiery political one-upmanship from Joey and his opposition—such as the confederation debates or the later conflicts with a young John Crosbie.

In his evaluation of the play, Pittman rightly thought the writing of the "serious" moments of the work unequal to the comic ones. He also regretted that the script did not support what he perceived to be actor Kevin Noble's potential for giving "glimpses of Smallwood none of us have ever seen." One can understand from this why director Donna Butt had wanted the play *written*. However, there is one element in *Joey*, also noted by Pittman, in which a different kind of theatre briefly obtains. Pittman spoke of Smallwood himself as a natural performer "who spent a great deal of his life playing the role of the person he envisioned himself to be." He therefore appreciated the allusion to this in the opening presentationalism of the play: the present-day Joey enters the stage from the auditorium and welcomes the audience to the play about *him* (and to the Arts and Culture Centre he has built—the original venue of the play in St. John's). Although quick to brag about his gifts as an orator, Joey modestly disclaims any pretences as an actor. But predictably, he is not impressed by the young actor who is about to impersonate him either.

The device whereby the eponymous character comments from outside the main body of the action, presented openly as a *performance* of his life, hints of Salutin's own *Nathan Cohen: A Review*, premiered at the beginning of the same year in Toronto. In the latter, technically a memory play, this establishes performance conceptually and structurally as a continuing metaphor integral to the protagonist's function as theatre critic. In *Joey*, however, the logistics of the play's mimetic convention prevent an explicit theatrical through-line on the theme of Joey as a political *performer*. The "live" presence of the subject of the play serves only as a casual frame, an opening flourish to establish the actor in *his* role. However, it also shows comic deference to the still living person and playful recognition that Joey is more than capable of self-dramatization.

When Joey is finally encouraged to sit down in the audience—quite pleased with the opening send-up scene of God's preparing the three wise fisherman for their journey to Gambo (where Smallwood was born on Christmas day) and insistent that they start at the beginning of his career rather than leap instantly into the IWA strike—he disappears until the end of the play. There, he pops up one more time to assert his own importance to history and to demand that the company conclude the evening by singing "Ode to Newfoundland." Despite the comic relief of *Joey*, the company's inevitably sketchy nod at dramatic realism under the dictates of chronological necessity is no substitute for collective creation's more characteristic exploratory transformational style. Nor is the mimetic mode itself—particularly as practised here in the double focus of the play—really adequate to the potential of the subject. To probe the ambitions of such a hero—and to integrate the consequences of his choices on the populace whose lives he affected—invites a play beyond the means of collective creation.

As late as 1987, Donna Butt still found it necessary to urge—in a brief—that theatre in Newfoundland should expand beyond its too habitual reliance on this mode of playmaking: "We need plays written by playwrights, plays that are enduring and tough, plays that are willing to look at Newfoundlanders, warts and all."[61] In the 1970s, collective creation filled "a very real need" at the seminal stage of a developing indigenous theatre in Newfoundland as elsewhere; but performers and their audiences enjoyed the collective play too much to prompt an analogous development of scripted plays in the 1980s.[62]

David LeReaney as Billy Bishop and Jan Randall as the pianist in the 1983 revival of *Billy Bishop Goes To War*, directed by Gerry Potter at Workshop West Playwrights Theatre. Photo: Gerry Potter.

Chapter Four
John Gray's Local Heroes

On the public platform of the mid-eighties and elsewhere, John Gray often recalled his first awareness of the impact of Canadian content on a theatre audience. The play was the revised *1837: The Farmers' Revolt* in performance at the Listowel auction barn in May 1974. There, he marvelled at the farmers in plaid jackets and John Deere caps who were cheering—some tearfully—the vindication of their ancestors, which Salutin and Theatre Passe Muraille were giving them. What astonished Gray most was that the enthusiasm came from people very like those he knew back home in Truro, Nova Scotia—"practical people who, I assumed, thought culture had something to do with germs and must be controlled, not encouraged."[1]

The eventual effect of this changed his life in the theatre from that of a director interested in contemporary theatre styles (derived from American and British counter-culture influences) to that of Canada's most popular indigenous musical playwright. The seminal step in this direction came through his working association with Theatre Passe Muraille—as composer, musician and sometimes director of their shows. This led to the creation of his own work: *18 Wheels*, 1977; *Billy Bishop Goes to War*, with Eric Peterson, 1978; *Rock and Roll*, 1981; and *Don Messer's Jubilee*, 1984. Their most characteristic elements, in the best Passe Muraille tradition, are informed by Gray's perception at Listowel of the popular appeal of the substance of Canadian culture to an audience that did not traditionally go to the theatre.[2]

Gray's earlier career had followed in a fairly standard Canadian pattern of the time. Upon completing his theatre training at the University of British Columbia, he quickly discovered that the only way to acquire professional credentials was to start his own company. From 1971 to 1974, he was founding director of Vancouver Theatre Workshop, later renamed Tamahnous (Chilcotin for "magic"), in collaboration with UBC associates such as Peterson, Larry Lillo, and Jeremy Long. Like other young Canadian theatre companies of that day, Tamahnous did indeed begin by modelling its work on the styles and texts of the radical counter-culture companies of Britain and more particularly of the United States. The first production was *Dracula II*, based on a Bram Stoker improvisation created by the Stable Theatre, Manchester; and the second, *The Bacchae*, evolved in the intense ritualistic manner of Schechner's Performance Group.[3] They were "Grotowski-like" out of necessity, Gray said later: "We had to explore what we could do with just the voice and the body in an empty space, because that was all we could afford."[4]

In its first years, Tamahnous worked towards a flexible ensemble method that allowed for experiment "within the widest possible range of theatre forms."[5] The text was fluid and, through group improvisation, the work evolved in subsequent productions.[6] Soon the company was working with its own adaptations—for example, Jeremy Long's violently physical *Medea* in 1973 and, in the same year, a group adaptation of *The Tempest* as projected through the mind of Prospero. The company also explored original material, including *Bill Durham* by Jeremy Newsome—a vaudevillian satire on the American western, which Gray described to an interviewer as shaped from "a terrible script with a wonderful plot."[7] Gray, denoted by Christopher Defoe as a perfectionist, had already taken the work through at least three different treatments at Tamahnous and was now restaging the show at Global Village in Toronto. At this point in his career, Gray had no thought of becoming a writer.[8] Jeremy Long was Tamahnous' resident playwright, following his version of *Medea* with his *The Final Performance of Vaslav Nijinsky*, featuring Eric Peterson as the great Russian dancer.

Gray's retrospective view of his approach to theatre in these years was stated bluntly in an interview with Alan Twigg in 1981:

> I used to be quite the little elitist. I went to university for seven years. Nothing will hone an elitist like seven years in a university. So I tended to do shows for formalistic reasons. Content wasn't that important. New theatre forms and staging were just as important as what a play said.[9]

The environmental type of theatre done by the Performance Group, from which Tamahnous took its initial model, was intended to break down the conventional barrier that the proscenium places between audience and performers. For Gray, however, it required Paul Thompson's populist experiments at Theatre Passe Muraille to make him recognize that "the event of having a particular audience becomes just as important as what's happening on the stage." He was discovering, as he told Twigg, a kind of theatre where "it's not like there's a little glass cube around the stage and everybody sits there and admires the work of art on display."[10] The connection between the audience and the subject matter became for Gray the major element of a contemporary Canadian play. "People go to a Canadian play for its content," he told another interviewer at that time, even though the work "can be rougher, not as clean and stylish and glintsy [sic] as one would sometimes hope for." Audiences go to a British or American play, he added, "for the production values"—sometimes the only element that makes a mediocre piece "workable."[11] In *Billy Bishop Goes to War*, he was to turn homespun legion-hall informality into a stylistic virtue.

Over the years, Tamahnous gradually moved away from its experiments in ritualistic theatricality, where gesture and movement are as important as language, to the more popular and direct social appeal. This began even before Gray's departure with Larry Lillo's production of Jeremy Long's *Salty Tears on a Hangnail Face* (1974). Gray wrote the music for this cat's-eye view of the vicissitudes of hippydom in a Kitsilano commune—a work described by reviewer Bob Allen as showing every possible variety of popular music-theatre style.[12] Eventually, Tamahnous was to produce the Vancouver premiere and the British Columbia tour of Gray's *18 Wheels*, his first original work for Theatre Passe Muraille (premiered in 1977). In 1978, Tamahnous and the Vancouver East Cultural Centre also co-produced the premiere of *Billy Bishop*, workshopped at Theatre Passe Muraille. In their separate ways, both Gray and his original company were moving to more popular contact with Canadian audiences, although the signs were already there in *Bill Durham* and *Salty Tears*. From UBC and Tamahnous, Gray learned the theatre craft that helped him "to write things which work on the stage."[13] But from Theatre Passe Muraille, he acquired that new feeling for the popular audience, which became the catalyst for his inherently musical creativity.

Gray moved to Toronto in 1975 and began composing and performing the music at Theatre Passe Muraille. His first work was for Rick Salutin's *The False Messiah*, premiered in March of that year at the cavernous St. Paul's United Church. In this sharply criticized play and production, Gray's Jewish liturgical music was nevertheless noted approvingly in one review.[14] Later, he composed a country-music score for a revival of *1837* and a brilliant pastiche of sacred and secular songs (which he performed on the electric organ) for *The Horsburgh Scandal* (1976), the play by Theatre Passe Muraille and Betty Jane Wylie, which he also co-directed. The same year, he did the music for the belated premiere of Hershel Hardin's *The Great Wave of Civilization*, directed by Paul Thompson at the Lennoxville Festival. In the meantime, Gray kept in contact with the west-coast theatre scene. In May of 1975, he and Eric Peterson were both in Vancouver performing in the New Play Centre's premiere of Thomas Cone's *Herringbone*, which they presented at the Du Maurier Festival as a one-actor multiple-character piece with piano player. Naturally, this work was important as a precursor to *Billy Bishop*.

1. *18 Wheels*

The idea for *18 Wheels* originated in actor Booth Savage's suggestion for a Passe Muraille collective creation on the life of long-distance truckers. In a manner similar to the development of his earlier hitch-hiking show, *Free Ride* (1971), Thompson gave the actor seed money to cross the country in a truck with a tape-recorder to gather material that could be developed later by a collective of actors, director and composer. Gray remained behind to write the songs. The documentary investigation proved too depressing for Savage, so the plan for a collective was abandoned.

But Gray, inspired by the myths about North American truckers with their country-and-western sentiment, continued to write the songs.[15] The result was "a conceptual piece"[16] structured as a three-set evening entertainment by a group of musicians playing in a local beer parlour. The cast includes four singers of a country-and-western band, who alternately perform the feature and support roles in each of the three musical sets. These consist of sung narrative poems about trans-Canada trucking life interspersed with shorter songs, occasional dialogue, and sung or spoken narration.

Through musical format, Gray was beginning to apply the basic principle of accessible indigenous theatre, which Thompson and Theatre Passe Muraille had developed. Yet, in recognizing the creative strengths of Passe Muraille's collective playmaking, he was personally averse to the "anarchy" and last-minute panic of the process (Preface 20). More particularly, he criticized the "jumble" of language: its quality "varies with the performers" and "obviates the existence of language as an arrangement of words and sounds that has a consistent mind behind it."[17] Yet he was strongly indebted to Theatre Passe Muraille for showing him "how powerful a monologue can be."[18] Observing from his position on stage during his tours with the company through the small towns of southern Ontario, he noted that, among audiences with no tradition of the invisible fourth wall,

> whenever an actor played directly to the audience in the manner of a story-teller or sang in the manner of a beer-parlour act, the audience members caught in the spill of the stage light suddenly relaxed, watched the stage closely, slapped their knees and laughed.[19]

In the balladry of *18 Wheels*, whose audiences are fans of country-and-western music rather than truck drivers, Gray develops variations on Passe Muraille's raconteur style. His concept of the show's theme also provides for a variation on that company's interest in Canadian geographical identities as reflected in their travels. Thus, *18 Wheels* is a trucker's-eye map of the country in motion. Its opening song, "Do You Wanna Know the Country?", carries the metonymy of Canada as an asphalt river "stretching out from shore to shore" (31). Although individual themes, temptations, romantic sorrows, and dangers of life on the road echo Nashville, the map is particularized as stories and songs that discover places and people along the route. These discoveries are lightly informed by regional and nationalistic ironies to which a Canadian audience can readily respond.

Sadie, a Nova Scotia miner's daughter, is "the nicest waitress on the highway." She alternates from lyric, rock and country swing, song and rhythmic speech to render a long balladic account of the mistakes of her youth. Having rejected her devoted trucker for the temptations of Upper Canada, she now works in the greasiest spoon in Alberta for the pleasure of serving these "good honest men of the road," represented by Lloyd and Jim (39-44). Lloyd is the typical Canadian loser, an "independent" trucker who, in an *entr'acte* song, resentfully tells about his role in the "Canadian balance of trade": he gets to haul the offending chicken guts while "The Colonel gets the money" (46).

The third and most dramatically extended set, tells the story of Lloyd's loss of his long-suffering wife and trucking partner, Molly, to the American driver of "a Kenworth rig." This romance is an object lesson in Canadian complaisance and American enterprise. This time, two raconteurs (the Jim and Sadie of the previous sets) guide the audience through the tale, interspersed with dramatized moments from the principals in either speech, song, or mimed comic illustration. As the plot thickens, the narrators play other brief roles in the familiar style of Passe Muraille. They also become chorus to the repentant Lloyd's futile search for his Molly across all of the United States. An American citizen and herself one of the best truckers on the road, she is now lost forever.

The second set, "Night Driving," is closer in substance to a Passe Muraille episode. It's the true story of James New, a trucker who suffers from the dark memories of a highway pile-up during a white-out on Ontario's Highway 400. (Savage had provided coroners' reports of this incident.) Initially, James New addresses the audience directly and factually before breaking into a ruminative song about stark nights on the road. The documentary detail behind his memories of the accident is alternately narrated by the other three. They speak to a musical background occasionally suspended for effect—for example, during their litany of the names of all those who died (54). The focus alternates between the two narratives: the haunted reflections of James New in the dramatic present as he drives cautiously along his route, and the narrators' retrospective account of the harrowing events of two years before. The two lines merge towards the end as James reveals himself to be the trucker involved. They are also mediated in the concluding up-beat mood of "Ridin' with Jesus," a gospel song inspired by Gray's discovery of a truck driver's magazine called *The Highway Evangelist* (Preface 22).

2. Billy Bishop Goes to War

Overall, *18 Wheels* shows Gray already working towards the structural flexibility and tonal variety that was to challenge him further in the storytelling of *Billy Bishop Goes to War*. In this musical play, the proportion of music to speech is reversed. Through this important shift of format, the play most precisely reflects the influence of Theatre Passe Muraille—in its spoken monologues, in its transformational characterization, and in its close attention to Canadian speech textures—through the collaboration of Eric Peterson, a gifted improvisational actor from Theatre Passe Muraille.

In subject matter and tone, this play is the natural descendant of the successful collaboration of Theatre Passe Muraille and Rick Salutin in *1837: The Farmers' Revolt*. Gray told Robert Wallace that he came to dislike what he called "the tragic aspect of Passe Muraille plays," alluding to *1837: The Farmers' Revolt* in this respect.[20] Yet the two works share the same mocking view of textbook history which characterizes the sensitivity of Theatre Passe Muraille in the 1970s to the issue of lingering colonial dependence. The difference in Gray's work is his rejection of the loser theme that ultimately could not be ignored in the other play. He chooses a hero who wins "because he was the best," thereby presenting "one image of Canada we don't often see."[21]

The germination of *Billy Bishop Goes to War* began in November 1976, when Gray was still completing *18 Wheels* and also performing in Ottawa, along with Eric Peterson, for Theatre Passe Muraille. Peterson discovered Bishop's autobiography, *Winged Warfare*, in an Ottawa bookstore. Over the next year, he and Gray became immersed in Billy

Chapter Four: John Gray 187

Bishop's extraordinary record as a fighter pilot in the First World War. They decided on a raconteur one-man approach for a play about Bishop as a war ace with an amazing capacity for killing and surviving. Peterson would perform all the parts and Gray would play the music—in the general manner of their production in 1975 of Tom Cone's *Herringbone*, a play that has some interest as a precursor to *Billy Bishop*.

Gray reports that Cone had originally written *Herringbone* for a large cast (there are 14 characters and speakers in the published text[22]) but was persuaded by director Gray and actor Jim McQueen to reconceive the work as a one-actor play.[23] Thus in a bizarre show-biz demonstration, star performer George Herringbone, age 35, accompanied only by an onstage piano player, re-invents himself, his relatives and their associates. He demonstrates how, when he was only 10 years old, his Albee-like parents turned him into a 35-year-old vaudevillian midget, only to discover too late for George that child stars had now become the rage. John Gray's songs, by the sheer typicality of their vaudeville sound and sentiment, accent the black absurdities of George's peculiar loss of selfhood and his sole destiny as the comic performer of his own life story.

In essence, *Herringbone* is the rather studied unfolding of a black literary conceit. The audience, as the only verification and *raison d'être* of George's existence, is manipulated into both shocked recognition of and amused participation in his perpetual performance act. By contrast, *Billy Bishop* is presented simply as "a champion story" told by "a champion story-teller."[24] The play's comic ironies and exhilarations are stated frankly and in large measure are shared directly by the speaker with his audience.

Early in 1978, Gray began the writing, completing a script in March. Theatre Passe Muraille offered him a three-week workshop of this script while Tamahnous offered a co-production with the Vancouver East Cultural Centre. Through joint research, Peterson made an important contribution with his interest in the technology of the time and his discovery of the popular expressions of the period. Reversing Passe Muraille's usual method of evolving the text from actor improvisation, they worked from Gray's written speeches, which were then "trimmed and shaped to Eric's speech patterns."[25] Eric Peterson's versatility as a performer was central to the success of the conception. The 17 additional roles embellishing the flying adventures of Billy Bishop posed no particular difficulty for him: unlike *Herringbone*, no more than two characters are in dialogue at once.

Like Passe Muraille's young Donnellys before him, Billy Bishop is depicted as a typically unruly small-town boy lacking a constructive channel for his energies. His cadet life at Royal Military College is a fiasco: he joins the army only because he is about to be expelled for cheating on exams. As a cavalry initiate in England, he is an accident-prone disaster. His one bright moment occurs at first sight of a single-seater scout whose pilot, he thinks, is warm and free from mud, horses and officers.

That Billy Bishop is both a colonial and a hero is the comic contradiction of the work and the essence of the contemporary theme behind the aviator's story. For a Canadian audience, Gray's best laughs in the first half of the play come from his digs at colonials and imperialists. For example, Billy expresses the colonial inferiority complex:"How can I get into the Royal Flying Corps?" he asks of a cockney RFC officer. "I'm Canadian. I'm cannon fodder."[26] Lady St. Helier, the grand dame of Portland Place, typifies the imperialist position when she perceives beneath Bishop's "rude Canadian exterior" the "power that will win wars for you" (52-53).

If Gray's point is that "there is such a thing as a colonial attitude that makes you try harder,"[27] then this benign Lady Bracknell has efficiently tapped the resource when she takes the blundering Billy Bishop in hand—especially since the life expectancy for new fighter pilots is "about eleven days" (33). But by the end of the play, Billy is so good at killing and surviving that he has to be taken out of active service before the laws of chance against fighter pilots finally strike him down. The general staff cannot afford to lose a "colonial figurehead" since, says General Trenchard, "the problem with your colonial is that he has a morbid enthusiasm for life" (92). In Gray's view, the British "like their heroes/Cold and dead" (77).

The story telling in *Billy Bishop Goes to War* identifies the essential Canadian structural feature for Gray, although such story telling also has an origin in military life as Billy Bishop himself records it in *Winged Warfare*. Here, Bishop tells how the members of his squadron used to exchange stories of their air fights in the relaxed atmosphere of the officers' mess, which indeed is the opening setting of the play. What is particularly relevant is the way they used to tell these stories:

> It was typical of the attitude of these comrades of mine that, when a man had been in an exceedingly tight corner and had managed to squeeze out of it, it was later related as a very amusing, not as a very terrible incident. And as the narrator would tell his story, the others would shriek with laughter at the tale of how nearly he had been hit and how "scared" he had been. It was such a wonderful way to take life, that upon looking back at it I feel that nothing the future can ever hold for me can excel those wonderful days.[28]

This is exactly the tone that Gray is so successful at achieving through his legion-hall version. The difference from what the real-life Bishop described is only in degree.

The Billy Bishop of the play, with the musical accompaniment of the piano player, takes the story telling further—into song as well as speech with characters he gleefully caricatures. But the important thing, specially in the first act, is the note of irreverent complicity with the audience. Everyone participates in the camaraderie of waggish offhandedness and exaggeration. Of course, this is a traditional way of dealing with essentially dark matters like war. Here, a colonial's perspective intensifies the audience's sense of Billy's personal involvement in an imperial war.

As a device for sharing intimacy with the audience, the raconteur technique of the play functions thematically in at least two dimensions that are shared between story teller and audience. This technique also explores a third dimension as far as the limits of the monologue will allow. In the last analysis, Gray's special achievement in this play is to acknowledge and transcend those limits through the irony of his songs. In *Billy Bishop,* he shows the capacity not merely to make a song "a natural extension of the narrative"[29] but also to put into a song something that "needs to be said that a character can't really say."[30]

First, there is the motif of acknowledged contemporary hindsight expressed in the play's pervasive comedy about colonialism. Of course, the historical Billy Bishop would not sense this in his own day with quite the same amusement as the stage character shares confidentially with us in ours. We laugh at his self-deprecation as a colonial bumpkin and at his caricatures of imperial condescension—for example, in Lady St. Helier's patronizing analysis of him as a "typical Canadian":

> I'm awfully sick and tired
> Being constantly required
> To stand by and watch Canadians
> make the best of it,
> For the Colonial mentality
> Defies all rationality.
> You seem to go to lengths
> to make a mess of it. (50)

Second, there is Billy's self-deprecating version of himself as the high-spirited bad boy who resents military discipline (especially when he is not having any fun). This motif fits well within Lady St. Helier's view of him. And he definitely lacks the proper war-time idealism of most of his contemporaries. His momentary enthusiasm, inspired by the patriotic fervour of embarkation at Montreal, is quickly deflated by the uncomfortable crossing on "the good ship Vomit" (28). His unheroic view of his circumstances, and of himself as a person swept along randomly on the tide of events, is expressed equally in caricatures of military figures he encounters. Billy is a winning story teller throughout the first act because of his robust sense of humour—not only at others' expense but at his own expense as well. He frankly confesses to incompetence as an aviator and to alternating fear, panic and exhilaration as he struggles for survival under the pressures of this frightening new type of warfare. Almost in spite of himself, he becomes one of the best fighter pilots of the Great War.

However, the disarming raconteur style is less adequate for the exploration of the third motif emerging in the second act. Certain ironies of self-unawareness also become evident in Billy's narration—such as the implications of his aggressive pleasure in killing and of his obsession with his rising score. To a point, Gray strives to incorporate this dehumanizing note within the theatricality of the legion-hall raconteur style. He tries to distance us from Billy's mounting enthusiasm for combat killing by using the stage language of adolescent games. However, this approach can provide the needed irony only by indirection, as we can see in two contrasting passages in Act 2 which comment inferentially on each other with respect to the motif of war as a game.

In the first passage, the famous one-man raid on a German aerodrome is deliberately "half told, half acted out" as "an adventure story" presented exuberantly "as a boy might tell a story, full of his own sound effects" (85).[31] At the end of the "adventure," he limps home, his plane in tatters, an exultant survivor who "never had so much fun in me whole life!" (91). Later, resentful that he is to be withdrawn from active service, Billy is eager to increase his score during the short time left. This leads to the sobering experience of witnessing his target plane disintegrate in the air with its two occupants still alive and falling. Here, Billy experiences his only qualms about the killing game, so he is "pretty glad to be going after all" (94). While not a sustained moment of moral awareness, it gives a certain balance to the character as a sensitive human being. Yet it deters us only briefly from our growing uneasiness about the nature of a military hero going off to enjoy the honours heaped upon him by his King.

A more detached perspective on events and attitudes emerges by considering the songs and the image patterns of their lyrics. While Gray argues that the play "does not address itself to the issue of whether or not war is a good thing or a bad thing" (Introduction 12), he is conscious nevertheless of the defence mechanisms needed for survival under wartime conditions. In the songs, these mechanisms are expressed ironically in two mythic motifs: the romance of war and the romance of imperialism. Sung sometimes solo by one of the performers, in duet or in choral refrain, the songs provide the foundation for an ironic technique that the spoken text by itself cannot sustain. In *Billy Bishop Goes to War*, Gray is more than merely reversing the proportion of song to spoken text, which had occurred in *18 Wheels*. While speech in the earlier play provided tonal variety within the narrative function of the music, the songs in *Billy Bishop* work more complexly. They function not only as personal response to event or situation but also as a more detached and counterpointing commentary to the spoken narration. The songs not only complement the monologue structure but also overcome its inherent limitations.

In the general movement from innocence towards experience in the first act, the songs speak ironically to a succession of evolving notions. Either held collectively or individual to Billy Bishop, these notions concern the heroic romance of war and its corollary, the pastoral romance of home, which surfaces in moments of stress. In the second act's concern with the realities of survival, the motif about the romance of war, expressed in the songs, takes a more sardonic turn. Gradually, it shifts in focus to what for Gray is the overall Canadian issue of the play: not the pros and cons of war, but the romance of imperialism as seen from our own ironic post-colonial perspective.[32]

The romance of war begins with the opening duet, "We are off to fight the Hun." This song describes and at the same time gently undercuts the naive enthusiasm of the inexperienced colonial boys, whose fighting sentiments are "correct" but whose perceptions and knowledge of war are faulty ("And it looked like lots of fun, / Somehow it didn't seem like war / At all...." 19). In comic counterpoint, progressively heightened in his descriptions of his own delinquent youth, Billy is neither "keen" nor idealistic, given his dislike of the military and his having volunteered simply as the lesser of two evils. Even his first awakening to the romance of flying is an escape from the hazards of basic army training and prompts a momentary lyrical nostalgia for home. "December nights / In the clear Canadian cold" are a comforting pastoral contrast to the alien world of mist and rain "far across the sea" (32).

According to the myths circulating when Billy Bishop is training as an observer, the rarefied camaraderie of life in the air is a world of a different order. The song "Champagne and Vermouth," prompted from Billy by the Piano Player, extols the chivalric *esprit de corps* of flyers on both sides of the conflict because they fight according to a more gracious code than the soldiers on the ground. The possibilities of death and destruction are not even mentioned: just the picture of one flyer forcing another to the ground after a virtuoso display of combat flying, the defeated enemy warmly toasted before his departure to prison camp (39-40). Of course, the reality is something else, as Billy soon discovers as an observer over the war zone. At a distance, Canada again looks romantic—with its "big blue sky" and "Northern Lights," a home of peace where "Nobody shoot[s] no one... / At least nobody they don't know" (44).

Billy's belated arousal to the romance of war—his personal equivalent to the opening song, "We're Off to Fight the Hun"—comes when he is finally accepted into pilot training (thanks to the influence of his patron, the redoubtable Lady St. Helier). The jingoistic "Gonna Fly" is sung with all the arrogant cockiness of the novice, but it soon dissolves into the hilarious anticlimax of his perilous solo flight. However, the haunting music and rueful lyrics of "In the Sky," the concluding song of the first act, offer a more subtle irony in the contradiction between the ideal and the reality. Billy Bishop has just enjoyed his first win in air combat, breath-takingly recounted in all its terrifying detail. Suddenly, his engine gives out and he finds himself floating down helplessly into the trenches to glimpse his first shocked close-up of the devastation below. The song, sung together with the Piano Player, begins by starkly contemplating the pathos and ignominy of such a scene. It gathers momentum in its expression of a collective yearning modelled on Bishop's own recognition earlier that his "only way out is up" (33)—into a cleaner and more heroic kind of war in the sky.

In effect, that romantic illusion reaches its climax at this point. The sustaining myth of the *esprit de corps* expressed in "Champagne and Vermouth" is now accommodated somewhat perversely to a new and starker experience. At the same time, this myth still insists on the special dignity of the whole flying enterprise, which is disallowed in the chaos of the fighting below. The possibility of death during the exhilaration of aerial combat is no longer ignored. Yet death is glossed over in the graceful pattern and intimacy of a dance performed by "the hunter" and "the hunted" ("Oh, let us dance together in the sky"). Like separating lovers, one partner waves a sad "goodbye" to the other in the *Liebestod* of his "last returning / to the earth" (65).

In the second act, as the pressure of air warfare becomes more severe for the RAF as a whole, the romance of flying becomes more contorted. The ironic undercutting of "In the Sky" becomes more stark with the black humour of the opening song, a perverse celebration of a macabre consummation in death of "the bold aviator" and his beloved plane. The *esprit de corps* takes on a grotesque self-sacrificial dimension in the dying aviator's cheerful orders to "the sobbing mechanics" for a toast to his memory from "six good airmen" and a resurrection of the machine from the bits now embedded in his broken body (167-168). Conversely, this song introduces the realities of survival as opposed to heroic gesture as far as the developing career of Billy Bishop is concerned. It also prepares the way for the ironies of Gray's thesis that, in contrast to the colonial's "Life-Wish" (92), "a decadent culture worships death."[33]

Time has passed and Billy Bishop has become extremely efficient in air-combat tactics: "If you want the machine to go down every time, you aim for one thing: the man. I always go for the man" (69). Background to this is the mournful musical theme "reminiscent of a French café" (69), establishing a contrasting setting and tone to Bishop's brisk factual accounts of triumph, on what is for him quickly becoming a totally depersonalized proving ground. Bishop is increasingly disassociated from the heroics of self-sacrifice and fatal statistics, as indicated by the mordant little eulogies on pilots who "didn't survive," sung on a bleak note of erotic fatalism in the *chanteuse* voice and gesture of "the lovely Hélène." While "Johnny," "George," "Geoffrey," and "Jimmy" suffer the consequences of emotional involvement in what they are doing, ranging from patriotism to cowardice, Billy has no such problem:

> You're part of a machine, so you have
> to stay very calm and cold. You and
> your machine work together to bring the
> other fellow down. You get so you don't
> feel anything after a while.... (71)

The choral advice to flyers is "Remember, war's not the place for deep emotion, / And maybe you'll get a little older" (70, 72, 73). One stanza, nevertheless, is reserved as a caution against over-confidence ("You may think you're something special," etc. 74).

The effect of the combined music and speech in this sequence is perhaps still ambivalent in its attempt to balance the negative impact of Bishop's increasing pleasure in the skills of killing with the pragmatic recognition that his cool mental attitude is a decided advantage in the circumstances. At the same time, the romantic notions of aerial combat, elaborated in Act 1 and reaching their zenith with "In the Sky," are held up to severer scrutiny in both the sung and spoken passages. There is nothing rarefied after all about either quick and violent death or determined survival in the air. But, within the context of the recurring ironic focus on the colonial/imperial relationship in time of war, Bishop's successes are positive.

The Albert Ball sequence makes a direct statement to this effect. Initially it's a dialogue, then turns into a haunting recitation of doomed fanaticism "performed like a Robert Service poem" (77) instead of a song. Here, Gray elaborates and contrasts the conception of heroism in a decadent imperial culture with that in a colonial culture. In the latter, he remarked to Wallace, the issue is survival and therefore "living for something has value"; in the former, "Dying for something is a value."[34] As a colonial boy, Billy Bishop is ultimately prepared to try harder to stay alive. Therefore, he is unamused by Ball's proposal that they should become "compatriots in glory" in the "grand gesture" of a suicidal plan to raid the German aerodrome at Douai; Billy wants a line of escape included in the plan (75). With Ball's death occurring before the feat can be attempted, Bishop later takes it up on his own, but more as a challenge to his own daring and skill than as a longing for martyrdom. "The Death of Albert Ball" is his tribute, an extended eulogy commemorating the tormented spirit of the young solitary with a record of kills Bishop has yet to match. Unlike Bishop, Ball "courted the reaper, / like the woman of his dreams," serving Gray's bleak argument that "the British like their heroes / Cold and dead, or so it seems" (77).

However, as the reciter, Bishop is infected as well as angered by the implications of Ball's story. He is bitter at the collective insanity of the martyr principle wherein "Just to be alive is something of a sin." Yet he himself is drawn into the fatal spell of the idealism Ball represents: "And my name will take the place of Albert Ball" (79). That the spell is pervasive is indicated in the subsequent "Friends Ain't S'posed to Die," a more comprehensive variation on the elegiac mood in which Bishop and the Piano Player sing a nostalgic lament for a whole generation of youth lost "back then." In short order, Bishop nevertheless recovers his buoyant colonial spirits in London, enjoying a respite from morbid thoughts as the now acknowledged "Number One" live hero—"Just a Canadian boy, / England's pride and joy, / My fantasies fulfilled" (84).

Ironically, however, after the success of his one-man assault on Douai and his rising score during that summer, Bishop gets his summons to retire for the sake of colonial morale (which "plummets" if the "colonial figurehead gets killed"). Significantly, this summons comes when he is one short of Ball's score (93). The personal trauma of his one bad moment preceding this departure—shooting down the still living enemy fliers from their shattered plane—seems insufficient in appropriate introspection (as suggested above). Yet this shortcoming is somewhat redressed by Gray's broadening the theme in the latter part of the act. The ironies of the romance of imperialism affect both Billy Bishop in his subsequent career "as a living colonial figurehead" and "us," the collective colonial society. Together, we sing a chorus to the imperial scheme of things through another world war.

The brief comic scene follows in which Bishop is honoured by the King who, in Lady St. Helier's word, is "amused" that the first person to receive three medals at once is "from the colonies." Then Bishop announces the celebratory dance as a tango, wryly entitled "The Empire Soirée." Unfortunately, the full effect of this song is diminished somewhat in the published text by the exclusion of its opening counterpart, "Canada at War."[35] In both songs, the dance functions as an ironic metaphorical inversion of the romance of war echoed in the dance motif of "In the Sky." The discarded opening ballad originally set the political stage of the play as a rousing series of courtly dances under negotiation among the "lovers," which is to say alliances, of Europe:

> Well Britain, France, and Russia
> Struck up a fine romance,
> And Germany asked Austria
> Oh would you like to dance:
> And all these fine old lovers
> Made their plans on bended knee,
> As befitted the Continental Aristocracy.

According to the jingoistic choral refrain, the unsophisticated and eager colonials, as a humble version of the romance of empire, naturally follow the lead unquestioningly: "If it's good enough for England, / Then it's good enough for us, / And the Colonial boys are linin' up, / We're linin' up, / We're linin' up for war!" In contrast, the victory dance of "The Empire Soirée" is sung "sotto and sinister" as the on-going "dance of history" (98-99). In this dance, an anonymous power behind the scenes is forever calling the ominous tune, making social requirements, as it were, like those Lady St. Helier makes of Bishop. These cannot be ignored—least of all by the Billy Bishop who is now imperially co-opted by royal recognition.

With the aid of the ironic substructure of the songs, the playwright takes the irony at Billy's expense further than in his one moment of fear in the air. In the end, Gray targets both the colonial and the imperial mentality, although the treatment of the former is somewhat softened in the context of the latter. Bishop's last spoken utterance in the play is a Second World War recruitment speech. So twenty years later, a new dance at the perpetual "Empire Soirée" has begun. But the tune is a repeat, so to speak, as indicated by the reprise of the play's opening "We Were Off to Fight the Hun" which precedes Bishop's imperialistic war rhetoric. As a figurehead, he has now become the useful colonial voice of the imperial romance, even though he seems a little weighed down by his medals when he speaks. His final personal note, although slightly bewildered, is ultimately complacent: "Makes you wonder what it was all for? But then, we're not in control of any of these things, are we? And all in all. [sic] I would have to say, it was a hell of a time!" (101).

The deeper irony rests in the concluding reprise of "In the Sky." No longer is this song a lilting reinforcement of the romance of flying but an enigmatic reminder of the seductive power of myth in the face of stark complexities of another war time reality. This ending was a modification of the original for Mike Nichols's production in New York. Lewis Allen, Nichols's partner, is quoted as saying "We feel it needs a better ending to point up what learning and liking to kill did to Billy. It needs more irony at the end."[36] Gray comments that the "documentary/factual feel" of the original was changed to the more dramatic and ironic ending because the play "had to work as fiction in the U.S."[37] But to Canadian audiences, the ironic ending comments less on the personal "fiction" of Billy Bishop than on the persistent recurrence of the ironies of a colonial condition that helps to perpetuate the imperial myth.

3. *Rock and Roll*

In a discussion about the destructive side of his Billy Bishop character, Gray remarked that he approached the play "as not being about Bishop but someone I knew in Truro—a type of person that is useless in peacetime but whose destructive urge is really useful in war if channelled rightly."[38] A preliminary stage direction notes that Billy Bishop's "speech pattern is that of a small-town Canadian boy who could be squealing his tires down the main street of some town at this very moment" (19).

Gray's memories of Truro and what the squealing tires imply emerge explicitly in his next work, the musical play *Rock and Roll* of 1981. Similar to *Billy Bishop,* this musical play focuses on the undisciplined and rebellious energy of late adolescence. Here, the restless young people of the fictional Mushaboom, Nova Scotia—the generic nowhere town of the 1960s—escape the stultifying restrictions of small-town life through the liberation of rock and roll. The Monarchs are a memory of Gray's own band, the Lincolns (in which he played from 1965 to 1968). The frenetic high-flying of the period is epitomized in the ghost figure of Screamin' John McGee. He's the presiding spirit of local rock and roll, whose destructive urge leads to his death in a spectacular car crash at the age of 19.

Gray was inspired to write the play after the popular success of a Lincolns' reunion and dance in 1978. The occasion was a catalyst of the same order as his Listowel experience of audience enthusiasm four years previously. The old fans loved the music because it was *"their band"* and evoked *their* collective memories. Writing in 1981, he called this kind of music-making "small-town Canadian culture"—a popular culture that, like the character Parker in the play, he had always assumed "you left home to find."[39] Only later, in a nationalist frame of mind, was he to emphasize the derivative nature of this Canadian institution of local rock-and-roll bands named after American cars. Borrowed or not, the popular culture that *Rock and Roll* explores—the raucous one-night gigs passing for musical performance—is whole-heartedly the characters' own way of being young, free and wicked before growing old and ordinary. The same applies to the fans. In the words of Shirly, the Monarchs' staunchest supporter, "there are a lot of people out there who think you're more important than the Beatles and the Rolling Stones combined" (149). Here in Mushaboom, at their reunion performance, the Monarchs have replaced Screamin' John McGee as local myth.

Framed in the present time (1980) with the Monarchs nervously gathering for their reunion, the body of the play is a retrospective of the 1960s. This central section traces the growth of the band, primarily through its rehearsals and performances, from eager and incompetent 16-year-olds to popular local success by the time they break up five years later. It shows the four Monarchs coming to terms individually with their past and present lives and, in the process, finding a collective meaning in the bond with their local audience. This bond is a reality that has nothing to do with riches, success or the lack of it in their personal lives. Gray has described the personal story lines of the performers as the Monarchs' "unsentimental examination or playing through of 'the time of their lives'" as they put the past and its unfulfilled hopes behind them in the reunion-night performance. By "completing something," he says, "the characters can go on." He cites the concluding song "Hello Tomorrow" as "the key to the play."[40]

As a play of character growth and articulated recognitions, the work is slight. The dramatic reality of the play lies in the needs the band has served in each character as an individual type, what each has brought to it, and the disagreements that comically divide them still. One point is clear throughout the retrospective scenes: that except for the sideliner Shirly, the music and the audience are a distant second to their more basic concerns. Volatile rich-boy Manny and cynical poor-boy Chink are in it for disreputable adventures of the road, aspiring Brent for the money, and Parker for the possibilities of becoming a star (132). Only at the end are these aims (and the ensuing disappointments of the next 15 years) made to seem less important than the fact of their audience's whole-hearted pleasure in their collective return. The playwright does not explore the ironies of personal failure that he raises in his characters. Rather, he leaves the four resting on their laurels in the final moment of union between the band and its audience.

As in Gray's previous work, the structure is clearly designed to establish immediacy with its audiences—in this case by specific address to the playwright's own generation (at the time of writing, between the ages of 30 and 40). They, like the characters, are being invited to share in what Martin Knelman refers to as "the ambivalent longings of adults looking back on the joy ride that didn't take them anywhere."[41] For his sense of place, Gray draws on the society and townscape of Truro, Nova Scotia. But he conveys the local colour of typical Canadian small-town life generally rather than by an argument for specific regional uniqueness explored, for example, by Christopher Heide in *Bring Back Don Messer*.

The music, of course, has the most direct appeal. Essentially, *Rock and Roll* is cast in the appropriate mode of popular performance and, as in *18 Wheels*, the music is integral to the subject and format of the play. The performers are characters who exist both within and beyond their musical material. However, this complication calls for a number of conventionally dramatized interactions of the characters behind the scenes. For these, songs often serve both narrative and thematic functions as expressions of individual personality. For example, Parker's "The Fat Boy" solo is essentially a well-placed response to derision about his appearance when he applies to the band as the much-needed singer. His point that one day "you" will be the same and the "fat boy" will have the last laugh is only one of the many pervasive allusions in *Rock and Roll* to the brevity of "the time of their lives" (125-126) and that of the audience to whom the song is actually addressed.

In the second act, Shirly and Brent—in the privacy of their favourite haunt, the graveyard—sing solo and in duet on the subject of their future together as "normal people, living in the normal world" (139-140). This song climaxes a predictable romantic relationship. Gray makes a livelier point through Shirly's private ruminations on the subject of the macho "Boys' Club," which in those days excluded girls from participating in the onstage excesses of rock and roll (117-118). Such motifs help to tell the story and to draw the audience into its own retrospection. In keeping with the general format of the play, such songs are presented as performance, since the play is enacted largely in some variation of a performance setting. Exceptions to this are two shifts in scene to the graveyard where Screamin' John is, in effect, both master of ceremonies and performer.

Integrating the recollective dramatization of the story into the actual event of the performance is Gray's most successful method of directly engaging his audience in the spirit of the times. For a play largely about performers performing, he incorporates *Billy Bishop*'s raconteur style into their rock-and-roll presentationalism. The work opens, in song and argument, as the rehearsal for the reunion. To initiate the retrospective history, each character—within the frame of the song "Just a Memory"—has a spotlight focus on him for an introductory personal monologue spoken in the manner of onstage patter of performers to audience (101-104). Over the course of the play, different characters alternate in this role of master of ceremonies and raconteur, introducing—through their personal accounts of their thoughts and actions—the succeeding phases in the band's development as demonstrated in the music of the scene.

The best example of musical performance as dramatic event is Parker's description in performance (the others playing "as though the band were at a dance") of his first night as lead singer. His actual singing is framed by his graphic narration of events before, during, and after that memorable occasion (126-129). Shirly is the more ruminative raconteur in the opening segment of Act 2. The scene begins with Parker's singing of "The King of Friday Night" to underline the point that the Monarchs are at the peak of their success. However, in the comments spoken by Shirly from her continual spot at the side of the stage, it is clear that their disintegration as a group is at hand. There are also several extended dramatic monologues that further the narrative from individual points of view. Manny's take the form of confession and prayer to a deity whose balance-sheet prerogatives resemble those of his resented father, the local rich man, D.B. (114, 140). Parker's is addressed to his widowed mum at supper, explaining that he has to go to Toronto because "I wanna be something a whole lot different than me" (145).

The enigmatic figure of Screamin' John McGee, identified as the local spirit of rock and roll, hovers nebulously between the performance and the dramatic dimensions of the play. Here, Gray seems to be moving ambivalently between the composer's urge to recover the rock-and-roll cult of his youth and the writer's retrospective compulsion to anatomize its components. Like the performers of *18 Wheels*, Screamin' John is a recurring theatrical rather than naturalistic presence, his role cast in song, in musical rhythms or in verse. As a local rock-and-roller, he is the hero to and inspiration of the band, giving them equipment and teaching them songs before his grisly accident—passing on the torch, as it were. As such, he fulfills his most coherently realized function in the play as archetypal performer, principally encapsulating the high energy of the rock-and-roll craze and at the same time infusing that whole scene with a cautionary edge. He is at once the explicit embodiment of the frenetic side of the *carpe diem* activity and the implicit warning of its disappointments and dangers.

At his first appearance (not yet a ghost), his warning song precedes his "Play a Little Rock and Roll." Seedily dressed in his 1950s performance costume, he sings about himself as a burnt-out joyrider, whose "visions of mortality" at the age of 19 include the awful possibilities of capitulation into boring suburban routine (110-112). In this surprising middle-class concern (despite the potential violence in his tone), he anticipates the doldrums of the later Brent, while his fear of lumps and "pitter-patter" in the chest suggests Manny. In his "shoot the shit" seediness and contempt for small-town restraints, he is closest in nature to the cynical and perennially unemployed Chink. His philosophy is that release from everyday tedium and adolescent stress is to be found, of course, through motion (112-113). Later, as a graveyard ghost, he reminds Chink—who is in despair after the band's breakup—that "When the situation's out of control / You better rock / You better roll" (143-144).[42]

At the same time, like Billy Bishop's flying-corps companions lamented by the lovely Hélène, he has not himself survived. In the words of his song in the penultimate scene of the original version of the play, he is "Stuck in time, in my prime, / the ghost of nineteen fifty-nine" (117)—a little reminiscent of the fading names on the statues of "Friends Ain't S'posed to Die" in the earlier play. Nevertheless, it is thematically fitting that his signature song, "Play a Little Rock and Roll," is sung at the reunion scene by all, including Shirly, who is initiated at last into full membership in the cult of local rock and roll (150). Not surprisingly, he makes a final appearance to sing a verse of "Hello Tomorrow." Thus, the spirit of Screamin' John is absorbed into the final performance as part of the process of completion that the reunion is intended to represent.

In a more intrusive manner, the Screamin' John figure also functions at random as a kind of choral commentator in various personal scenes. While his intrusion could be rationalized as appropriate, since he also embodies the particular spirit of rebellion that finds its outlet in the music, the effect overloads the retrospective irony in a rather belaboured effort to exchange reminiscent winks with the audience. Consider, for example, his presence as sardonic voyeur and pontificator in verse and song on the nervous gropings of Brent and Shirly (parked in the graveyard). Later he narrates the cautious negotiations of Parker, "the underage drunk" (he could as well be Parker himself speaking), sneaking conspiratorially into his churchgoing household at 6 a.m. on a Sunday morning (129-130). Again somewhat out of character, Screamin' John has the playwright's own sharp eye for textural detail and ironic juxtapositions—for example, when he describes the furnishings of Parker's home or when he establishes the setting for the second-act graveyard scene (Brent is about to propose to Shirly): "Oh, there's a bit of a view to the south of the Salmon River, lazily makin' its way to the Bay of Fundy / Carrying the crap from D.B.'s hat factory" (137). While his individual moments are often expressed vividly, his role as ghostly master of ceremonies to the audience on guided tour of Mushaboom is, dramatically speaking, redundant.

Gray has recently shed some light on the origins of the character (and therefore of the problem) as a "parody" of the Stage Manager in Thornton Wilder's *Our Town*: "In Screamin' John, I wanted to create that Stage Manager's nasty Canadian relative who has similar insights, but without all the pious wisdom, without all the answers" (Preface 91). This explanation also helps to account for Gray's choice of the graveyard as alternate setting. Unfortunately, the overall effect diffuses the primary intention of the figure as the spirit of rock and roll and perhaps truncates the dramatic potential of the individual living characters.

In the light of Gray's "Canadian-ness" (a term he finds more acceptable than "nationalist"[43]), his stated intention points to a burden of unresolved irony in *Rock and Roll*. It has less to do with the implicitly acknowledged "derivative sensibilities" of the local band; as in *18 Wheels*, Gray's ability to write his own popular music (often with just the smallest suggestion of parodic edge) frees him from the charge of being a colonial sycophant. Rather he uses popular music to reach his audience in familiar ways that, with the help of his lyrics, also remind it of Canadian differences. Since Gray had already learned how to break through the proscenium from his experience at Theatre Passe Muraille and in the writing and performance of *Billy Bishop*, the attempt to parody Wilder is itself redundant.

In *Rock and Roll*, he is trying to reach his audience on two levels of direct address—the immediate and the retrospective. But what he seems to have forgotten temporarily is the marked difference of effect on the audience between the informality of a good raconteur—for example, Chink or Parker—and the pseudo-literary commentary of a discursive narrator. The parody backfires. Not only does the work lose immediacy when Screamin' John becomes a voyeuristic word-painter, but Mushaboom is also diminished by the intimation of its being a Canadian *Our Town*, especially since the allusion points to a dramaturgical weakness in Gray's play.

4. *Don Messer's Jubilee*

Gray's next work, *Don Messer's Jubilee*, followed in 1985. Commissioned by Tom Kerr for Neptune Theatre,[44] this work is closer to *18 Wheels* in its musical format than to *Rock and Roll*. The piece is not a play but, in Gray's own words on the programme, "a fan letter," cast formally in an approximation of a typical Don Messer show.

Gray shows two specific intentions in the new work: first, to demonstrate that, in their nearly 40 years of radio and television broadcasting, Don Messer and the Islanders preserved and transmitted an "old-time" musical culture expressing the traditional values of ordinary Canadians everywhere; second, to advance a political point, characteristic of his platform stance of the period, that "Canadian institutions stifle Canadian culture by design."[45] In respect to the latter, his specific target is the CBC, whose abrupt cancellation of "Don Messer's Jubilee" in 1969, despite ten years of continuing top ratings, to him "symbolised the rejection of the whole of Canadian culture."[46] While either point may be debatable, the work is nevertheless of considerable interest for its theatrical methods of engaging audiences in a further variation of the performance mode that has been Gray's most constant form of creative expression. In this respect, *Don Messer's Jubilee* may be regarded as a Passe Muraille theatrical encounter writ large, a country-wide collective community of former Don Messer television fans.

Before discussing the point, however, it is useful to note some telling thematic connections with *Rock and Roll* that in hindsight seem to anticipate Gray's increasing cultural nationalism. One has to do with the Monarchs' discovery of their special place as a local band in their own generation's community mythology. Although Gray himself alluded subsequently to his own rock-and-roll days with the Lincolns as "basking in second-hand glamour and borrowed charisma,"[47] the general point still stands: a home-grown version has a more immediate appeal to an audience than an imported one. A related theme from *Rock and Roll* is Parker's insistence to his mother that he must go to Toronto if he is ever to become a singing star. He believes that in Mushaboom he will always remain just "the fat kid on the block," whereas away he can become "a whole lot different" (145). He also feels alienated from the solid small-town values of his parents, specifically expressed in the song "Mom and

Dad." In his eyes, parents belong to a simpler and more stable world ("And straight meant no lying. / And gay meant no crying") foreign to him (146).

Through the exploration in *Don Messer's Jubilee* of what he takes to be a rooted rather than a synthetic form of musical culture, Gray seems to be making a tacit apology to Parker's mom and dad on two accounts: his own generation's natural distrust of the traditional small-town world and that generation's contribution to the demise of the cultural tradition represented by Don Messer (Preface 159). He also demonstrates the fallacy of the common Canadian assumption that to be a successful artist one has to become (like the CBC mandarins of Toronto) a "culturally displaced person." Thus, the new work in effect begins where *Rock and Roll* ends—in down-home cultural territory. But this time it is rooted regionally, the musical and dance traditions brought from the old country by earlier generations and kept alive by rural fiddlers such as Gray's own grandfather. Performers become stars not by going away and trying to become "a whole lot different" but by staying home and remaining the same. Don Messer, the perennially smiling old-time fiddler; Marg Osborne, homely but wholesome; and Charlie Chamberlain, everybody's stout and slightly raffish uncle—they are celebrated here as modest Maritime performers who, by remaining local in their music and appearing as just plain folks in their stage personae, become "Canada in musical form" to a country-wide audience.[48]

Here, Gray is casting his popular entertainment net wider than ever before. Perhaps this causes him to make more sweeping assertions about the universality of British-Canadian down-home traditions than the multicultural complexity and regional disparities of the country warrant. Knelman writes: "For those who were urban and non-British, any old American sitcom seemed closer to home than Don Messer."[49] The point that the CBC killed Canadian culture when it cancelled the Don Messer show is satirically asserted more than convincingly explored—a dash of mother-corporation bashing that speaks resentfully of "culturally displaced persons" adorned in Nehru jackets and love beads who believe that programming should reflect "the correct aspirations of those in charge" (194). In the words of "The Corporation Reel," as performed by the Buchta Dancers: "We wanna hear the Beatles sing / Messer is embarrassing" (196-197). Otherwise, within the confines of the performance mode Gray has chosen, he is largely reinforcing sentimental memories about the popularity of the show itself and of the stage reality of the performers.

It is interesting to compare Gray's approach in *Don Messer's Jubilee* to Christopher Heide's earlier play *Bring Back Don Messer*, performed by the Mulgrave Road Co-Op in 1980. Gray is ostensibly simulating Messer-style performance. Within the performance structure, the Islanders' clarinetist and master of ceremonies, Rae Simmons, combines his colourful stage patter with an on-going, somewhat editorializing narration in which he recounts the origins of the band, the traditions from which it comes, and its subsequent history. His story is illustrated by back-projections of actual photographs. In fact, photographic icons are the only way in which the taciturn Messer is himself present in the show (see Preface 161); his part is otherwise fulfilled by the musicians.

Heide, in contrast, dramatizes the traditional Maritime song-and-dance culture as a living reality in the lives of one particular (fictional) family; over the decades of increasing threat to the indigenous culture pressured by technological and social change, the Don Messer programmes help keep that culture alive. The actual Messer performers never appear in the play but instead have their counterparts in the characters. On one occasion, when the family can't get the sound working on their new television set, they all join to make the familiar music themselves. When the show is cancelled, the negative effect on the creative dynamic of family and community life is all too clear.

On one hand, Gray is evoking the Messer era by recreating the connection between performers and audience as an actual theatre experience of the nation-wide show. On the other hand, Heide is mimetically dramatizing its meaning to representative characters within the immediate culture from which the show derives. Heide invites identification with a representative fictional world of which performance is an essential ingredient; Gray invites participation in a live performance.

However, audience participation in Gray's musical is more than merely foot-stomping, applauding, singing "Smile Awhile," and approving the sarcasm towards the CBC. Despite the emphasis on clever simulation, there is a degree of difference between what Gray and his cast effect on stage and an actual Don Messer television evening. It is on this level of difference that *Don Messer's Jubilee* best demonstrates Gray's ability to draw the audience actively into the performance. As a community theatrical encounter and as a myth-making enterprise, the work demonstrates its descent from the collective creations of Theatre Passe Muraille. The community is of course a very large one. Defined not by regional geography but by airwaves and television signals, it consists of all the people who were once fans of the Don Messer show. As a large element of Gray's audience also, they are invited into a familiar world of popular performance personalities, who in their stage representations are not entirely like either the pictures on the back-projections or the remembered figures and voices of the originals. For example, Jodie Friesen in the cross-Canada tour was a disconcertingly slim Marg Osborne; but in the words of one reviewer—"in the way she carries herself, sets her feet, and cups her hands...she is Marg Osborne."[50] The same sense of recognition is familiar among audiences of community collective creations: when an actor like Eric Peterson may feel that his "line drawing" of an actual person is "nowhere close," yet the audience supplies the rest.[51] In such cases, the creative encounter between actor and audience is the important form of the participatory process.

Similarly, the songs have the familiar sounds and many of the familiar sentiments; but they are, of course, written by John Gray in an approximation of the Messer repertory. This gives the composer/playwright a certain leeway, for example, to articulate the popular performance personalities, particularly of Marg and Charlie, through songs about themselves. In this respect, Gray is fulfilling his aim to "mythologize"[52] the Messer group. As a result, even audiences who never knew them (like the subsequent audiences of the community collectives) can respond to the characteristics the Messer performers came to represent in the collective mind of their public.

The unglamourous Marg is a model in her own way ("Never give up hope, girls / even I became a star" 172), but she also shares the unhappiness of all the "Plain girls in love with / conceited young men" (186). Charlie, with his "voice like a New Brunswick spring," singing his "songs of old emotion" (such as "My Little Flower"), pumps gas in the summer, presumably to keep himself in beer money (175-177). There is a duet of comic behind-the-scenes discord ("It's Been Going on For Years") between the prim Marg ("If she's ever perspired / I would be very much surprised" 194) and the earthy "slob" Charlie ("Droolin' on my nice dress / And snappin' my brassiere" 192) which is not entirely in keeping with the soulful tranquility of their regularly featured "Quiet Time" gospel song. Messer's physical absence from the show may also be considered as part of the myth-making, specifically alluding to his role as all-Canadian victim to corporate insensitivity. Certainly by the end of his show, Gray exceeds himself on this score by insisting that, in the aftermath of the CBC cancellation, Don, Marg and Charlie virtually died not of heart trouble but of broken hearts.

In two general respects, Gray's dramatic themes may be seen to take a point of departure from Theatre Passe Muraille: in his focus on Canadian geographical identities, and in the ironic myth of colonial dependence and imperial exploitation. With regard to the first, *18 Wheels* is a country-wide overview with an emphasis on distances between people and places. *Rock and Roll* posits a fictional Maritime town with its own concretely rendered physical and social configurations and textures.

However, it's offered as a generic representation of society for the Canadian rock-and-roll generation as a whole, whereby historical time foregrounds the specific place. In *Don Messer's Jubilee*, the geographical emphasis is on the cultural origins of what is seen as a national institution, recognizing that Don Messer was for many "Canada in musical form." The occasional images of Canadian place in *Billy Bishop Goes to War* are appropriately general and romantic in their nostalgic context. But as indicated earlier, Billy's character type belongs to the same cultural milieu as *Rock and Roll*.

Although, in the introduction to his collection of musicals, John Gray denied that "any deeply-felt political nationalism" (14-15) motivates his creative work, certain variations of the nationalistic theme in *1837: The Farmers' Revolt* find their way into his work. For example, "The Canadian Farmer's Travels in the U.S.A." is satirically inverted for a latter-day setting in *18 Wheels*' cautionary tale of the complacent Lloyd and his enterprising trucking partner and wife, Molly. Both pieces are parodies of Canadian apathy in contrast to American enterprise, self-reliance and friendly assimilation. The difference is that Davis, the farmer, returns from his journey inspired but not seduced (like Molly) by what he sees; whereas for Lloyd, the loser, it is too late. In vain, he speeds his "old and rusty Mack truck" across the border to try to recover what has been lost to the driver of the American Kenworth rig, who is "ready to take it all away." Canada as consolation prize ("If I must live alone / It will be in my native land") makes its own sardonic point.

As an historical play, *Billy Bishop Goes to War* is in a more direct line from *1837*. The satirical and anti-imperialist tone of the latter has some of its best moments in burlesque and caricature—such as "The Head," "The Family Compact," "The Dummy," and "The Lady in the Coach." In *Billy Bishop,* the tone translates into a colonial comedy of manners, with the "imperial ventriloquist" John Bull, as it were, still in control of Peter Stump. More specifically, Lady Backwash (the lady in the coach, who is usually played by a male actor) as the intrepid

Chapter Four: John Gray 213

investigator of quaint and uncouth colonial local colour now emerges in the full flowering of Lady St. Helier. She is the patronizing London society matriarch with a shrewd sense of the usefulness to empire of the power beneath the rude colonial exterior of the young man from Owen Sound. Gray's point—that Billy Bishop becomes the best because colonials have to try harder and have a stronger instinct for survival than older cultures—results in a witty example of the virtue to be made out of colonial necessity. The 1837 story, to the regret of its creators, could only tentatively provide this in Lount's "We haven't won yet." Gray seized the opportunity to temper the current hero repertory of Canadian drama with a winner for a change.[53]

In *Don Messer's Jubilee*, the political line of attack is from within the society, directed at a cultural institution for whom imported media trendiness is more desirable than what is identified here rather sweepingly as national cultural expression. In this case, however, Gray may be confusing two separate and more complex issues: commercial media marketing on the one hand, and urban take-over or marginalization of rural culture on the other. What Gray sees as manifestations of specifically Canadian colonized cultural displacement in the executive branch of the CBC might be better understood as a sign of the inevitable response to shifts in the sensibilities of that day. His interest in writing *Rock and Roll* makes an obvious example. *Don Messer's Jubilee* therefore succeeds better on the level of popular media myth than as a convincing analysis of national cultural politics. Unfortunately for the fate of indigenous Canadian culture, the question of "who killed Don Messer?" has no such simple or single answer.

To this point in his career as a playwright/composer, John Gray's most notable work has been informed by his desire to reach a popular audience for Canadian theatre. In three of the four works under discussion here, he has drawn on his particular gift for witty musical pastiche as the initial point of cultural contact with his specifically identified audiences: the fans of country-and-western music in *18 Wheels*, the sixties generation in *Rock and Roll*, and the mom-and-dad generation still lurking in the ancestral memories of all Canadians in the old-time music of Don Messer. Thus, his most important contribution to Canadian drama and theatre has been in the exploration of Canadian themes and character through popular entertainment modes: the legion-hall and tavern entertainment, the rock-and-roll dance band, and the television variety show.

Gray's singular ear for popular music has been a major factor—notably, as in *Billy Bishop Goes to War*, in combination with the wit and irony of his lyrics. *Billy Bishop Goes to War* is undoubtedly his strongest dramatic work, showing his capacity to work collaboratively with an actor of like mind on the potentials of creative storytelling. In the years following, however, musical theatre seemed to be his more characteristic form of expression than drama. After *Don Messer,* he continued in this vein with a musical version of John Buchan's *Thirty-Nine Steps* (its hero is a Canadian!). Yet his most recently produced work, *Health, The Musical* (premiered at the Vancouver Playhouse on February 24, 1989), once more featuring Eric Peterson in multiple roles, recalls that fruitful collaboration—this time in combination with a new popular music score and a back-up chorus.

The 1984 revival of *O.D. on Paradise*, directed by Gerry Potter at Workshop West Playwrights Theatre. From left to right: Dennis Robinson, Francis Damberger, Earl Klein, Christine McInnes, Jane Heather and David McNally. Photo: Gerry Potter.

Chapter Five
Linda Griffiths' Transformations

The lines of demarcation between collective playmaker and individual playwright diminish in the work of Linda Griffiths. Among the several playmakers who began working with collectives and who have since become playwrights in their own right—Ted Johns, Cindy Cowan, Sharon Stearns, for example—her work most consistently reflects the collective process: in the genesis and development of its subject matter, or in its completed form, or in both. Transformation is a key concept in her work, both as an actress highly skilled in the transformational acting required of collective creation and as the maker of her own plays, where transformation is a form of expression and increasingly a theme. Like Rick Salutin in one respect, Linda Griffiths has always worked on her own plays in some form of collaboration: with Paul Thompson for *Maggie & Pierre* (1980), with Patrick Brymer for *O.D. on Paradise* (1982), and with Paul Thompson and Maria Campbell for *Jessica*, which also premiered in 1982. Initially, the latter was a collective creation but was revised extensively in 1986 by Griffiths in consultation with Campbell and Clarke Rogers, the dramaturge and director.

Griffiths began collective creation at 25th Street Theatre in Saskatoon with *If You're So Good, Why are You in Saskatoon?* Thompson directed this production during Passe Muraille's visit in 1975 to create *The West Show*. Griffiths had come to 25th Street Theatre from Montreal at the end of the previous season, playing a role hastily invented for her in Andras Tahn's equally hastily written play, *The Ballad of Billy the Kid*. For Tahn, founding artistic director of the three-year-old theatre, this was a last-ditch effort to save a failing season. Written by Tahn in only three days, the play was a resounding success, thanks to the collaboration of director Christopher Covert and the company in reworking the play and developing their characters from "raw script."[1] Griffiths played the fictional character of Angela, Billy's wistfully romantic girlfriend.

In the comic physicality of *If You're So Good...*, Griffiths created Bev, the disaffected reporter for a university newspaper. This character is bored to desperation with the same old distractions—beer, pot and seduction—and exacerbates her black moods by decorating her apartment with an over-sized noose. Bev is the first to escape from the ennui of life in the so-called "Paris of Saskatchewan." But homesick for stubborn prairie skepticism and the empty landscape, she soon returns from bland Vancouver, bringing the moral of the play and with it, the title. She is more than ready to shake her fist at the next person who asks the sneering question.[2] Griffiths later explained, "we made heroes out of people who stay in a place that isn't the centre of the country and who love that place, but who are crazy and modern and mixed up. They're a type of anti-hero."[3]

Tahn's guiding principle at 25th Street was to provide a theatre to keep the local talent at home as well as "to raise the calibre and widen the scope of local and regional culture."[4] His association with Thompson was a large step in that direction, because the introduction of collective creation to his theatre opened up new possibilities for the exploration of that regional culture. The first production of *Paper Wheat*, about the struggle of Saskatchewan pioneers to found the wheat pool, opened on March 18, 1977, in Sintaluta, Saskatchewan. It was the prime example of that thrust.[5] Here, Griffiths' versatility as a comic performer and inventiveness as a collective creator came to the fore. The play was much revised in its second and best-known version for provincial tour in the fall by a predominantly new collective (except for Sharon Bakker and Michael Fahey) directed by Guy Sprung. Yet Griffiths' original contribution is still in some evidence in that version.[6]

Since the first collective was composed of two men and four women, Griffiths helped to adjust the gender balance with her atypical character of Jean Shirley, a Scottish mail-order bride who adjusts very well to independent homesteading when her groom fails to show up. She's the one who teaches the first lesson in neighbourly co-operation, offering a spare ploughshare in return for some good home-cooking. She's the one with the team of oxen, which nearly breaks *her* in her stubborn attempt to break the prairie. In the revision, the ideas remain but they are transferred more appropriately to male characters. Griffiths also wrote the earthy "Smells" monologue, created the witty lyrics of "Grain Exchange Rag," and originated the old sod-buster's nostalgia that sums up the meaning of the play. This episode brought Saskatchewan audiences to their feet every time. With her vivid language and talent for turning a dramatic parable, the writer in the performer was already becoming apparent.

In the winter of 1978, she rejoined the collective-creation enterprise at 25th Street Theatre for *Generation and 1/2*, also directed by Sprung. This commissioned sequel to *Paper Wheat* has a semi-futuristic plot that examines the present critical state of the co-operative movement from the vantage point of A.D. 2028. In this play, Griffiths created Kathy somewhat on the model of Jean Shirley. The character is a Saskatchewan farm girl who resents the stereotyping of women and longs to return from her "voc ag" training to work the family farm in the modern way. The following summer, Griffiths joined Paul Thompson's collective project in

Montreal, *Les maudits anglais*, with writer Gary Geddes. The play is a satirical piece performed in French to show the *Québecois* audience how they are viewed by English Canadians outside Quebec. Here, Griffiths showed a gift for parody: first as Myrna Potash, a Ukrainian reporter from western Canada compulsively in search of the separatist story; and then briefly as Trudeau, performing behind a cut-out figure of the prime minister.[7] This second characterization led to Thompson's suggestion for a play about the Trudeaus with Linda Griffiths playing both principle characters. Like Thompson, she was always interested in developing the collective creation in new directions.

1. Maggie & Pierre

Maggie & Pierre previewed at Theatre Passe Muraille on November 30, 1979. Griffiths' collaboration with Thompson differed from the usual collective process only in intensity and concentration, not in kind. Thompson has described Griffiths as the improvisational source of "all of the verbal work, all of the character work" and therefore the author. But the programme clearly designated the work as a collaboration "with Paul Thompson." Thompson explained, "if I'm not there, it can't happen." This collaboration involved not only shaping the work and making the choices of what must go or stay (at one time, the collaborators considered incidental characters) but also following Thompson's characteristic practice of suggesting improvisational situations for strengthening character, whether the scenes were used or not.[8]

Griffiths refers to the method as "mind-track," which she describes as "like a seance" in which she would take on the personality of the character in a given situation "and say and do whatever happened." The third character of Henry, the ubiquitous journalist, "evolved from me asking questions about Trudeau because he's such an enigmatic character and the Trudeau character would answer."[9] Before the nine-week-long process began, she had spent months gathering both archival and first-hand material. But rehearsals started with only a few speeches and notes written down. As the rehearsal process went on, they taped and transcribed. Eventually, they introduced a stenographer who took down the various versions of scenes for them to compare on the spot. The more than two hours of play that they had developed by this point was finally reduced by a third.

As one-person plays, the most obvious of several differences between *Billy Bishop Goes to War* and *Maggie & Pierre* is the latter's multiple points of view. Besides the two protagonists, there is the observing reporter—in effect, the myth-maker who shapes their story for us (the public who is the audience). This reporter also becomes personally connected, sometimes as confidante, to his subjects. *Billy Bishop* presents the single point of view of the narrator and raconteur who tells his own story—in part by transforming into other, often incidental, characters along the way. *Maggie & Pierre*, in contrast, requires a continuing focus on three principals. With the exception of Henry's occasional speeches of direct address to the audience—as the teller and enactor of the play in which he is also a participant—the individual scenes observe the convention of the fourth wall. They are performed in sketched-in settings with backdrops and with back-up rock music and other sounds.

Thompson—as scenarist the year before at Blyth for Ted Johns' written monodrama for seven characters, *The School Show*—had already been working on the development from raconteur structure to the illusion of a transparent fourth wall, which the multiple point of view invites.[10] In Johns' play, however, the connection between the characters is thematic rather than interactive. Each of a series of characters depicts his separate perspective on the issue of the recent teachers' strike in Huron County. The result is a virtuoso exercise in both dramatic monologue (the second speaker is implied) and intricate impersonation (the monologuist enacts all the conversations he is reporting to the audience) within a mimetic structure. One character is even provided with a dummy companion.[11]

Maggie & Pierre relies more closely on refinement of the presentational techniques developed for and by collective creation. These techniques include characterization through suggestive language and movement (rather than insistent mimesis) as well as consistent, although modified, transformational acting. There are frequent costume changes (engineered discreetly rather than openly), but these do not occur at every point, depending on which character has the focus of the scene. For example, Pierre is represented wittily by a black sleeve on Maggie's arm when they talk and dance on their first date. The organization of the individual scenes within Henry's narrative frame provides a full range of dramatic expression within the one-person format: from interior soliloquy, to dramatic monologue sometimes shifting into dialogue, to fully dramatized scenes of two speakers. During one occasion—a *tour de force* at a journalists' bar—all three characters are engaged in argument.

The play is a chronology of juxtaposed scenes ranging over 11 years of the Trudeau era—up to the Liberal Party's defeat in May 1979. However, it is not a political play but, in the playwright's words, a play about "emotional connections to politics"[12]: those of the media, as represented by Henry (and by extension the media-oriented public), and those of Maggie and Pierre in relation to their public and to each other. The episodes selectively highlight the progress and decline of Trudeau's political romance with the country through the personal romance, marriage and parting of Maggie and Pierre. In effect, the personal story emerges as the metaphor of the public one. Altogether, says Griffiths, the play is "a metaphor for much larger concerns going on in the country and with people" related to politics, marriage and the idealism of both (Introduction 10).

In its selection of material and in its manner of presentation, *Maggie & Pierre*—like the best collective creations of Thompson and Theatre Passe Muraille—is consciously informed by its intended audience. In principle, it is a community collective writ large in its

Chapter Five: Linda Griffiths 223

nation-wide appeal (confirmed by its successful trans-Canada tours) that comes essentially from its witty and intimate characterization of familiar media stories of the time. To complain, as did some reviewers, that the play offers no more than what we already knew about the eponymous characters is in some way to miss the point. Like *The Farm Show*, but in a more urbane manner, *Maggie & Pierre* takes its audience through a discovery and a myth-making process (Henry's, which is the media's) as indicated by the subtitle, "a fantasy of love, politics and the media." In effect, the play is a post-media event in which the playwright is imagining from the inside those familiar media versions of Canada's most public private couple of the day.

Behind Henry is the authorial point of view—Griffiths' discovery, in the personal and public conflicts of the Trudeau story, of a parable of the hopes and uncertainties of Canada in the 1970s. In the first scene, when Henry is deciding to tell that decade-long story "one more time" in order to get it out of his head, he says to the audience:

> There's something at the centre of the story, something that affected everybody deeper than they're willing to admit.... Certainly something that offended everybody! (16)

Griffiths is interested not only in the public perceptions projected vicariously on the Trudeaus but also in the way the protagonists contribute actively to the myth-making (and to their personal difficulties). This is accomplished through their own consciousness of themselves as media performers and their continual manipulation of the media audience.

This realization comes only gradually to an unformed Maggie who, nevertheless, spends her early adulthood ingenuously trying on the available identity roles of the day. These range from preppy to hippy to flower child—all of which combine comically in her first dinner date with Pierre. Even more absurdly, her role playing blossoms with increasing confusion in the composite last scene of the first act, where she is the prime minister's young bride on duty among the sedate and famous of the diplomatic world. Here as the self-appointed voice of the "now" generation, she tries unsuccessfully to "show them what a little love is all about" (47) while, to her horror, she discovers that "they think I'm one of them" (49).

By contrast, the middle-aged Pierre, alternately gratified by Trudeaumania and skeptical of it, is already a skilled performer with his public image in place. He reinforces his political principles, using a charismatic pirouette and a rose (21-22). Tellingly, one of his fascinations for Margaret at that first dinner is his shifting image: "He changes, frame to frame to frame. It's like watching television!" (37). Public disillusionment comes later, after the imposition of the War Measures Act ("The very things they loved of me six years ago, they can't stand in me now"). That's when his shifting image is revealed as calculated political strategy. ("The only way to stay alive is to avoid their wish to define you" 64.) By this time, his shiftiness has lost its fascination for Maggie, who is "freaking out" with boredom and the incompatibility between her autocratic philosopher/king and his "little jolt of electricity" (57).

At this point in the play Maggie, always alert to the press's intrusions on her awkward moments, begins to stage her own media events. She tells "all" at the bar to her sometime defender Henry, interrupted but not inhibited by Pierre who, in Henry's books, has become the villain all around. (Maggie tells him later: "You're starting to look like those cartoons" 81.) In the penultimate scene, which combines the fatal election-night results and Maggie's escape to a New York disco (and to the Rolling Stones), she turns for the first time to the actual audience, the surrogate of her now offended media audience. The always thin lines between public and private, image and reality, disappear in her taunting performance of "the woman who gave freedom a bad name":

along comes little Maggie Trudeau, doodle-doodle-doo...and she falls apart right in the middle of your television set.... And we don't like that, do we, ladies? Noooo. And we don't like that, do we, gentlemen? Nooooo. Because if Maggie Trudeau, with all the advantages, falls apart, where does that leave us? In the same boat...Welcome aboard. (95)

Occasionally, reviewers have suggested that the play could be performed better by three actors instead of one. (Griffiths herself has speculated on that possibility and, indeed, the ill-fated New York production placed Eric Peterson in the role of Henry.) However, this might raise expectations of the play on the level of psychological realism, to which it never seems to aspire. As a play about living people, it presumes to explore only the public perception of those people. It is less an examination of the psychological intricacy of a personal relationship than a theatrical analysis of popular media psychology from both the giving and the receiving ends. In essence, the journalist Henry is the key figure of the play—both as its storyteller and as its interpreter—by depicting his characters in action.

2. *O.D. on Paradise*

At a glance, there seems little obvious connection between *Maggie & Pierre* and Griffiths' next work, *O.D. on Paradise*. This was a writing, not an improvisational collaboration, with actor Patrick Brymer. In Griffiths' words, "there were pieces of paper before there was a life on stage."[13] It had its premiere at 25th Street Theatre in the winter of 1982, during the period when Griffiths was co-artistic director at the theatre along with Layne Coleman and Andras Tahn. At this time in the theatre's history, Coleman, acting artistic director of the previous season, was trying to excise the grassroots populist image continued by Tahn after the success of *Paper Wheat*. His idea was to move into "contemporary things" with scripted plays; he no longer wanted to "romanticize the West" but rather to look "at things more the way they are, in a naturalistic, more documentary style."[14]

Griffiths and Brymer got the idea for *O.D. on Paradise* during a vacation in Jamaica before the opening of *Maggie & Pierre*. There were "characters and situations knocking at the door," she said in 1982.[15] She later explained more fully, "There was a kind of group energy that happened among us as we kept pushing and pushing to experience a 'full' vacation."[16] The play explores the situation of eight Canadian travellers determined to enjoy their one-week tour package in an exotic place and shows how little or how much they can shed of their normal selves in the process. It was performed in workshop, directed by Clarke Rogers at Theatre Passe Muraille, before the opening at 25th Street Theatre and then revised for a remounting at the Toronto theatre, where it won a Dora Award for the best new play of 1983.

Although the play's genesis is not collective creation, the process resembles collective creation in one way and the play itself is like others that *are* the product of collective creation. It originates in the personal base that Thompson always advocated for his actors and that Griffiths expressed through the character of Henry in *Maggie & Pierre*. The co-authors of *O.D. on Paradise* also found this base in the group energy of "people desperate to relax."[17] It also reflects a general pattern, often found in collectives, where an alien situation prompts the characters' comic assertion of their native social identities—as in *Les maudits anglais* and *Paper Wheat*. More specifically, there is the democratic stress on individual characterization. In *O.D. on Paradise,* there are eight characters (distinct types beneath the textures of personal idiosyncrasy) given equal attention, in contrast to the more usual designation of central and subordinate characters in literary naturalism. Also like the collective, there is less a plot than a general unifying theme in episodic format—in this case, the experience of a tour package itself: six days of fun in the sun

Chapter Five: Linda Griffiths 227

and, ideally, a quick melting of tensions and inhibitions.

The liveliest and most unpredictable characters are the working-class family of four: Fred, the overbearing boozed-up father, determined to get his money's worth in good times; his new wife Peggy, an overweight "Queen of Sheba" who plays the fool but clearly is not; the diffident Joan, frightened of the tropics and of her new husband; and Vic, Fred's browbeaten son, newly married to Joan. Vic is the one who mysteriously overdoses on the joys of sun, sea and tropical creatures. The urban sophisticates are Joey and Candy, a married ex-hippy couple; he is now an upwardly mobile lawyer while she, Maggie-like, is an ex-flower child offended by Joey's new conventionality, including the tour package itself. Other vacationers include Karen, guilt-ridden by her "very good job" and her "cuisine art" in the face of the world's poverty, Jamaica's included, and her "gigolo" Robin, a trendy, rootless Englishman quick to "go native" (originally performed by co-author Brymer).

In the first script, characters lean toward talkiness, either about themselves or about the situations of the moment, leaving little to the power of suggestion or innuendo. This is a vestige of the downside of the collective process, when loose and wordy speech patterns pass sometimes for contemporary dialogue.[18] It is a problem Griffiths alludes to herself in speaking of the "slightly heightened" language she looks for when she "writes" collective plays (and found from listening to journalists while researching *Maggie & Pierre*).[19] In the revision of *O.D. on Paradise*, the dialogue was tightened while the language became more lyrical at key moments.[20]

The play is loosely structured on character interaction over the six-day period, heightened by comic collisions between the travellers and the allurements of the tropics: reggae, rum, a little pot, Rastafarianism, and the beach life generally, to which each becomes increasingly susceptible. Because of its inherently episodic nature, critics of the version at 25th Street Theatre tended to pronounce the play formless and disjointed—in one reviewer's words, "lacking a strong developmental line."[21] For *Maggie & Pierre*, Thompson had worked structurally according to collective creation's principles of highlighting and juxtaposing rather than attempting to contrive a naturalistic cause-and-effect continuity. For *O.D. on Paradise*, therefore, Griffiths relied on Brymer for the appropriate sense of structure she claimed to be lacking.[22] This meant resolving the problems of moving eight characters plausibly in and out of the scene under the restrictions of a fairly tight chronology, of maintaining comparable dramatic attention to each, and of providing each with a clear line of action. One characteristic way in which Griffiths was able to contribute to this, however, was to take a role (Joan) in the first version—"because only as an actress could she get inside the play to acquire an instinctive feel for the areas that needed improvement."[23]

In revision, the scenic structure became increasingly cinematic —with rapid shifts in focus enhanced by overlapping dialogue and speeches trailing off. Although characters were modulated more subtly in their conflicts and growth, *O.D.*'s essentially naturalistic mode (emphasized by a full load of sand and exotic beach elements on stage[24]) is still at odds somewhat with the play's quirky risk-taking ending. This relates to the character of Vic whose naive fascination with the tropics—a refreshing contrast to Robin's faddish transformation into dreadlocks and Rasta—gives him the fortitude to free himself at the age of 36 from the domination of his father.

However, even this altered state of mind does not quite prepare us for the mystical dabblings inherent in Vic's strange death in the penultimate scene of the play. Through the week, he has become fascinated with the beauties of underwater life. Now, having successfully completed a series of spectacular dives from a nearby cliff, Vic inexplicably loses consciousness; he is lying on the beach with his family ineptly trying to cope, mostly by fending off the others. During these moments, Vic "speaks" three times, which nobody actually hears except the audience, although the other characters are supposedly sensing the oddness of his condition. He soliloquizes in a manner that expresses his identification with the sea and its life—a message of mystical fulfillment strangely at odds with the comic naturalism of the play. This scene was modified in a later emendation: Vic's words are spoken before he takes his last dive; some are repeated by his wife Joan as he lies dead on the beach.

Interestingly, however, this hints at the direction that Griffiths was beginning to take during the summer following the *O.D.* premiere, when she began to work with Maria Campbell and Paul Thompson on a dramatic version of the former's autobiographical *Halfbreed*. This collaboration would lead to a more daring form of dramatic risk-taking in the matter of altered mental states, the possibilities for which the collective mode was more directly responsible.

3. *Jessica*

As early as 1979, Paul Thompson had conducted an improvisational workshop with Métis writer Maria Campbell, attempting to create a dramatic version of *Halfbreed*. They used material cut from this published autobiography and also concentrated "on her journey since its publication" in 1973.[25] For Thompson, this workshop was a further expression of his abiding interest in western-Canadian material, increasingly in its potential for fantasy and surrealism on stage. The latter interest began with the three historical ghosts of *Far As the Eye Can See* and continued in 1981 with the Passe Muraille improvisation on Robert Kroetsch's *The Studhorse Man*. Campbell's interest in theatre was first sparked by Clarke Rogers' seed-show collective in 1974, *Almighty Voice*, and soon after by *The West Show*. Her collaboration with Thompson was an opportunity to learn a theatrical process that she felt would educate and empower native audiences.

Campbell and Linda Griffiths first met in 1980 during the tour of *Maggie & Pierre*. They agreed that Griffiths would improvise the central character, who was to be drawn from Campbell's own life. In the spring and summer of 1982, the *Jessica* project began in earnest. The two women met in Campbell's home at Gabriel's Crossing to assemble basic material. They also travelled to native communities in Saskatchewan and Alberta and even attended a native ceremony conducted by Campbell's spiritual teacher. A three-week-long collective workshop followed at Theatre Network in Edmonton. The participants were Thompson, Campbell, Griffiths, Bob Bainborough (from the original *Paper Wheat*), and native actors Graham Greene and Tantoo Martin (now Cardinal).

By the end of the workshop, Griffiths records, "we had characters, situations, but little material which could be used verbatim." This terse programme note from 1986 indicates nothing of the complexity of the initial process as recounted in 1989 by Griffiths and Campbell in *The Book of Jessica*. The other actors made lasting contributions to characters created to that point—notably Cardinal's Vitaline, Bainborough's Crow and the lawyer Bob, and Greene's Sam—but the major challenge was Griffiths' Jessica. Thompson had set up a volatile creative situation at the opposite extreme to the genial impersonations of the people of Clinton in *The Farm Show*. Both Griffiths and Campbell were keenly sensitive to the inevitable tensions arising when a white actor attempts to portray a native role, especially one dealing in a very personal way with racial suffering and abuse.

For Griffiths, the situation was intensified by the fact that the major resource person of the play was also its main character. "For sheer audacity this couldn't be beat," writes Griffiths. "I stood up and acted out my impression of Maria Campbell to her face."[26] Under the circumstances and despite her considerable experience as an improviser, Griffiths—like so many Passe Muraille actors before her—began to long for the writer to write. This would rescue them from "the wide-open terrors of improvisation" with "some nice safe scenes for us all to play." Meanwhile, Thompson told Campbell "that you couldn't control what happened in this kind of rehearsal, that all you could do was put out the information and see what the actors did with it."²⁷ One of the characteristically daring suggestions from Thompson was an improvisational exercise in which the actors played animal spirits. Griffiths' Wolverine was to become the most potent dark force in the eventual play. The increasing emphasis on the sacred world of native spirituality was becoming a delicate issue—no less from Griffiths' point of view, it seems, than from Campbell's.

The next phase of development was unique. Instead of reassembling an acting collective or (as in the case of Wiebe and *Far As the Eye Can See*) of sending the writer home to write a script from the improvisational tapes, Thompson negotiated with Campbell to allow Griffiths to improvise the whole play herself. The improvisation was to occur at Theatre Passe Muraille's BackSpace in the early fall; the opening of the play was already scheduled for November at 25th Street Theatre. No doubt, Thompson had confidence in this plan because of his experience with Griffiths in developing *Maggie & Pierre*. However, this process introduced the writer-on-her-feet in a new way. It placed a playwright's responsibility on the key performer for material she would not necessarily be performing herself. That this was a further stimulus to Griffiths' own creativity is evident, for example, in her invention (through the role of Vitaline) of the mixed-blood spiritual ceremony that became central to both theme and structure in subsequent developments of the play.²⁸

In this phase, the work became a collaboration rather than a collective creation. Griffiths built on the characters and scenes from the Edmonton workshop while Thompson and Campbell continued "to direct, hone and feed in new ideas."²⁹ The taped results of the three-week effort were transcribed into the rough script presented to the cast at rehearsal. Three of the four members of the original collective were included, with Thomas Hauff replacing Bainborough. While the actors all made some further contributions to the play, the director's note on the programme at 25th Street Theatre credits Campbell with the subject matter, Thompson with the structure, and Griffiths with the dialogue.

The acknowledgement of the division of labour three ways—an acknowledgement more specific than any other for collective creations—gave some reviewers a handy prod into flaws they thought were to be expected from a play patched together by a committee. Reviewer Caroline Heath was more alert to "the deeper than sociological intentions" and appreciative of the playfulness of the Métis sensibility at the core of the play. But in noting the need for further work, she reported from a discussion with Maria Campbell that the co-creators planned "to return to the play in a few months."[30] However, for personal reasons (aired much later by the collaborators), months turned into years.

Griffiths recounts that she finally returned to *Jessica* in 1984 after working with Caryl Churchill on *Fen* at the Public Theatre in New York. Churchill's brief mixture of real and super-real in that play suggested the even greater potential for "an entire play in dream and shadow"[31] waiting to be fully realized in *Jessica*. Over the next year or so, she rewrote *Jessica* by herself and eventually persuaded Campbell to renew their collaboration, with "the final elements coming in during a two-week session" at Gabriel's Crossing[32] in the fall of 1985. The play, now subtitled "A Transformation" and billed as having been written by Linda Griffiths in collaboration with Maria Campbell, opened at Theatre Passe Muraille in April 1986 under the co-direction of Griffiths and its latest dramaturge, Clarke Rogers, who was then artistic director of the theatre. For Campbell, Rogers' participation marked a full circle from the days of her admiration for his approach to native themes in *Almighty Voice* more than a decade earlier.

Even in the first phase of its play development, *Jessica* is a vividly concrete rendering of a feminine journey of self-discovery and spiritual growth.[33] On its simplest narrative level, it recovers in flashback crucial highlights of Jessica's story: from broken childhood and marital desertion to the traumas of prostitution, drug addiction and, later, to native activism and spiritual discontent. In its naturalistic dimension, the material derives roughly from *Halfbreed*. But the play goes well beyond the "familiar tale of native oppression" and "schizophrenic cultural dilemma of the Métis" noted by a national magazine reviewer at the time of the opening at 25th Street Theatre.[34]

Campbell's "journey" since the writing of her autobiography was the inspiration for something far more radical in theme and dramaturgy. The mixed-blood ceremony conducted by the old shaman, Vitaline, provides the basis for the flashbacks and for the introduction of the four animal spirits evoked by the ceremony. Essentially, the play is a mystical journey towards the recovery of the spirit forces embodied as animals, which Jessica has the gift to see but has been rejecting since childhood. That she is half-white creates particular conflicts. In Indian terms, Jessica is struggling to summon the visionary power to sing her own song; in universal terms, she must go back in order to go forward.

In a 1988 interview with Doris Hillis about the background of *Jessica*, Campbell speaks of her increasing awareness over the years of the "strength" and "profound spirituality" of women. Here, she speaks openly of her own return to the religion of her great-grandmother—a theme she excised from *Halfbreed*.[35] Even so, her depiction in the latter of Cheechum (her great-grandmother Campbell, a non-Christian who was also a niece of Gabriel Dumont) as the emotional support and spiritual teacher of her childhood hints at that direction.[36] In hindsight, Cheechum suggests the prototype of Vitaline and perhaps also of the grandmother who appears in Jessica's dream vision of childhood to offer her the gift of her guardian Crow.[37] Further to the "power of women," in her children's book *People of the Buffalo* (1976), Campbell distinguishes between the spiritual gifts of Plains Indian women and those of the men.

"Some people," Campbell writes, "think that in the Indian way of life the boy was glorified; on the contrary, the girl was considered the stronger spiritually because, like the earth, she gives life." She outlines how, at puberty, a boy had to go on a quest for the vision of his guardian spirit, revealed through fasting and meditation. For a girl, in contrast, "power to communicate freely with the spirits" came with the menstrual cycle. Because the spirits around her were uncontrolled at the time of menstrual onset, a girl was placed apart in a teepee, "guarded for four days by an old medicine woman who could communicate with and control the spirits."[38] In the play, these spiritual gifts are latent in Jessica; she has been seeing the animals all her life but has tried to ignore them, particularly Crow. She's had no guidance in her youth concerning the knowledge and power to accept and control the spirits. Only in her chronological maturity does she begin to value her natural gifts. As the process of vision intensifies under Vitaline's ceremonial direction, control becomes most difficult; for example, her spirit goes wild and destructive when possessed by Wolverine.

Combining with Campbell's emphasis on the ancient spiritual power of women is a feminist social theme. The latter was mildly evident in Griffiths' previous work in collective theatre and built gradually in her own plays. In a 1983 interview she noted:

> It was in the collective that I got encouragement to go for the female perspective. That was part of the populist ethos of collective theatre, which aimed at capturing the perspectives that the mainstream culture was likely to ignore.[39]

Her typically untypical women in the plays at 25th Street Theatre are witness to this direction. So is her essentially sympathetic interpretation of Maggie, broken but still defiant in her conflict between flower-child notions of love and freedom and Pierre's male-centred rationality and sense of public decorum. In *O.D. on Paradise*, Candy, the ex-hippy wife of a career-anxious lawyer, is trapped in the double role of beguiling and nurturing female. Karen, her opposite, is a liberated professional woman who theorizes that the feminine fight for mutual independence is a necessary and heroic struggle.

In outline, Karen anticipates Jessica's struggle with her native activist lover Sam. In his discouragement over the bureaucratic frustrations of his political crusade, he expects ego-stroking solace from her. He jokingly notes how he best likes the look from her that tells him "I'm your Iroquois brave and you're my vermin-infested halfbreed" (150). In the parlance of old Vitaline, with a little assistance from Unicorn and Wolverine, the whole earth is suffering from an imbalance between sun and moon dating back thousands of years since women were persuaded by "glory in sacrifice" to submit to the dominance of men:

> He took and she gave and gave until there was nothing left but migraine headaches and sacrifice.... The whole earth has to do with that balance, the tides and the winds and the growth of everything. Nothing can be right again without it, nothing. (170)

In *Halfbreed*, Maria Campbell makes only one incidental reference to the women's wisdom that Sam fears from Jessica's tutelage under Vitaline—but in an anti-Christian, not in a feminist, context. The narrator is seeking to explain to herself why a supportive male Indian friend changed his attitude towards her when she ventured to speak out in public meetings.

> The missionaries had impressed upon us the feeling that women were a source of evil. This belief, combined with the ancient Indian recognition of the power of women, is still holding back the progress of our people today. (168)

Through the collaboration on *Jessica*, however, she is able to speak openly of this modern conflict between male and female elements, both in society and within the individual, and to suggest their resolution in the wisdom of "The Old Way."

Integral to Jessica's spiritual journey, of course, is its basis in the very specific circumstances of the Métis struggle between two worlds. In several ways, Jessica makes the point that she is naturally drawn to the white world. Vitaline's canny acknowledgement of the conflict initiates her supreme ceremonial effort with a modern medicine "bundle" contained in Jessica's suitcase. Her high heels are laid out to mark the four sacred directions, papers from her work lie at the centre of the circle, and she herself is instructed to don her bathrobe and to plug her Walkman into her ears. This is hardly highfalutin obscurantist shamanism but rather a spiritualism rooted pragmatically in the facts of the modern world. The sense of this is reinforced by the earthy, often humourous tone of the whole ceremonial venture and is sustained by the idiomatic texture of the dialogue at all levels.

In the first version of *Jessica*, the present-time ceremonial moments upon which the play is structured are intercut with both naturalistic and supernaturalistic flashbacks. The ceremony itself has its own supernatural elements, with Vitaline's evocation of Bear as presiding spirit and of the comical Crow, Jessica's ubiquitous guardian, who as such plausibly enters several of the flashback episodes as well. But more vivid as a theatrical moment than coherent in structural terms is the late one-episode introduction of the full animal-spirit pantheon (in the flashback context) halfway through the play. Not only does this introduce new animal-spirit characters, Coyote and Wolverine, but it rather belatedly sets up a whole new convention in the play—the explicit identification of the spirit figures with human counterparts. However, this one "Group Spirit Scene" is the basis for the play's development, in Griffiths' later and inspired formalization of the structure into a mythological parable of supernatural intervention, for which the animal spirits *perform* human roles.

A comparison of the two versions shows how *Jessica* evolves in complexity of theme and structure from the two most characteristic elements of the collective process. One is the multiple-characterization that transformational acting provides, used in *Maggie & Pierre* more as an interpretive rather than a mimetic technique. The other is the episodic structuring: the usual collective play, as indicated elsewhere, grows through the juxtaposing of individually improvised units rather than through a closely integrated developmental format. *Jessica*'s flashback structure lends itself to the collective method because the flashback process is by its nature discontinuous. Also, as elsewhere in Thompson's later work, the lines between fantasy and actuality can be drawn less sharply than in conventional naturalistic drama. In *Jessica*, the combined elements of multiple-characterization and discontinuous structuring paradoxically provide the means for giving concrete dramatic reality to the governing concept of the play. This is the Cree belief in the unity of spirit life, or soul, in all living things, which Jessica must re-learn in and through the presence of the animal spirits who are each part of her being.

In the first version, the play establishes a thematic relation between some, but not all, of the natural and supernatural characters performed by the same actors. Explicitly identified are Bear and Sam, Jessica's activist lover; Coyote and Vitaline; Wolverine and, for a time, Jessica. But the structural rationale for other identifications is rather hit-and-miss, suggesting the expediency characteristic of small-cast collective creations. Thus, while there is a rough irony in the Vitaline actor also playing the prostitute friend Liz, this has no thematic bearing on the Vitaline/Coyote identification. Nor is there any clear connection established by the Crow actor's multiple performances of a jeans salesman in a more or less naturalistic scene of sado-masochism and Bob, the white power-broker lawyer, who helps bring out the voracious "wolverine" side of Jessica.

In revision, the partial identifications of human and animal spirits disappear as such into a governing fabular mode of supernatural intervention. The flashbacks emerging from the ceremony are Jessica's "shadow dream of what has happened" (125); they are visions of her past, not their naturalistic reconstruction, although some scenes are still played naturalistically. The animal spirits evoked by Vitaline's ceremony agree to take Jessica back in time by engaging in a series of interventions, for which they transform themselves appropriately into the people of the dream visions of the past and perform *their* roles in Jessica's life. In other words, the human guise of the animals is part of the ceremony, whose purpose is to provide Jessica with clear parables of meaning from certain key people and moments of her life.

Thus, Coyote plays Vitaline; Bear, Sam; Wolverine, Bob; and a newly created Unicorn plays Liz. Jessica's feckless childhood guardian spirit, Crow, with his passion for poolhalls and racetracks, is mostly but not always himself. The only human characters actually on stage are Jessica and Vitaline, while the animal spirits collectively represent the discordant components of Jessica's own soul, which she must recognize and finally bring into equilibrium. Thus, the play uses multiple-characterization not only to its full conceptual capacity but also to its full presentational capacity. In this way, the spirits function both as audience and performers as the need occurs—as if they were party to the discovery process of their own collective creation, in which they improvise ways of interpreting Jessica to herself.

Since the animal spirits are a full and continuing presence in the play, the actual audience is always privy to their actions and their views about the actions of others. Far from solemn and remote "deities," they chat and argue among themselves as they determine who should be next to enter Jessica's dream moments. To participate as people, they remove their animal masks and enter the human areas of the stage. The design has varied in production. For instance, at the Theatre Passe Muraille premiere, on Griffiths' instruction there were three stage levels, the highest suggesting a kind of Cree Olympus; the middle, the Métis world of Vitaline's kitchen, once Jessica's family home; the bottom level variously a whore-house, Sam and Jessica's apartment, and the city world of white encounters. For a remounting by Northern Light Theatre in

Edmonton, directed by Larry Lewis on a thrust stage, most of the dream-vision scenes took place in a roughly circular ceremonial space downstage. This space took the shape of an earthpit surrounded by a ramp usually inhabited by the animal spirits and giving a more immediate sense of their hovering presence at all times.

In the revised play, the idea of ancient feminine power under seige through the millennia is intensified by Griffiths' addition of a bold mythological appropriation. This is added to Jessica's Cree pantheon in the form of a female Unicorn, a fabular beast, traditionally a male, noted for ferocity except at mating time. Here the figure expresses the spirit of archaic *female* mysteries: "...wildness. And lunacy. And ecstasy" (118). While Unicorn appears to be one of "the final elements" to emerge in the last phase of the collaboration between Griffiths and Campbell at Gabriel's Crossing, yet the need for such a figure was implicit, even at the initial stages of collective creation back in 1982. At that time, according to Campbell's recollections in *The Book of Jessica*, she was wondering rather desperately why her white collaborators were failing to draw on their own traditions of historical oppression and related cultural repression (Celtic tradition, for example) instead of leaning so heavily on hers. For Griffiths, Unicorn emerged to restore the balance in response to talk "about the unexplored white side of Jessica."[40]

Structurally, this provides a spirit counterpart to the character Liz, especially suitable if the latter is played as a white woman. Narratively, Unicorn introduces herself to the other spirits as "what's been missing" (125) in the ceremony so far. Her incongruity in the context of the Plains Indians is confronted comically in the other animals' amazement at her appearance and particularly by Coyote's matter-of-fact statement: "I saw you at the Bay, you had a big pink bow and you were sitting on a candy-cane rainbow" (119). However, Bear slowly begins to recognize Unicorn as "a relative, part of us that was left behind long ago" (123). As Liz, she is Jessica's instructor in the wiles of prostitution. As Unicorn, she is "a bit of the goddess left over" (128).

In her first intervention as Liz, she is assisted by Bear and Crow who perform as clients for a session of presumably kinky sex. Here, in an initially comic continuation of the emphasis on mythological incongruity, the familiar feminist point emerges that prostitution was in ancient times a sacred and cleansing act. Bear gropes a little for his lines about "the round-bellied goddess" (132) while the more facile Crow enjoys the obvious confusion of the girls, who think they are servicing "weirdos." But the purpose of the intervention is "to take away the shame" by evoking the ancient meaning of the oldest profession.

The disguised spirits (confusingly "disguised" as themselves in the Toronto production) place the blindfolded Liz and Jessica back-to-back and teach them how to chant the "whore's prayer," an evocation of the goddess in a litany of her several names. As the "clients" vanish, the two women are briefly possessed by the spirit power of the chanting. Jessica is on the verge of singing her own song but abruptly pulls back; there is more degradation yet to come. To the degree that the scene confronts its own absurdity, it works (it was revised after the production in Toronto). Yet, unlike the other interventions, this one still imposes its broader feminist meaning rather self-consciously instead of letting it emerge spontaneously from the context.

Nevertheless, in this play, Griffiths has written a work that is remarkably performable from stories of Jessica's journey towards wholeness. Through the fabular interchange of animal and human, she has developed a powerful externalization of an essentially interior struggle. Already in *Maggie & Pierre*, particularly in the characterization of Maggie, she had shown signs of moving beyond collective creation's habitual focus on public or social depictions of personality. An example is Maggie's brief attempt at escape from the confines of 24 Sussex Drive for a walk along the river in the rain. Here, Griffiths explores behind the media-enhanced public personality of her character, coming to a tentative recognition of the split self. The scene begins with the fanciful self who longs for a little freedom from the intrusion of security guards and the strict rationality of her husband. It ends with reference to the self who beckons down from the window of the house: the "me, all dressed up in my Yves St. Laurent gown, a monument to good taste" (64).

Maggie's frenetic dancing, building through her ingenuous attempts at "diplomacy" and later punctuating her public scorn at the New York disco, reveals another self who anticipates Jessica more particularly. The latter's most threatening time occurs when she must confront the destructive Wolverine. Indeed, for several chilling moments, she becomes the Wolverine (alluded to in the first version as the Wolverine dance). In comparison to such moments, the naturalism of *O.D. on Paradise* makes the resolution of Vic's crisis state at the end seem merely odd. With Maria Campbell as mentor, *Jessica* represents a considerable growth in the experimental directions that Griffiths' experience in collective creation initiated.

Linda Griffiths in the original production of *Paper Wheat* (1977), directed by Andras Tahn at 25th Street Theatre. Photo: 25th Street Theatre.

Chapter Six
Seminal Theatre

This study has been concerned with the importance of a particular mode of theatrical performance central to the growth of indigenous Canadian theatre and drama during the 1970s. By concentrating on the work of one particular theatre, Theatre Passe Muraille, and of one director, Paul Thompson, it has been possible to trace certain lines of development in the performance of collective creation as an indigenous dramatic form. This in turn provides a basis for enquiry into the plays of individual playwrights who have been associated with this playmaking process at Theatre Passe Muraille and elsewhere. This is not to assume, however, that collective creation signifies a type of proto-literary subgenre aimed directly towards the development of a new dramatic literature. The primary purpose of the collective enterprise is performance, not text.

It is difficult to accept the unqualified sweep of Robert Wallace's recent statement that "Thompson clearly eschewed the idea of literature as valuable in the theatre."[1] Admittedly, Thompson's interests as a director have always been focused on the potential of actors for creating theatre, not of writers for creating dramatic literature. Even in his off-duty time at Stratford, Thompson was beginning to use texts as points of departure rather than as objects of performance. In the early 1970s, the absence of a flourishing literary drama gave him a special freedom to work with Canadian material in ways that were new in intention and substance, allowing him to pioneer a distinctly Canadian theatre among potentially new audiences. Rather than an outright rejection of dramatic literature as such, however, this was Thompson's particular way of challenging the predominance of foreign plays and the attendant pretensions of establishment theatre.

At that time, Thompson's discontent was akin to Salutin's later discontent, alluded to previously in this study. That individual playwrights emerged directly from the collective process, while a by-product of the primary goal, was nevertheless often a matter of some satisfaction to Thompson—especially when their plays, such as *Billy Bishop Goes to War* and *Maggie & Pierre*, so effectively vindicated his collective principles. But, of course, he has been pleased even more that a collective play such as *The Farm Show* proves to have a continuing life as theatre—for example, as demonstrated in its popular revival, produced in 1985 by citizens of the Clinton district with most of the original cast.[2]

Of the collective plays selected here for discussion, each illustrates a variation, and often a new development, in the performance techniques of Theatre Passe Muraille during the 1970s. The first major creative breakthrough, acknowledged universally by Canadian theatre historians, was of course *The Farm Show*. Yet there is a tendency to isolate that work from its context in the other collective playmaking of the time at Theatre Passe Muraille. The integration of subject matter and its audience-oriented forms of presentation was an on-going objective from 1970. With the changing scope of subject matter and with new audiences to win, there was a continuing challenge to theatrical development and innovation which shifted in some respect with every configuration of collective participants. Only Thompson is the constant

Chapter Six: Seminal Theatre 245

element in the collective work under examination here.

Yet there are various patterns of development to be observed in this group of plays. For example, a comparison between *Doukhobors* and *1837: The Farmers' Revolt* illustrates a change from insistent imagistic statement—seen in the former's images of work, nakedness and fire—to satiric analysis through theatrical analogue, present in the latter's metaphors of conjury, ventriloquism and historical tableaux. In both plays, ensemble body language is the primary expressive vehicle. A parallel development may be observed in *Buffalo Jump* and *The West Show*, this time in the expressive emphasizing of scenic properties. The one features the visual images of John Boyle's cutouts while the other explores the metaphoric scope of Joe Fafard's farmscape puzzle pieces. A further and more complex line of development in performance language can be seen by comparing *Jessica* to *Far As the Eye Can See*. The animal spirits and the Regal Dead are of the same order of verbal conceit. But in the later play, this rhetorical device combines with the extended theatrical metaphor of the mixed-blood ceremony, which is the performance vehicle of the heroine's necessary journey into her past. Of the plays discussed, only in the evolution from *Them Donnellys* to *The Death of the Donnellys* is there a reductive rather than an exploratory element in evidence—specifically in the shift from theatrical imagism to literary moralism.

Although the influences of collective creation on the writers discussed here have been very different, examination of the particular elements to which each has responded offers an important critical context for their work as individual playwrights. For Salutin, the experience of *1837: The Farmers' Revolt* provided initial access to the polemical as well as the satiric possibilities of stage metaphor in its condensed form; this he was able to expand with success later in *Les Canadiens*. He also cultivated a good sense of how to draw audiences into issues through entertainment values. Thus, with help from other members of the Passe Muraille collective, his convictions about history translate effectively into the quite remarkable audience strategies of *1837: The Farmers' Revolt*. The timely and entertaining demonstration of hockey as history in *Les Canadiens* was a coup in its day—so entertaining, in fact, that the heavy bits of Act 2 were hardly noticeable in performance.

Yet subsequent individual plays suggest a certain ambivalence, perhaps justified in the case of *Nathan Cohen*, about "show" techniques. Here, the conflict between his advocacy of "dramatic" techniques (as in the essays on documentary) and collective theatre's presentational practices becomes more evident. The metaphor of the critic as a performer himself, while providing an often lively documentary survey of Cohen's critical encounters, is not altogether adequate to the comedy of ideas to which the play seems to aspire. Salutin may have had his experience of this play in mind when he later observed to an interviewer that "Paul's speciality is the collective...not the scripted stuff."[3] If he is alluding to new play development, *The Death of the Donnellys* seems an earlier case in point. Yet when Salutin tried to resolve his apparent dilemma by moving to literary collaboration for *S: Portrait of a Spy*, the shift away from sustained theatricalism to dramatic realism was also problematic.

As a playwright, Salutin requires an association with a theatre company prepared to collaborate (not merely to function as a workshop) in the development of his particular social vision of theatre as timely community-oriented dramatic expression. On the two occasions in which he worked with an actors' theatre in Newfoundland, he helped the respective companies to express *their* vision much more than his own. Since the kind of theatre that might serve him best in his maturity as a playwright is no longer (in his view) available to him, he has unfortunately, and one hopes temporarily, relegated himself to a minor theatre of occasion which, inexplicably, he still refuses to identify as political.

For John Gray, the popular appeal of the informal raconteur style, initiated by Theatre Passe Muraille in *The Farm Show* in combination with illustrative physical gesture, was a major influence—especially on *Billy Bishop Goes to War*. Related to this is the note of irreverent conspiracy with the audience on the colonial theme, also strong in the first act of *1837: The Farmers' Revolt*. Gray's particular contribution to the Theatre Passe Muraille principle of creating theatre for a non-theatre-going audience is through his adaptations of the *mise en scène* of popular musical performance. In the musicals *Rock and Roll* and *Don Messer's Jubilee*, popular musical entertainment is his subject as well as his mode of expression. In each case, the work is informed by a special relationship to audience in the manner, although not the substance, of the community collective creation. Gray differs from Thompson in one major respect. He has the writer's respect for language and rejects its "jumble" in collective creation when actors of unequal verbal skills are involved in the process. Gray's own verbal and musical wit is his most distinguishing quality as a playwright and composer. In the musicals after *Billy Bishop*, he has worked creatively on an independent basis.

Linda Griffiths is the playwright connected most consistently and most directly to collective creation. Her improvisational work at 25th Street Theatre first demonstrated her talent for lively depiction of character. There and later, she consistently involved herself in collectives that required a degree of narrative development of character rather than just individual portraiture—an interest that perhaps prefigures her playwriting. Still in the context of the collective's researched (and in some way) documentary theme, she continued to be challenged by the potential of *theatrical* characterization, not by the literary variation that emerged, for example, in *The Death of the Donnellys*. Judging by *Maggie & Pierre*, she found a personal base, expressed in the character of Henry, for a richer improvisational exploration of the more traditional dramatic elements of character interaction and conflict.

In the process, however, Griffiths also helped to bring something new both to Canadian theatre and to Canadian drama. This was the play's skilfully sustained character interaction within the format of a one-person show and also its clever variation on the myth-making aspect of the collective process. The play thus becomes a nation-wide community encounter, building its metaphoric analogues (the disillusionments of personal and political romance) out of the insistent image-making of the electronic media. In this respect, *Maggie & Pierre* is a more sophisticated work than *Don Messer's Jubilee*. In her continuation in *Jessica*, Griffiths' creativity as a transformational performer opens up the structural potential of the dramatic material of the original collective creation. At its best, *Jessica* does so in a manner that integrates what Thompson sometimes calls "the theatre of it"[4] with the spiritual vision of Maria Campbell.

Perhaps the most important general influence of Thompson's enterprise at Theatre Passe Muraille lies in its emphasis on the role of theatre in its own community. As already indicated, other theatres followed Passe Muraille's model of local collective creation, either as an initial or as a continuing means of establishing a relationship with specifically identified audiences. Filewod, in the context of collective documentary drama, describes this as a principle of "a shared historical or community experience" transformed into art.[5] Depending on the mandate of the particular company, the principle of the shared experience may also evolve into a theatre of shared discovery and development.

The most interesting of the smaller regional companies in this regard is The Mulgrave Road Co-Op, a company touring to the small and large towns of Nova Scotia. Over the years, its work shows an unusual pattern of organic growth rooted in its collective playmaking. The company began in 1977 on the Passe Muraille model of theatre for new local audiences—in this case to create theatre for the small communities of Guysborough County. The first play was a comprehensive collective creation, *The Mulgrave Road Show*, exploring the past and present of a given community. In turn, this production provided a thematic and sometimes scenic basis for the further discovery of promising local and regional material through collective playmaking—for example, *Let's Play*

Fish, *The Coady Co-Op Show*, and *One on the Way*. The subjects of Mulgrave's collective creations have also provided ideas for individual plays by certain performer/playwrights. Plays by Robbie O'Neill (*Tighten the Traces / Haul in the Reins*, 1982) and Cindy Cowan (*Spooks: The Mystery of Caledonia Mills*, 1984) were expanded from material discovered for the collective creation, *Guysborough Ghosts* (1981). Christopher Heide, participating playwright on the *Coady Co-Op Show* (a Nova Scotian variation on *Paper Wheat*), has also written individual plays for the company—*Bring Back Don Messer*, discussed earlier, and more recently *The Promised Land* (1988). Mulgrave still produces a collective creation most seasons; one notable production was *Ten Years After*, a playful recollection of their own work in their 10th anniversary year.[6]

Theatre Network of Edmonton, founded in 1975 by Mark Manson, also began operating with a touring mandate of collectively created plays. Following closely on the example of *The Farm Show* and other community collectives by Theatre Passe Muraille, Theatre Network moved into communities selected as the subjects of its plays to work and to participate in the local life. The first collective work of note, *Two Miles Off: Elnora Sunrise with a Twist of Lemon* (1976), examined the declining life of a small Alberta town two miles off the highway to the city of Red Deer. For its next work, Theatre Network moved to Fort McMurray to explore the impact of the tarsands boom and to trace the origins of that community through early discoveries of black gold. The play, *Hard Hats and Stolen Hearts: A Tarsands Myth* (1977), after much touring in Alberta and other parts of Canada, eventually played at the Performance Garage in New York. That same year, while in residence at Simon Fraser University, Theatre Network created *Tracings* in collaboration with playwright Sharon Pollock. This is a play about the life and explorations of Fraser himself.

In an effort to extend its theatre network to the north, the company—this time under the direction of David Barnet—moved to

Inuvik in 1978 for the development of *Kicker*. Once the company found a permanent space in Edmonton, it gradually shifted from an actors' to a playwrights' theatre. Its last work of improvisational origins, with text developed further by Geoffrey Le Boutillier, was the 1981 *Rig*, about life and work in the Alberta oil patch. In the meantime, two members of the company—Tanya Ryga and Sharon Stearns—had written a play of their own. This was a feminist musical fantasy, *A Trip to the Farm* (1979), revised and toured as *Sarah and Gabrial* the following year. Stearns continued to develop as a playwright with *Hooking for Paradise* at Workshop West in 1981 and *Enemy Graces* at Prairie Theatre Exchange in 1985. In her own plays, she has continued her historical research into the western-Canadian past, which she had initiated in her collective work. Among the western-Canadian companies that have established themselves largely through collective creation, Theatre Network has the longest history of consistent adherence to the principle of theatre for the immediate community. During the 1980s, under the artistic directorship of Stephen Heatley, the theatre continued to support this principle through the development of new local plays and playwrights.[7]

It has often been observed by critics and reviewers that collective creation is an important influence on the development of Canadian theatre and even of Canadian drama. The usual rider—that it is probably too early to judge—may be the most critically sound position in the long term. Yet time is passing, and memories in the theatre are remarkably short—given how the pressure of the next project naturally takes precedence over retrospection on the last. Besides, fashions in theatre (and in the ways of thinking and talking about theatre) change quickly in Canada as elsewhere. This study attempts to recover in a critical context one important aspect of a seminal era in the development of modern Canadian theatre and drama which, with all its pristine hopes and enthusiasms, is probably over now. Professionalism may be necessary, but it lacks the spontaneity of commitment to change by those who used to exist on 30 dollars a week or less. The attempt to recover and evaluate even so recent a past—while fraught with the difficulties of that recovery at every step of the way and no doubt permeated with the predictable failings of premature judgement—may at the very least draw attention to the need for the further study of Canadian theatre history and drama. The subject clearly deserves this attention.

Chronology of Principal Dramatic Works

Note: please see Index for location of pages in text.

1970:

May, *Notes from Quebec*, collective creation directed by Paul Thompson at Theatre Passe Muraille in Toronto.

1971:

Feb., *Next Year Country* by Carol Bolt, directed by Ken Kramer at the Globe Theatre in Regina.

April, *Doukhobors*, collective creation directed by Paul Thompson at Theatre Passe Muraille (Toronto: Playwrights Co-op, 1973).

Oct., *Free Ride*, collective creation directed by Paul Thompson at Theatre Passe Muraille.

1972:

Jan., *Fanshen*, adaptation from William Hinton by Rick Salutin, directed by George Luscombe at Toronto Workshop Productions.

May, *Buffalo Jump*, a collective creation with Carol Bolt, directed by Paul Thompson at Theatre Passe Muraille (*Playwrights in Profile: Carol Bolt*, including *Buffalo Jump, Gabe, Red Emma,* Toronto: Playwrights

Co-op, 1976).

Sept., *The Farm Show*, collective creation directed by Paul Thompson at Theatre Passe Muraille.

1973:

Jan., *1837*, collective creation with Rick Salutin, directed by Paul Thompson at Theatre Passe Muraille.

Mar., *Pauline*, collective creation with Carol Bolt, directed by Paul Thompson at Theatre Passe Muraille.

Sept., *Under the Greywacke*, collective creation directed by Paul Thompson at Theatre Passe Muraille.

Nov., *Them Donnellys*, collective creation with Frank McEnaney, directed by Paul Thompson for Theatre Passe Muraille's tour of southwestern Ontario.

1974:

Feb., *Adventures of an Immigrant*, collective creation with Rick Salutin, directed by Paul Thompson for Theatre Passe Muraille on tour in Toronto.

Mar., *Naked on the North Shore* by Ted Johns, directed by Paul Thompson at Theatre Passe Muraille.

Mar., *The Farm Show* (revised), directed by Paul Thompson at Theatre Passe Muraille (Toronto: Coach House Press, 1976).

June, *1837: The Farmers' Revolt* with Rick Salutin (revised and remounted for a tour of southwestern Ontario), directed by Paul Thompson for Theatre Passe Muraille (*Rick Salutin and Theatre Passe Muraille*, Toronto: James Lorimer, 1976).

June, *Oil*, a collective creation directed by Paul Thompson at Victoria Theatre, Petrolia, for Theatre Passe Muraille.

Oct., *Them Donnellys* (revised), directed by Paul Thompson at Theatre Passe Muraille.

Oct., *Almighty Voice* (originally titled *Sir, I have the Honour to Report...the Voice has not yet Stopped*), seed-show collective creation directed by Clarke Rogers for a cross-country tour.

1975:

Jan., *I Love You, Baby Blue*, collective creation directed by Paul Thompson at Theatre Passe Muraille (Erin: Press Porcépic, 1977).

Mar., *The False Messiah* by Rick Salutin, directed by John Palmer at Theatre Passe Muraille (Toronto: Playwrights Canada, 1981).

April, *Canadian Heroes Series #1*, collective interpretation of paintings by John Boyle, directed by Paul Thompson at Theatre Passe Muraille.

Oct., *The West Show*, collective creation directed by Paul Thompson for Theatre Passe Muraille on tour (in *Three Prairie Docu-Dramas*, Edmonton: NeWest Press, 1982).

Oct., *Prairie Landscape or...If You're So Good, Why Are You in Saskatoon?*, collective creation directed by Paul Thompson at 25th Street House Theatre in Saskatoon.

Oct., *IWA: The Newfoundland Loggers' Strike of 1959*, collective creation with Rick Salutin, directed by Chris Brookes for the Mummers Troupe in St. John's.

1976:

Feb., *The Horsburgh Scandal*, collective creation with Betty Jane Wylie, with music by John Gray, directed by Paul Thompson at Theatre Passe Muraille (Windsor: Black Moss, 1981).

June, revivals of *The Farm Show* and *1837: The Farmers' Revolt* for Habitat Festival in Vancouver.

Oct., *Canadian Heroes Series #2: John Hornby*, collective creation directed by David Fox for Theatre Passe Muraille.

Nov., Theatre Passe Muraille in repertory at the National Arts Centre Studio in Ottawa with *Hornby*, *1837: The Farmers' Revolt*, and *The Blues* by Hrant Alianak.

1977:

Feb., *Les Canadiens* by Rick Salutin, directed by Guy Sprung at Centaur Theatre in Montreal.

Feb., *18 Wheels* by John Gray, directed by John Gray at Theatre Passe Muraille (in *Local Boy Makes Good: Three Musicals by John Gray*, Vancouver: Talonbooks, 1987).

Mar., *Paper Wheat*, collective creation directed by Andras Tahn at 25th Street [House] Theatre.

April, *Far As The Eye Can See*, collective creation with Rudy Wiebe, directed by Paul Thompson at Theatre 3 in Edmonton (in *Three Prairie Docu-Dramas*, 1982).

Sept., *Paper Wheat* (revised), directed by Guy Sprung for tour by 25th Street Theatre (*Paper Wheat: The Book*, Saskatoon: Western Producer Prairie Books, 1982).

Sept., *Shakespeare for Fun and Profit: A Canadian Dream*, collective creation at the St. Lawrence Centre in Toronto, music by John Gray, directed by Paul Thompson for Theatre Passe Muraille.

Oct., *Les Canadiens* (revised), directed by George Luscombe at Toronto Workshop Productions (Vancouver: Talonbooks, 1977, assist Ken Dryden).

1978:

Mar., *Generation and 1/2*, collective creation directed by Guy Sprung for 25th Street Theatre.

Aug., *Les maudits anglais*, collective creation with Gary Geddes, directed by Paul Thompson for Theatre Passe Muraille on tour (Toronto: Playwrights Canada, 1984).

Nov., *Billy Bishop Goes to War* by John Gray with Eric Peterson, directed by John Gray for Vancouver East Cultural Centre in association with Tamahnous Theatre (Vancouver: Talonbooks, 1981).

1979:

Aug., *The Death of the Donnellys* by Ted Johns and Theatre Passe Muraille, staged by Paul Thompson in co-production with the Blyth Summer Festival (Toronto: Playwrights Canada, 1982).

Nov., *Maggie & Pierre* by Linda Griffiths with Paul Thompson, directed by Paul Thompson, preview at Theatre Passe Muraille.

1980:

Jan., *Coming Through Slaughter* by Michael Ondaatje, directed by Paul Thompson at Theatre Passe Muraille.

Feb., *Maggie & Pierre*, opening at Theatre Passe Muraille (Vancouver: Talonbooks, 1980).

July, *Bring Back Don Messer* by Christopher Heide, directed by Ed McKenna for Mulgrave Road Co-op in Guysborough, Nova Scotia.

1981:

Jan., *Nathan Cohen: A Review* by Rick Salutin, directed by Paul Thompson at Theatre Passe Muraille.

Mar., *Rock and Roll* by John Gray, directed by John Gray at the National Arts Centre in co-production with the Vancouver East Cultural Centre (in *Local Boy Makes Good*, 1987).

May, *The Studhorse Man*, collective creation with Frank Moher from the novel by Robert Kroetsch, directed by Paul Thompson at Theatre Passe Muraille.

Sept., *Joey*, collective creation with Rick Salutin, directed by Donna Butt at Rising Tide Theatre in St. John's.

1982:

Feb., *O.D. on Paradise* by Linda Griffiths and Patrick Brymer, directed by Clarke Rogers at 25th Street Theatre.

Nov., *Jessica* by Linda Griffiths, Maria Campbell and Paul Thompson, directed by Paul Thompson at 25th Street Theatre.

Chronology 257

1983:

Jan., *O.D. on Paradise* (revised), directed by Clarke Rogers at Theatre Passe Muraille.

1984:

Feb., *S: Portrait of a Spy* by Rick Salutin and Ian Adams, directed by Patrick McDonald at Great Canadian Theatre Company in Ottawa.

1985:

Jan., *Don Messer's Jubilee* by John Gray, directed by Tom Kerr at Neptune Theatre in Halifax.

1986:

Mar., *Spirit of '85*, collective improvisation directed by Paul Thompson at Theatre Passe Muraille.

Mar., *Jessica: A Transformation* by Linda Griffiths in collaboration with Maria Campbell, co-directed by Linda Griffiths and Clarke Rogers at Theatre Passe Muraille (in *The Book of Jessica: A Theatrical Transformation*, Toronto: Coach House Press, 1989).

Endnotes

Chapter One

1. Bob Wallace, "Paul Thompson at Theatre Passe Muraille: Bits and Pieces," *Open Letter*, 2nd ser. 7 (1974): 64; Wallace's first of two interviews with Thompson (conducted 9 Nov. 1973) is subsequently referred to as Wallace I.
2. See C.D. Innes, *Erwin Piscator's Political Theatre* (Cambridge: Cambridge UP, 1972) 60-61.
3. John Willet, ed., *Brecht on Theatre* (New York: Hill and Wang, 1964) 78.
4. e.g., Innes 68.
5. See Arthur Arent, "The Techniques of the Living Newspaper," *Theatre Quarterly*, 1.4 (1971): 57-59.
6. Alan Filewod, *Collective Encounters: Documentary Theatre in English Canada* (Toronto: Toronto UP, 1987) 54.
7. See Howard Goorney, *The Theatre Workshop Story* (London: Methuen, 1981) 125-26.
8. John Elsom, *Post-War British Theatre* (London: Routledge, 1976) 102.
9. Introduction, *The Knotty* (London: Methuen, 1970) xii.
10. Introduction, *John Ford's Cuban Missile Crisis* (London: Methuen, 1972) 7, 9.
11. Albert Hunt, *Hopes for Great Happenings: Alternatives in Education and Theatre* (London: Methuen, 1976) 111.
12. Catherine Itsin, *Stages in the Revolution: Political Theatre in Britain Since 1968* (London: Methuen, 1980) 49-50.

13. Arthur Sainer, *The Radical Theatre Notebook* (New York: Avon, 1975) 17.
14. Theodore Shank, "Collective Creation," *Drama Review*, 16.2 (1972): 3-4.
15. Full studies of these theatres and their work may be found in Arthur Sainer; Theodore Shank, *American Alternative Theatre* (London: Macmillan Modern Dramatists, 1982); C.W. Bigsby, *A Critical Introduction to Twentieth-Century American Drama*, vol. 3 (Cambridge: Cambridge UP, 1985). My account draws on these sources for the American experimental theatre except where otherwise indicated.
16. For succinct commentary on the theories of Artaud see Margaret Croyden, *Lunatics, Lovers and Poets: The Contemporary Experimental Theatre* (New York: Delta, 1974) 55-71.
17. Stuart W. Little, *Off-Broadway: The Prophetic Theatre* (New York: Coward, 1972) 185; for an informal account of Café La Mama, see Ellen Stewart, "La Mama Celebrates 20 Years," *Performing Arts Journal*, 6.2 (1982): 7-28.
18. See Peter Ansorge, *Disrupting the Spectacle: Five Years of Experimental and Fringe Theatre in Britain* (London: Pitman, 1975) 47-51 and Rob Ritchie, ed., *The Joint Stock Book: The Making of a Theatre Collective* (London: Methuen, 1987) 11-32.
19. Henry Lesnick, ed., *Guerilla Street Theater* (New York: Avon, 1973) 250.
20. Lesnick 195.
21. Lesnick 91-92.
22. Lesnick 147.
23. Lesnick 13.
24. John Hirsch, "Healthy Disengagement," *Canadian Theatre Review*, 4 (1974): 30. This account of regional theatre relies on my essay "The Regionalism of Canadian Drama," *Canadian Literature*, 85 (1980): 7-19.
25. Quoted by Mark Czarnecki in "The Regional Theatre System," *Contemporary Canadian Theatre: New World Visions*, Anton Wagner ed. (Toronto: Simon & Pierre, 1985) 35, 36.
26. See Rex Deverell, "Medicare! as a One-Man Collective," *Showing West: Three Prairie Docu-Dramas*, Diane Bessai and Don Kerr, eds. (Edmonton: NeWest, 1982) 176.

260 *Playwrights of Collective Creation*

27. Renata Usmiani, *Second Stage: The Alternative Theatre Movement in Canada* (Vancouver: U of British Columbia P, 1983) 69, 71.
28. "Workshop's Technique: Building a Play," Toronto Workshop Productions release [1967].
29. Filewod 51.
30. Wallace I 57.
31. For example, see Don Kerr, "Three Plays," *next year country*, 2.5 (1975): 42-43.
32. Robert Wallace & Cynthia Zimmerman, *The Work: Conversations with English-Canadian Playwrights* (Toronto: Coach House, 1982) 240. This interview, by Robert Wallace, is subsequently cited as Wallace II.
33. Paul Thompson interview with David Barnet and Diane Bessai, Edmonton, 20 Aug., 1986, subsequently cited as Barnet/Bessai.
34. Herbert Whittaker, "Come wrecker's ball or poverty, Theatre Passe Muraille means to survive," *Globe and Mail*, 21 Oct. 1972; Wallace II 240.
35. Barnet/Bessai.
36. Barnet/Bessai.
37. From Theatre Passe Muraille file, Arts Section, Metropolitan Toronto Reference Library (MTRL).
38. Merle Shain, "Pursuing the need for a guerrilla theatre," *Toronto Telegram*, 1 Mar. 1969.
39. From a brief prepared by Garrard for the 1969-70 season, MTRL.
40. Nathan Cohen, "A story that needs to be plainly told," *Toronto Star*, 22 Nov. 1969.
41. "Nude Memories Swing About Jungle Gym," *Globe and Mail*, 6 Nov. 1969.
42. See "Jim Garrard & Theatre Passe Muraille," an interview with William Lane, *Theatre*, 2, special section, n.d. [Jan. 1976].
43. Barnet/Bessai.
44. "Theatre Passe Muraille: History of Productions," 22 Jan. 1976, from TPM archive, now at the University of Guelph.
45. Elaine F. Nardocchio describes the function of the *animateur* in Quebec collective creations of the 1960s and 1970s as "the job of noting the best improvisations and of making suggestions for changes and additions." *Theatre and Politics in Modern Quebec* (Edmonton: U of Alberta P, 1986) 82. In a

discussion of Germain's work as animateur/playwright, Renata Usmiani says that for this, the company's first play, "improvisation provided a starting point, but Germain soon took over and eventually produced a complete script" (*Second Stage*, 138).
46. Usmiani 141.
47. Barnet/Bessai.
48. Usmiani 108.
49. James Reaney, "Ten Years at Play," *Dramatists in Canada: Selected Essays*, William H. New, ed. (Vancouver: U of British Columbia P, 1972) 72.
50. R.D. MacKenzie, "Theatre Passe Muraille, Paul Thompson," *Alive*, 39 (1974): 8.
51. Wallace I 63.
52. Ted Johns, "An Interview with Paul Thompson," *Performing Arts in Canada*, 10.4 (1973): 30.
53. Linda West, "Passing Comment on Passe Muraille," *That's Show Business*, 25 Sept. 1974: 5.
54. West 5.
55. MacKenzie 8.
56. Rick Salutin, *1837: William Lyon Mackenzie and the Canadian Revolution* (Toronto: Lorimer, 1976), Preface to *1837: The Farmer's Revolt*, 186-87.
57. Wallace I 65, 55.
58. "Betty Jane Wylie: The Playwright as Participant," *Canadian Theatre Review*, 38 (1983): 117; Barnet/Bessai; Salutin 190; Wallace II 245-246.
59. Wallace I 55; Wallace II 248.
60. Wallace II 245, 246. Here, he was referring specifically to the characterization of living or historical figures.
61. Frank Moher, "Flying a Kite," *Interface*, 4.6 (1981): 14.
62. Johns 30.
63. Forsyth Hardy, ed., *Grierson on Documentary* (London: Faber, 1966) 13.
64. In principle, documentary drama emulates the scope of the camera eye in its function of relaying material reality "through the dynamic and sequential transmission of physical evidence in a manner that (in theory) 'never lies'." It transmits and authenticates its information theatrically or presentationally rather than mimetically or representationally. See my

262 Playwrights of Collective Creation

      "Documentary Theatre in Canada: An Investigation into Questions and Backgrounds," *Canadian Drama*, 6.1 (1980): 12-13.
65. See Robert C. Nunn, "The Meeting of Actuality and Theatricality in *The Farm Show*," *Canadian Drama*, 8.1 (1982): 44.
66. Salutin 194.
67. "Notes Towards a Definition of Documentary Theatre," *Theatre Quarterly*, 1.1 (1971): 41-43; especially see section x.
68. Wallace II 240.
69. Herbert Whittaker, "The pioneer expounds on the documentary," *Globe and Mail*, 28 June, 1972; Filewod 18-19, and 190, note 18.
70. Johns 30.
71. Wallace I 58.
72. Wallace II 241, 240.
73. Wylie 115.
74. Wallace I 55.
75. Wallace I 69.
76. Richard Schechner, *Public Domain: Essays on the Theatre* (New York: Avon, 1970) 133-143.

Chapter Two

1. *Doukhobors* premiered at Theatre Passe Muraille on April 2, 1971, with Bob Aarron, Jeanette Collins, Alan Jones, Larry Mollin, Michael Rudder, Karen Sanderson and Phil Savath.
2. Thompson says that Toronto Doukhobors did not want to be associated with a play sympathizing with The Sons of Freedom (Barnet/Bessai).
3. "General Notes by Paul Thompson on the production of *Doukhobors*," in *Doukhobors*, Paul Thompson and cast, transcribed and collected by Connie Brissenden (Toronto: Playwrights Co-Op, 1973) 2, hereafter cited in parenthesis as "General Notes." Textual reference to this play and those to follow is cited in parenthesis. Emphasis is in the original unless otherwise indicated.
4. Barnet/Bessai.

5. This is a precis of "Autobiography of a Fanatic," *in Terror in the Name of God* (Toronto: McClelland and Stewart, 1964) 217-238; cf. *Doukhobors* 37-40.
6. Barnet/Bessai.
7. Barnet/Bessai.
8. Wallace I 63.
9. Wylie, "The Playwright as Participant" 115.
10. The idea had an even earlier phase, initiated the year before in a company compilation entitled *Songs and Stories of the Dirty Thirties*.
11. Gail Smith, "Author of Globe depicts life in the 1930s," Regina *Leader-Post*, 25 Feb., 1971.
12. The Globe Theatre archives contain a relatively clean typescript identified by artistic director Ken Kramer as the original, plus a revised, cut-up and pinned-together version edited by Sue Kramer.
13. *The Work*, interview with Carol Bolt, 267.
14. Premiered at Theatre Passe Muraille on May 14, 1972, with Anne Anglin, Larry Benedict, Michael Bennett, Peter Boretski, Brenda Darling, Howie Cooper, Richard Farrell, Alan Jones, Gordon May, Miles Potter, John Smith.
15. Sandra Souchotte, "Introduction," Carol Bolt, *Playwrights in Profile: Buffalo Jump, Gabe, Red Emma* (Toronto: Playwrights Co-Op, 1976) 8.
16. Herbert Whittaker, "An ingenious Buffalo Jump," *Globe and Mail*, 19 May, 1972.
17. Particularly from Ronald Liversedge, *Recollections of the On-to-Ottawa Trek* [1963] (Toronto: McClelland and Stewart, 1973) and *The Dirty Thirties: Canadians in the Great Depression*, edited by Michiel Horn (Toronto: Copp Clark, 1972).
18. Herbert Whittaker, "Artist's sets give play unique look," *Globe and Mail*, 22 May, 1972.
19. *The Work* 267.
20. Robin Endres, "Not Fully Realized," *Canadian Forum*, 57.671 (1977): 38.
21. The original collective consisted of Janet Amos, Anne Anglin, David Fox, Al Jones, Fina MacDonell, and Miles Potter. According to Robin Endres' general comparison of the play to the American street theatres of the 1960s, the Passe Muraille

originality lay in their method "of interviewing and observing people and reproducing them as *characters* on stage." Cited from "Many authors make a play," *The Globe and Mail, TVOntario* (advertising supplement) 14 Nov., 1975. Of all the collective groups of Europe and the United States whose work was described by Theodore Shank in 1972, the closest resemblance to the Passe Muraille method at Clinton is that of younger members of the Royal Dramatic Theatre in Stockholm, who spent several weeks in 1969 living among the foundry workers of Norrbotten, Sweden, interviewing and creating a play from their collected material ("Collective Creation" 15).
22. Filewod 35.
23. West, "Passing comment on Passe Muraille" 5. Cf. Lois Wheeler Snow, *China On Stage* (New York: Vintage, 1973), "Do-It-Yourself Theatre," 307-310. Cf. the earlier suggestion that the CBC and the NFB provided the Canadian models for creating "a kind of living community portrait or photograph" (Johns, "An Interview with Paul Thompson" 30).
24. Barnet/Bessai.
25. Urjo Kareda, "Free Ride fine ironical glimpse of hitchhiking," *Toronto Star*, 11 Sept., 1971.
26. Terms applied by David Barnet (Barnet/Bessai).
27. Quoted by Max Wyman, "Passe Muraille defies tidy definition," *Vancouver Sun*, 25 May, 1976.
28. Paul Thompson, "The Farm Show," *The Farm Show: A Collective Creation by Theatre Passe Muraille* (Toronto: Coach House, 1976) 1. Hereafter, reference to the text is cited in parenthesis.
29. Ted Johns, "The Farm Show" 1.
30. Nunn, "The Meeting of Actuality and Theatricality in *The Farm Show*" 47.
31. Nunn 45.
32. He refers to this as "the sharing of work and the sharing of art" 49.
33. That auction barns were often the company's performance venues during its subsequent tour of the play through southwestern Ontario makes its own point about the inherent theatricality of this commonplace rural event. See "The Space Show," *Canadian Theatre Review*, 6 (1975): 14-27.

34. Wallace II 241.
35. Nunn 51.
36. Nunn 50.
37. This emphatically includes the drama, as pointed out by Alexander M. Leggatt in "Playwrights in a Landscape: The Changing Image of Rural Ontario," *Theatre History in Canada*, 1.2 (1980): 135-148.
38. Leggatt 144.
39. Chris Johnson, "Theatrical Scrapbook," *Canadian Literature*, 85 (1980): 132.
40. Wallace II 240.
41. Johnson 133.
42. In the Clinton community revival of *The Farm Show* in 1985, actor Anne Anglin, struck with the changes from the younger to the older Alison Lobb, developed a contemporary persona of the character, which she incorporated into the original portrayal (Barnet/Bessai).
43. Wallace II 240.
44. Barnet/Bessai; also see Filewod 48.
45. Filewod 45.
46. Barnet/Bessai.
47. Brian Boru [Brian Arnott], "The Spirit of '37: history as hypothesis," *That's Show Business*, 14 Aug., 1974: 5.
48. Urjo Kareda, "History Comes to Life," *Toronto Star*, 18 Jan., 1973.
49. The play premiered at Theatre Passe Muraille on 17 Jan., 1973. The original actors were David Fox, Janet Amos and Miles Potter of *The Farm Show* as well as Suzette Couture, Clare Coulter and Neil Vipond; others subsequently participating in the development of the play were Doris Cowan, Eric Peterson and Terry Tweed.
50. Rick Salutin, Preface to *1837: The Farmers' Revolt*, 186, 200, hereafter cited in parenthesis (as are references to the play).
51. Herbert Whittaker, "1837 engrossing handling of history," *Globe and Mail*, 19 Jan., 1973.
52. Herbert Whittaker, "Passe Muraille becoming top touring company," *Globe and Mail*, 29 May, 1974.
53. Wyman, "Passe Muraille defies tidy definition."
54. Rick Salutin, "Was Sartre Smartre? Occasional Theatre, on Occasion," *This Magazine,* 21.3 (1987): 35.

55. Arnott [Brian Boru], "The Spirit of '37" 5.
56. Rick Salutin, "The Great Canadian History Robbery," *Maclean's*, 86.4 (1973): 64.
57. Salutin, "The Great Canadian History Robbery" 64.
58. In this he is following historian Stanley Ryerson, author of *Unequal Union*, 1968, "our only historian who writes from the viewpoint of the ordinary working people of the country." ("The Great Canadian History Robbery" 62).
59. Wallace I 58.
60. First published as "1837—Diary of A Canadian Play," *This Magazine* 7.1 (1973): 11-15.
61. Wyman, "Passe Muraille defies tidy definition."
62. Urjo Kareda, "History comes to life," *Toronto Star*, 18 Jan., 1973. In a general way, the pattern carries over from *Fanshen*, not only in *1837*'s treatment of the rebellion as revolutionary conflict but also in its focus on the people rather than the leaders (Mackenzie, like the all-purpose Red Soldier, is presented as teaching them the ideological skills they need, cf. Preface 194), and in its agitprop characterization of traditional power figures.
63. cf. Wallace II 245-246.
64. For illustration, see *Canadian Theatre Review*, 6 (1975): 24-25, 58-59.
65. Wallace I 65; cf. Preface 188, 193, 195, 197.
66. Mary Jane Miller, "The documentary drama of Paul Thompson," *Saturday Night*, 98.7 (1974): 36.
67. Johns, "An Interview with Paul Thompson" 32.
68. Wallace II 241.
69. Marlynn Jollife, "Victoria Playhouse Petrolia: The Building Burden," *Canadian Theatre Review*, 6 (1975): 35-36.
70. Performers in the two collective developments of *Them Donnellys* were Janet Amos, Ian Amos, Lynn Cartwright, Clare Coulter, Barry Flatman, Craig Gardner, Dean Hawes, Shannon King, Geza Kovacs, Maureen MacRae, Larry Mollin, Bob O'Ree, Eric Peterson, Miles Potter, Gary Reineke, Booth Savage, Phil Savath, Phil Schreibman and Terry Tweed; designer was Paul Williams and participating writer was Frank McEnaney.

71. The Thompson connection in the development of the theatre at Blyth goes back to *The Farm Show* tour of 1972 in which the play was performed successfully in the basement of the Blyth Memorial Hall. The occasion demonstrated to Keith Roulston, the Festival's eventual founder, the feasibility of restoring the upstairs of the building for the use of a summer theatre company. Although Thompson was not free to participate in developing the festival, in the spring of 1975 he recommended James Roy to Roulston as the first artistic director. Even before Janet Amos succeeded Roy in 1980, Passe Muraille performers, directors and writers frequently participated in the Blyth productions. For the founding and development of the Blyth Festival, see Jim Hagarty, "Blyth—the little festival that grew," *Stratford Beacon Herald*, 22 Sept., 1983; Gillian Pritchard, "Janet Amos: artistic director/actress," *Scene Changes*, 8.5 (1980): 19-21.
72. Herbert Whittaker, "The Black Donnellys are riding hard again," *Globe and Mail*, 10 Nov., 1973.
73. Sources for my study of *Them Donnellys* are a typed transcription of the second version lent to me by Ted Johns, from which I quote, and a semi-audible tape of the first version copied in 1976 from the original with the permission of Paul Thompson. In the transcription, each act is separately paginated.
74. Wallace I 59.
75. MacKenzie, "Theatre Passe Muraille, Paul Thompson" 8.
76. "The Black Donnellys are riding hard again."
77. Brian Arnott [Brian Boru], "History, Mystery, and Myth: The Donnellys," *That's Show Business*, 12 Dec., 1973: 4.
78. In distinguishing his own style from Keith Turnbull's gestural technique in the Reaney trilogy, Thompson noted in an interview that when Turnbull puts an actor-as-horse on stage he is striving for the "effect of horses," starting with coconut shells (for hoof-beats) rather than physical bodies (Barnet/Bessai).
79. See note 73 for pagination of typescript.
80. "Them Donnellys in need of editing," [unsigned] *Globe and Mail*, 5 Dec., 1973.

268 Playwrights of Collective Creation

81. At Blyth, the opening barn-raising was redesigned by Bob Pearson from the use of ladders to beams. These were extended over the audience "from balcony to stage providing interesting entrances and playing areas for later scenes." Ted Johns with Theatre Passe Muraille, *The Death of the Donnellys* (Toronto: Playwrights Canada, 1982) 1.
82. Johns's spelling.
83. The collective itself was similarly constituted to include Passe Muraille regulars David Fox, Anne Anglin, Ted Johns, Eric Peterson and Janet Amos, along with newcomers Paula Jardine and Connie Kaldor (the latter had worked earlier in the year with the Mummers Troupe in Newfoundland on *Buchans: A Company Town*).
84. Robert Nunn, "Fibre/Optics," *Canadian Literature*, 102 (1984): 104.
85. Frank Rasky, "Theatrical vagabonds dig up prairie sagas," *Toronto Star*, 2 Dec., 1975.
86. The people they acknowledge for research assistance include Maria Campbell, Joe Fafard, Andras Tahn, Ron MacDonald of Rosthern Mennonite College, Juliet and Napoleon Perret of Duck Lake.
87. Foreword to *Showing West: Three Prairie Docu-Dramas*, edited by Diane Bessai and Don Kerr (Edmonton: NeWest Press, 1982) 11. Reference to individual plays is cited in parenthesis.
88. Foreword 8, drawn from Johns' unpublished introduction to the manuscript [np].
89. In addition to illustrations in the published text, see Don Kerr, "The West Show," *next year country*, 3.3 (1976): 21-25.
90. Johns' unpublished introduction.
91. Kerr 22, 24.
92. Rudy Wiebe, *Showing West* 89.
93. Wallace II 243.
94. These were David Fox, Janet Amos, Connie Kaldor, Layne Coleman, Ted Johns, with Eric Peterson, who was engaged in the Centaur Theatre premiere of Salutin's *Les Canadiens*, and Dennis Robinson joining later; three other actors—Graham McPherson, Gordon Tootoosis, Betti Trauth—were hired to complete the cast for the Edmonton premiere.
95. Betty Jane Wylie, "The Playwright as Participant" 115.

96. Wylie 115.
97. Wylie 117.
98. Years later, for the onerous task of compiling a text for publication (Windsor, Ont.: Black Moss, 1981), she acquired half ownership of the play over her original one-twelfth (115).
99. Wylie 118.
100. Actor Donald Harron comments on his own "kinship" to Horsburgh for Frank Rasky in "A minister's tragedy helps actor find courage for self-discovery," *Toronto Star*, 6 Mar., 1976, in which he notes "I've never intended to impersonate him, but to recapture the spirit of the man...."
101. Wylie 118.
102. Wiebe 91.
103. Ron Chalmers, "Insults to Democracy during the Lougheed Era," *Socialism and Democracy in Alberta: Essays in Honour of Grant Notley*, edited by Larry Pratt (Edmonton: NeWest, 1986) 133.
104. Quoted by Rudy Wiebe (from "On stage everyone for a rousing curtain call!", *Edmonton Journal*, 6 May, 1977) 92.
105. "Alberta-based play fails to reach heart of the issue," *Edmonton Journal*, 2 Dec., 1977, a Canadian Press report on Gina Mallet's review in *The Toronto Star*.
106. Johns, "An Interview with Paul Thompson" 32.
107. Filewod 31.
108. Usmiani misses the point when she describes the device as "artificial and quite unnecessary" (57). Filewod, in comparison, finds "their scenes the most effective in performance but the most awkward on the printed page" (31).
109. Wallace II 245.
110. Muriel Leeper, "Linda Griffiths: The Actress as Playwright," *Canadian Theatre Review*, 38 (Fall 1983): 113.
111. Kerr 23-24.
112. Ronald Bryden, "The critic as artist," *Books in Canada*, 17.2 (March 1988): 17.

Chapter Three

1. "Was Sartre Smartre? Occasional Theatre, on Occasion" 38.
2. "Occasional Theatre" 36.

3. Introduction, *Les Canadiens* (Vancouver: Talonbooks, 1977) 19-21. Reference to the play is cited in parenthesis.
4. No transcription exists.
5. Urjo Kareda, "Not ready for the stage," *Globe and Mail*, 26 March, 1975. Directed by John Palmer, the play is about the Jews who flocked to Turkey to claim Shabtai Zvi as Messiah, only to witness his conversion to Islam to save his own life. (Toronto: Playwrights Canada, 1981).
6. "Shaping the Word: Guy Sprung and Bill Glassco," *Canadian Theatre Review*, 26 (1980): 35.
7. The transcription of *IWA* was made available to me in 1976 by Lynne Lunde of the Mummers Troupe; this and other Mummers' playscripts such as *Gros Mourn* and *Buchans: A Company Town* are at the Provincial Library, St. John's. The manuscript of *Joey* was provided through the courtesy of Donna Butt, artistic director of Rising Tide Theatre.
8. Sprung 35; cf. Mary Jane Miller, "Two Versions of Rick Salutin's *Les Canadiens*," *Theatre History in Canada*, 1.1 (1980): 58, 60.
9. "Hockey fans can cheer for Les Canadiens on stage in Montreal," [unsigned] *Globe and Mail*, 12 Feb., 1977.
10. Gail Scott, "Centaur half saviour, half sheep," *Globe and Mail*, 18 June, 1977.
11. See Peter Copeman, "Rick Salutin and the Popular Dramatic Tradition: Towards a Dialectical Theatre in Canada," *Canadian Drama*, 10.1 (1984): 26.
12. Miller 67.
13. Miller speaks of the original inclusion of representations of "real players whose playing styles were familiar to the audience: Lafleur, Shutt, Bouchard" as well as Dryden himself (60).
14. Miller 65.
15. "Documentary Style: the Curse of Canadian Culture," *Marginal Notes: Challenges to the Mainstream* (Toronto: Lester & Orpen Denys, 1984) 94.
16. cf. Miller 68.
17. John Bentley Mays, "Taking time on the road," *Maclean's*, 92.23 (1979): 62.

Endnotes 271

18. Cited respectively by David McCaughna, "Nathan Cohen in Retrospect," *Canadian Theatre Review*, 8 (1975): 31, and by Wayne Edmonstone in *Nathan Cohen: The Making of a Critic* (Toronto: Lester and Orpen Denys, 1977) 67-69.
19. Edmonstone 260; among critics who took this line, he refers to John Hofsess and Ross Stuart.
20. Mary Land, "Nathan Cohen: A Review: Cohen would have killed it," *the newspaper* (an alternate student newspaper at the University of Toronto), 4 Feb., 1981 (clipping in Theatre Passe Muraille file No. 7, MTRL).
21. Jamie Portman, "Douglas Campbell: actor plays role of his harshest critic," *Calgary Herald*, 12 Jan., 1981.
22. Rosemary Sullivan, "From Cohen to Salutin to You," *Canadian Forum* 60.708 (1981): 37.
23. Rick Salutin, *Nathan Cohen: A Review*, published in *Canadian Theatre Review*, 30 (1981): 45-105. Citations of the play are noted in parenthesis.
24. cf. Copeman 31.
25. cf. Edmonstone's quotation (172-182) of Cohen's response in *The Critic* (Oct. 1950) to Moore in *The Canadian Forum* (Aug. 1950).
26. Audrey M. Ashley, "Salutin breaking from docu-drama in new 'Spy' play," *Ottawa Citizen*, 3 Feb., 1984.
27. Ian Adams, *S: Portrait of a Spy* (Toronto: Virgo, 1981) xxiii.
28. Retired RCMP counter-espionage director, Leslie James Bennett, obviously thought he was justified in initiating a libel suit charging the author with basing the character of S on him; as a result, the work was withdrawn from circulation for three years pending court rulings. Salutin's interest in Adams' predicament led to his publication of an article in *This Magazine*, Dec. 1980, in which he printed letters from journalist Peter Worthington to Bennett demonstrating the former as instrumental in Bennett's decision to sue. Bennett ultimately settled out of court.
29. Ashley, "Salutin breaking from docu-drama."
30. Rick Salutin and Ian Adams, *S: Portrait of a Spy* (Toronto: Playwrights Canada, computer script [1985]). Pagination is by act.
31. Ashley.
32. Sherie Posesorski, *Books in Canada*, 15.3 (1985): 41.

33. Posesorski 41.
34. Salutin, "Documentary Style" 97.
35. Salutin 94.
36. Salutin 97.
37. Doug Bale, "Playwright turned from lonely novel writing," *London Free Press*, 8 Nov., 1978.
38. *The Work*, interview with Rick Salutin 257.
39. "Documentary Style: the Curse of Canadian Culture," reprinted in *Marginal Notes*, is drawn from two Culture Vulture columns of *This Magazine*: the first, titled "Front Page Challenge and the Curse of Canadian Culture," Nov.-Dec., 1976, p. 26 (dated October, 1976 in the reprint); the second, "More on Documentaries," July-Aug., 1977, 23-24 (dated June, 1977 in the reprint). For convenience, the reprint is quoted here.
40. Salutin 91-92. This is a manifestation of "people who have trouble taking their own experience seriously" and need the "assurance" of what "feels like fact" (92). Much later Salutin moderated this view, specifically in relation to docu-drama: "There was a need to be very clear about who we were and what our society was about, and establish that Canada really was a plausible setting for drama" (Ashley, "Salutin breaking from docu-drama").
41. Salutin 95.
42. Salutin 94-95.
43. Alan Filewod, "The Political Dramaturgy of the Mummers Troupe," *Canadian Drama*, 13.1 (1987): 65. This issue also contains the script of *Buchans: A Company Town*.
44. She is a co-founder and artistic director of Rising Tide Theatre, a splinter group from the Mummers Troupe founded in 1978 and now serving St. John's subscription audience at the Arts and Culture Centre.
45. Telephone conversation with Donna Butt, June 11, 1987, and subsequent correspondence.
46. Conversation with Rick Salutin, Aug. 6, 1985.
47. An important model for him, he stated, was a Memorial University Extension Department interactive film project on Fogo Island in the 1960s. (John Fraser, "Those Mummers of Newfoundland just won't keep their traps shut," *Globe and Mail*, 18 Oct., 1975.)

48. Sandra Gwyn, "The Newfoundland renaissance," *Saturday Night*, 91.2 (1976): 40.
49. Filewod, *Collective Encounters* 130.
50. "Send the IWA About Their Business," newspaper text of Smallwood's speech reprinted in the *IWA* programme.
51. Alan Filewod (the Mummers' dramaturge of the time) reports that he and performer Rhonda Payne had together assembled a preliminary body of material during a field trip in March, 1975, to Grand Falls and Badger. Filewod shifted to another project, putting his notebook of research, including bibliography and a strikers' song he had written in tribute to Landon Ladd, at their disposal; other research material, including interviews, was assembled by Donna Butt, Rick Boland and Chris Brookes. A typescript of the play is in the Provincial Archives, St. John's, and was made available to me in 1976 with permission of the theatre.
52. Members of the collective included Rick Boland, Donna Butt, Ron Hynes, Ray Landry, Pamela Morgan, Rhonda Payne and Jeff Pitcher.
53. Paddy Warrick, "Writing a play together," *St. John's Evening Telegram*, 19 Sept., 1981.
54. *A Public Nuisance: A History of the Mummers Troupe* (St. John's: Institute of Social and Economic Research, Memorial University of Newfoundland, 1988) 147-148.
55. Gwyn 38.
56. Salutin 94.
57. *I Chose Canada* (Toronto: Macmillan, 1973), specifically "Shall Might be Right?" 396-413. cf. Richard Gwyn, *Smallwood: The Unlikely Revolutionary* (Toronto: McClelland and Stewart, 1968 [rev. 1972]), especially "'We Are Only Loggers,'" 199-211.
58. Al Pittman, "Joey: A genuine hit from Rising Tide," *Western Star*, 25 Sept., 1981.
59. Gina Mallet, "Joey's spirit certainly charms," *Toronto Star*, 13 Jan., 1982.
60. Paddy Warrick, "'Joey' biggest challenge for Rising Tide Group," *St. John's Evening Telegram*, 5 Sept., 1981. The members of the collective also included Brian Downey, David Fox, Sheilagh Guy, Kevin Noble, Jeff Pitcher and David Ross.
61. From a typescript lent to me by Donna Butt.

62. For analysis of collective creation in Newfoundland of the 1980s, see Denyse Lynde, "The Wake or the Awakening," *Canadian Theatre Review*, 55 (1988): 48-52. For the recent emergence of playwright Janis Spence from the collective process, see Joan Marie Sullivan, "Giving voice to those who take care of the world," *Globe and Mail*, 23 July, 1988.

Chapter Four

1. Martin Knelman, "Roots," *Saturday Night*, 100.12 (Dec. 1985): 70.
2. An earlier version of the material in this chapter appeared as "Discovering the Popular Audience," *Canadian Literature*, 118 (1988): 7-26.
3. Usmiani, *Second Stage*, 69.
4. *The Work*, interview with John Gray, 46.
5. Max Wyman, "Total Theatre," *Vancouver Sun*, 19 Mar., 1976.
6. See Christopher Defoe, "The Tamahnous Theatre: scripts are a point of departure," *Vancouver Sun*, 5 Feb., 1974, on their retrospective season of that year.
7. Herbert Whittaker, "A Western myth with Canadian point of view," *Globe and Mail*, 20 June, 1974.
8. *The Work* 46.
9. Alan Twigg, *For Openers: Conversations with Canadian Writers* (Madiera Park: Harbour, 1981) 102.
10. Twigg 102.
11. Audrey Johnson, "Distinguished visitor doesn't mince his words," *Victoria Times-Colonist*, 28 Nov., 1981.
12. Bob Allen, "Talent in light vein," *Vancouver Province*, 9 May, 1974. Jeremy Long continued along this line with what was now projected as a musical trilogy, the second of which was *Eighty-Four Acres*, premiered in March, 1976. This was a light focus on the threats of land developers in the British Columbia wilderness. In 1978, Bruce Ruddell and Glen Thompson wrote *Liquid Gold*, also a musical, telling the story of the formation of a British Columbia fishermen's union.
13. Twigg 103.
14. Daniel Dematello, University of Toronto's *The Varsity*, 26 Mar., 1975.

15. Preface to *18 Wheels*, in John Gray, *Local Boy Makes Good: Three Musical Plays* (Vancouver: Talonbooks, 1987) 19, 21. Reference to the plays in this text is noted in parenthesis.
16. *The Work* 50.
17. *The Work* 49.
18. Twigg 102.
19. Introduction, *Local Boy Makes Good* 12.
20. *The Work* 48.
21. Viveca Ohm, "John Gray," UBC alumni *Chronicle* (Spring 1979): 28.
22. In *Three Plays by Tom Cone* (Vancouver: Pulp, 1976).
23. *The Work* 46-47; cf. interview with Tom Cone 37.
24. David McCaughna, "Billy Bishop Goes to War," *Toronto Star Week*, 17-24 Feb., 1979.
25. Letter to D.B., 22 Nov., 1987.
26. *Billy Bishop Goes to War* (Vancouver: Talonbooks, 1981) 34, hereafter cited in parenthesis.
27. John Lekich, "The co-pilot brings Bishop in smoothly," *Globe and Mail*, 13 Nov., 1982.
28. *Winged Warfare* (New York: George H. Doran, 1918) 169.
29. Introduction, *Local Boy Makes Good* 13.
30. Twigg 104.
31. Billy has already demonstrated the fears and triumphs of his solo flight in a similar manner (57).
32. "I think the whole notion of war being futile and a bad thing is a smoke screen.... It's a device to divert people from the real issue which is imperialism," he told Lekich.
33. *The Work* 52.
34. *The Work* 52.
35. The song was removed on the advice of Mike Nichols for the New York production on the grounds that it "climaxed too early." Gray, letter 22 Nov., 1987. It may be found on the audio recording of excerpts from the play, *Ottawa: Good Day Music*, 1979.
36. Judy Steed, "Mike and Eric and Chris and John," *The Canadian Magazine*, 26 May, 1979: 4.
37. Letter, 22 Nov., 1987.
38. *The Work* 51.

39. Author's Note to *Rock and Roll*, published first in *Canadian Theatre Review*, 35 (Summer 1982): 68. See also Preface to the revised text (1983) in *Local Boy Makes Good* 89-90. Unless otherwise indicated, references to this play are from the second publication and are indicated in parenthesis.
40. *The Work* 53.
41. Martin Knelman, "The King of Friday Night," *Saturday Night*, 96.5 (1981): 71.
42. Cf. the original "It's the rhythm of life, rock and roll. / Follow the beat and save your soul" (113). Gray's later explication of the title relates to this advice: "the combination of words implied an approach to life; an alternating rigidity and flexibility, both of which seem essential if one is to survive life's inevitable and various transitions. Sometimes you have to be a rock; sometimes you have to roll with it. The trick is to know when" (Preface 90).
43. Introduction, *Local Boy Makes Good* 14.
44. In 1983, Tom Kerr had premiered Gray's only completely non-musical play, a comic murder/mystery/thriller of mistaken identity (among four Santa Clauses), *You Better Watch Out, You Better Not Cry*, set on Christmas Day in Victoria's Empress Hotel.
45. Keynote address, "Theatre in Atlantic Canada," Mount Allison University, 4 April, 1986.
46. Nora Abercrombie, "Love song: Messer by Gray," Edmonton *Bullet*, 1 Feb., 1986: 8.
47. Knelman, "Roots" 70.
48. Knelman 70.
49. Knelman 71.
50. Bill Robertson, "Islanders Remembered," *NeWest Review*, Mar., 1986: 17.
51. Eric Peterson in conversation with R.H. Thompson, CBC, "State of the Arts," 12 July, 1987.
52. Sherri Aikenhead, "Spotlight on a down-home hero," *Maclean's*, 97.4 (1984): 71.
53. Contrast Theatre Passe Muraille's *Canadian Hero Series #1*, 1975, in which Gray was a performer. This depicts the leaders and landscapes of defeat in the Rebellion of 1885, based on painter John Boyle's *Batoche Series* (see *Artscanada*, 198/199 [1975]: 32-37). The second in the series was *John Hornby*,

directed by David Fox, 1976, a collective creation on the extraordinary life and death on the northern Barrens of an eccentric English explorer and hunter, with Eric Peterson in the title role.

Chapter Five

1. Christopher Covert, "Saskatoon Vision," *Canadian Theatre Review*, 7 (1975): 130.
2. The play is preserved on video in the 25th Street [House] Theatre archive, University of Saskatchewan, Saskatoon.
3. Introduction, *Maggie & Pierre—a fantasy of love, politics and the media* (Vancouver: Talonbooks, 1980) 10. Citations from the play appear in parenthesis.
4. "25th Street House," undated statement [1972] of aims, signed by Tahn, Gerry Stoll, Sharon Bakker and others in 25th Street [House] Theatre archive.
5. For Don Kerr's history of the evolution of this collective creation and for its final (composite) text, see *Paper Wheat: The Book* (Saskatoon: Western Producer Prairie Books, 1982).
6. This and other 25th Street plays referred to below are in the 25th Street [House] Theatre archive. At this time, Griffiths was participating in Paul Thompson's collective creation, *Shakespeare for Fun and Profit* (with music and lyrics by John Gray).
7. Gary Geddes in collaboration with Diana Bellshaw, David Fox, Linda Griffiths et al, *Les maudits anglais* (Toronto: Playwrights Canada, 1984).
8. Wallace II 245, 247, 248.
9. Judy Rudakoff, "Maggie and Pierre and Linda," *Scene Changes*, 8.4 (1980): 15-16.
10. Linda Manning, "the twenty-two sides of Ted Johns," *Scene Changes*, 8.4 (1980): 21.
11. Ted Johns, *The School Show* (Toronto: Playwrights Canada, 1979).
12. Rudakoff 15.
13. Muriel Leeper, "Linda Griffiths: The Actress as Playwright," *Canadian Theatre Review*, 38 (1983): 113.

278 *Playwrights of Collective Creation*

14. Don Perkins, "Coleman relishes new role...", *Saskatoon Star-Phoenix*, 26 Aug., 1980. Other collective plays at 25th Street Theatre include *Prairie Psalms*, Oxcart Summer Players, 1977; *Don'tcha Know, the North Wind and You in My Hair*, 1978, a look at contemporary Cree communities in Northern Saskatchewan. Coleman himself contributed to the prairie-hero genre with *Queen's Cowboy*, 1979, a written collaboration with William Hominuke. See my "Drama in Saskatchewan," in *Saskatchewan Writing*, edited by E.F. Dyck (Regina: Saskatchewan Writers Guild, 1986) 227-231.
15. Jamie Portman, "...and Linda's learned her lesson," *Vancouver Sun*, 4 Mar., 1982.
16. Leeper 114.
17. Leeper 114.
18. About Layne Coleman's *Conversations with Girls in Private Rooms* (1980), CBC Radio's reviewer Ron Markham remarked that to imitate "the way they talk down at the Ritz beer parlour" is not necessarily enough to make art. ("Stereo Morning," 28 April, 1981.)
19. Rudakoff 15.
20. Typescripts of the two versions are held in the archives of 25th Street [House] Theatre [1982] and Theatre Passe Muraille [1983], respectively. An emended second version was released later by Playwrights Canada [nd].
21. Portman, "...and Linda's learned her lesson."
22. Leeper 113.
23. Henry Mietkiewicz, "Will Lovely Linda Griffiths O.D. on Success?" *Toronto Star*, 23 Jan., 1983. It may be no coincidence that over half of the original cast, including Griffiths, were experienced in collective creation: Michael Fahey, Dennis Robinson, Wendell Smith and Sharon Stearns.
24. See Mira Friedlander, "Paradise revised, revisited," *Globe and Mail*, 13 Feb., 1984.
25. Linda Griffiths, "A Transformation," Theatre Passe Muraille programme note to *Jessica: A Transformation*, 20 Mar., 1986.
26. Linda Griffiths and Maria Campbell, *The Book of Jessica: A Theatrical Transformation* (Toronto: Coach House, 1989) 31.
27. *The Book of Jessica* 37.
28. *The Book of Jessica* 44.
29. Griffiths, "A Transformation."

30. Caroline Heath, "'Jessica' mixes mythology and reality," *NeWest Review*, Dec. (1982): 5.
31. Griffiths, "A Transformation."
32. Griffiths, "A Transformation."
33. A typescript of the 1982 version is in the 25th Street [House] Theatre archive. Typescript of the Toronto version is courtesy of Linda Griffiths. The final version is published in *The Book of Jessica*.
34. Mark Czarnecki, "Cultural schizophrenia," *Maclean's*, 95.46 (1982): 78.
35. Doris Hillis, "You Have to Own Yourself: An Interview with Maria Campbell," *Prairie Fire*, 9.3 (1988): 51-52.
36. Maria Campbell, *Halfbreed* (Toronto: Seal Books, 1979) 82.
37. For other elements in the Vitaline character, see *The Book of Jessica* 41, 44.
38. Maria Campbell, *People of the Buffalo* (Vancouver: J.J. Douglas) 21-22.
39. Alice Klein, "Griffiths' collective works," *Now Magazine*, 17-23 Feb., 1983: 7.
40. *The Book of Jessica* 35-36; 59.

Chapter Six

1. Robert Wallace, "Towards an Understanding of Theatre Difference," *Canadian Theatre Review*, 55 (1988): 11.
2. The play has also become a classic source for training actors at all levels.
3. Peter Copeman, "Rick Salutin: The Meaning of it All," *Canadian Theatre Review*, 34 (1982): 195.
4. Barnet/Bessai.
5. Filewod, *Collective Encounters* 183.
6. I am indebted to Professor Richard Paul Knowles for access to his archive of Mulgrave plays.
7. Theatre Network material was made available to me by Stephen Heatley, current artistic director, and Professor David Barnet.

Index

Aberhart, William (Bible Bill) 114, 119
Adams, Ian 134, 136, 155, 156, 161
Adams, Jimmy 95
Adventures of an Immigrant, The 135
Advocate, The 86, 87
Agitprop Street Players 18
Allen, Bob 182
Allen, Lewis 199
Almighty Voice 30, 107, 227, 229-230, 251
Alternative Theatre 13, 19, 22, 24, 26, 27, 29, 35, 134
   Britain 22, 26
   Canada 13, 24, 26, 27, 29, 35
   United States 19, 22, 23
American guerrilla street theatre 23
Amos, Janet 75, 87, 120, 127, 129
Anglin, Anne 127
Arden, John 32
   Armstrong's Last Goodnight 32
Arent, Arthur 16

Arnott, Brian 81, 98
Artaud, Antonin 20, 31

Bacchae, The 180
Bainborough, Bob 230, 231
Bakker, Sharon 219
Ballad of Billy the Kid, The 218
Bennett, Leslie James 155
Berton, Pierre 146
Bessai, Diane
   "Documentary Theatre in Canada: An Investigation into Questions" 39
Bill Durham 180, 182
Billy Bishop Goes To War 10, 11, 45, 128, 180-183, 185-188, 191, 199, 206, 210-212, 219, 221, 242, 245, 253
   as comedy of colonialism 190, 197, 212
   complicity with audience 189
   echoes of 1837 186, 212
   ironic function of songs 190, 192, 214
   participation of Eric Peterson 186

Index 281

precursor in *Herring-
  bone* 187
  story-telling 189
Bishop, Billy (William A.) 186,
  189, 190
Black Donnellys, The 94
Blyth Festival 11, 30, 44, 94, 128
  association with Victoria
    Playhouse Petrolia
    93
  Roulston, Keith 94
  Thompson, Paul 94
Bolt, Carol 44, 62, 101
  at Globe Theatre
    (*Next Year Country*) 57
  at Great Canadian Theatre
    Company (*Buffalo
    Jump*) 62
  at Theatre Passe Muraille
    31, 44, 57, 58, 61
  Buffalo Jump 31, 44
  Pauline 44
Book of Jessica, The 230, 239
Boyle, John 57, 61
Bread and Puppet Theatre 35
Brecht, Bertolt 15, 16, 31
Brenton, Howard 22, 46
  Hitler Dances 22
Bring Back Don Messer 202, 209
Brissenden, Connie 51
Broadfoot, Barry 57
Brook, Peter
  Royal Shakespeare
    Company 18
  US 18
Brookes, Chris 135, 166, 167,
  169-171
  theatrical political satire
    171
Bryden, Ronald 130
Brymer, Patrick 46, 217, 225, 228
Buchan, John 215
Buchans 167, 170

Buchans: A Company Town 107,
  135, 136, 164-166
Buffalo Jump 9, 31, 44, 49, 56
  -65, 83, 92, 98, 101, 114, 126,
  161, 243, 250
  analysis 57
  audience participation 60
  Bolt's contribution 57
  compared to *Doukhobors*
    60
  origins in *Next Year
    Country* 56, 57
  Ottawa revision 63
  popular folk history 59
  treatment of historical
    figures 59
Butt, Donna 135, 165, 168, 172,
  176, 177

Café La Mama 21, 34
Campbell, Maria 46, 127, 217,
  229-235, 239, 241
  association with Griffiths
    217, 229
  collaboration with
    Thompson 229
  on women's spirituality
    233, 235
Canada Council 6, 24, 25, 32,
  106
  Council's *1961-62 Annual
    Report* 25
Canadian Place, The 33
Cardinal, Tantoo 230
CCF 114
Centaur Theatre 116, 135, 136,
  139, 142, 253
Chamberlain, Charlie 208
Cheeseman, Peter 40, 41, 50
  documentary style 16, 26,
    41
  Six into One 17

The Fight for Shelton Bar 17
The Knotty 17
The Staffordshire Rebels 17
Victoria Theatre, Stoke-on-Trent 16, 41
Churchill, Caryl 22, 46, 232
Cloud Nine 22
Close the Coalhouse Door 17
Cohen, Nathan 34, 136, 146, 163
Coleman, Layne 120, 225
Coming Through Slaughter 127, 254
Company Town 135
Cone, Thomas 183, 187
Coulter, Claire 35
Couture, Suzette 84
Covert, Christopher 218
Cowan, Cindy 217
Crosbie, John 174, 176
Croyden, Margaret 20

Davis, Robert 88
Death of the Donnellys, The 94, 101, 106, 126
"as a study in law" 106
attention to language 103
compared to *Them Donnellys* 101, 103
dramatic structure 103
written for Blyth Festival 94
Defoe, Christopher 181
Deverell, Rex 25, 26
Medicare! 26
Documentary 145, 164
"documentary" 142
collective documentary playmaking 165
documentary style 143
documentary theatricalism 169
Documentary Drama 39, 40, 82, 90, 140, 246
as corrective 40, 51, 82
as political 40
authenticating (presentational) style 40
community collectives 39
compared to film 90
compared to film (Grierson) 39
fidelity to source 41
Living Newspaper 16, 40
Don Messer and the Islanders 207
Don Messer's Jubilee 10, 45, 180, 205-208, 210-213, 215, 245, 246, 255
as a Don Messer show 207, 209, 210
audience as television community 207, 209
Donnellys Must Die, The 94
Doukhobors 9, 11, 38, 41, 49-56, 59, 60, 62, 64-66, 83, 86, 88, 92, 95, 99, 126, 243, 250
analysis 51
audience as adversary 54, 56, 126
images of purification and suffering 52
improvisational component 53, 54, 56, 88
selective depiction 50
Dracula II 180
Dryden, Ken 136

Edinburgh Fringe Festival 22

Edmonstone, Wayne 146, 153
  Nathan Cohen: The Making of a Critic 146
Edmonton Fringe Festival 44
18 Wheels 10, 45, 180, 182-184, 185, 186, 191, 200, 202, 204, 205, 210, 212, 213, 253
  as country-and-western 183, 184, 186
  origins at Theatre Passe Muraille 183
1837 134, 158
1837: The Farmers' Revolt 25, 30, 38, 40, 41, 44, 65, 78-81, 83, 92-94, 107, 117, 121, 123, 126-129, 134-137, 161, 164, 171, 179, 182, 186, 210, 213, 243-245 247, 251
  contemporary political perspective 79, 81, 88, 92
  dual-time relation to audience 85, 88
  pairing with *The Farm Show* 80
  popular performance metaphors 86
  revised 79, 90, 171, 245
Elsom, John 17, 26
Endres, Robin 61

Factory Theatre Lab 13
Fafard, Joe 109, 113
Fahey, Michael 219
False Messiah, The 182
Fanshen 22, 43, 82, 83, 250
Far As The Eye Can See 30, 42, 44, 106, 107, 114, 116, 118-121, 127, 227, 229, 231, 243, 253
  analysis 121
  contemporary action 121, 125
  history as fable (*The Regal Dead*) 121, 122, 127
  mimetic rather than presentational 121
  participation of Rudy Wiebe 115, 118
  sources of story and characters 115, 120
Farm Show, The 29, 30, 36, 44, 64-67, 72, 74, 79, 80, 93, 94, 97, 107, 108, 110, 120, 127, 130, 223, 230
  alternating themes and styles 69
  analysis 66
  as discovery process 66, 126
  audience as specific subject and object of performance 65
  community as co-creators 70
  double audience perspective 67, 78
  first-hand material 64, 65
  mythic element 72, 77, 108
  Passe Muraille method 69
  revision 76
  tractor as community icon 74
  use of songs 67, 72, 73, 76, 77
Farquhar, George 32
  The Beaux' Stratagem 32
Federal Theatre Project 16
Fen 232
Festival of Underground Theatre 35

Filewod, Alan 16, 77, 78, 127, 165, 166
Final Performance of Vaslav Nijinsky, The 181
Fisher, Red 138
Flanagan, Hallie 16
Foster, Paul 21, 34
  Tom Paine 22, 34
Fox, David 70, 76, 120, 127, 128
Free Ride 64, 183, 250
Freedman, Danny 35
Friesen, Jodie 210

Garrard, Jim 26, 33, 34
  "Statement of the Rochdale Theatre Project" 33
  at Rochdale 34
Gascon, Jean 33
Geddes, Garry 46
  Les maudits anglais 46
Generation and 1/2 219
Germain, Jean-Claude 35
  Diguidi, Diguidi, Ha, Ha, Ha! 35
  Si Aurore m'était contée deux fois 35
  Théâtre du Même Nom 35
Global Village 35, 181
Globe Theatre 8, 24, 26, 57, 109, 250
  The Kramers 26
Good Soldier Schweik, The 16
Gray, John (see also for individual titles) 15, 45, 128, 130, 179-183, 186-188, 190-193, 195, 198-202, 205, 208, 209, 211 213
  18 Wheels 45
  at Tamahnous Theatre 180
  at Theatre Passe Muraille 179, 182, 183
  audience interaction 190, 199, 201, 202, 210, 213
  Billy Bishop Goes to War 45
  cultural nationalism 200, 207, 212, 214
  Don Messer's Jubilee 45
  interaction with indigenous audience 179
  musical performance modes 183, 184, 186, 192, 203, 207, 210
  raconteur techniques 184, 190, 191, 202, 206, 209
  Rock and Roll 45
Great Canadian Theatre Company, The 62, 135, 255
Great Wave of Civilization, The 183
Greene, Graham 230
Grierson, John 39
Griffiths, Linda (see also for individual titles) 15, 45, 46, 127, 129, 130, 146, 172, 217-220, 223, 225-232, 234, 236, 239, 241
  as collaborating playwright 217
  association with Douglas Campbell 217, 229
  association with Paul Thompson 217, 219, 220, 229, 230
  at 25th Street Theatre 45, 218
  at Theatre Passe Muraille 46

growing feminism 234, 239
improvisational methods 220, 228, 230
Jessica 172
Gwyn, Sandra 166

Halfbreed 229, 233, 235
Hardin, Hershel 183
Hare, David 22, 43
 Fanshen 22
Hauff, Thomas 231
Hausvater, Alexander 27
Health, The Musical 215
Heath, Caroline 232
Heide, Christopher 202, 209, 210
Herringbone 183, 187, 188
Highway Evangelist, The 186
Hillis, Doris 233
Hinton, William
 Fanshen 43
Holt, Simma 51
Homemade Theatre 53, 95
Horsburgh Scandal, The 38, 128, 182
 a transitional play 118
 participation of Wylie 116, 118
 participation of Wylie compared to Wiebe 118
 Theatre Passe Muraille in transition 118
Hunt, Albert
 Bradford College of Art 17
 John Ford's Cuban Missile Crisis 17

I Love You, Baby Blue 106
If You're So Good, Why Are You In Saskatoon? 30, 45, 107, 120, 216, 218, 252
In His Own Write 34
Instanttheatre 33
International Woodworkers of America 167
Itsin, Catherine 18
IWA 136, 164, 165, 169, 171, 175
IWA strike 167
IWA: The Newfoundland Loggers' Strike of 1959 135
IWA; irreverent gestures of a theatrical approach 171

Jessica 10, 46, 127, 131, 172, 215, 217, 227-239, 241, 243, 246, 254, 255
 evolution from techniques of collective creation 236, 241
 origins in *Halfbreed* 229, 233, 235
 phases of development 230, 236, 237, 239
 theme of feminine spiritual growth 232, 236, 237, 240
Joey 135, 136, 164, 165, 168, 172, 175-177
 comic/ironic scenes of the outports 174
 mimetic convention 176
John Hornby 128, 211, 252
Johns, Ted 37, 44, 64, 65, 102, 105, 106, 110, 119, 124, 127, 217, 221
 editorial comments on *The Farm Show* 66
 editorial comments on *The West Show* 108, 110

Garrison's Garage 45, 128
He Won't Come in from the Barn 44
literary treatment of *Them Donnellys* 94, 101, 105
Naked on the North Shore 44, 128
portrayal of Aberhart 119, 124
St. Sam and the Nukes 45
The School Show 45, 129
Johnson, Chris 72, 74
Joint Stock 44

Kaldor, Connie 120, 129
Kareda, Urjo 78, 83, 135
Kelley, Thomas 94
Kerr, Don 112, 129
Kinch, Martin 31, 33-35
King, Shannon 100
Knelman, Martin 208
Kramer, Ken and Sue 24, 57
Kroetsch, Robert 127, 229

Laban, Rudolph 16
Ladd, Landon 167, 171, 174
Last Edition 16
Le Grand Cirque Magie of Paris 35
Lennon, John 34
  In His Own Write 34
Lennoxville Festival 183
Les Canadiens 9, 11, 93, 116, 134-139, 141-143, 145, 151, 155, 158, 161, 163, 164, 243, 244, 253
  documentary approach 141

dramatized didacticism 145
  mythic interpretation 141
Les maudits anglais 220, 226
Lesnick, Henry 23
Lewis, Larry 239
Lillo, Larry 180, 182
Littlewood, Joan 16, 28, 29, 40
  ensemble techniques 16, 28
  working-class theatre 16, 17, 28
Littlewood/Laban techniques of movement 28
Living Theatre, The 20, 23
  Beck, Julian 19
  Malina, Judith 19
  Paradise Now 20
  The Legacy of Cain 20
Long, Jeremy 181
Long, Larry 180
Lougheed, Peter 114, 121, 125, 126
Luscombe, George 28, 35, 43, 57, 59, 82, 140
  Buchner's *Woyzek* 32
  Chicago '70 35
  creating a play 28
  Hey Rube! 32
  Littlewood training 28
  Luscombe's ensemble method 30
  Ten Lost Years 28
  Toronto Workshop Productions 32, 35, 43, 140
  work with Littlewood 28

Mackenzie, William Lyon 86, 87
Maggie & Pierre 46, 146, 217, 218, 220, 226, 227, 231, 240, 254

as media fantasy   222
authorial point of view
    223
contrasts to *Billy Bishop
    Goes to War* and
    The School Show
    221
transformational
    characterization   237
Mallet, Gina   172
Manitoba Theatre Centre   24
    Hendry, Tom   25
    Hirsch, John   24
Man of La Mancha, The   147
Martin, Tantoo   230
Massey, Walter   33
McDonald, Patrick   135
McEnaney, Frank   95
McKeever, Andrew   45
McNally, Terence   34
    Sweet Eros   34
McQueen, Jim   187
Medea   180
Messer, Don   208, 212
Miller, Arthur   151
Miller, Mary Jane   90, 138, 142
Miller, Orlo   94
Moher, Frank   38
    Robert Kroetsch's *The
    Studhorse Man*   39
Mollin, Larry   53, 64, 95
Mr. Bones   59
Mulgrave Road Co-op   28, 29, 207,   246, 254
Mummers Troupe, The   27, 29, 44,   107, 135, 136, 165-168, 170, 252
    Buchans   169, 171
    *Buchans: A Company
    Town*   166
    collective theatre
        technique   171
    documentary   166

Gros Mourn   166, 169, 171
IWA   171
political satirists   171
popular theatre   166
Munro, Alice   31
    Lives of Girls and Women
    31

Nathan Cohen: A Review   134, 135, 145, 154, 155, 176
    a play of many styles
    153
    limitations of its structure
    153
    memory device   150
    pastiche structure   150
    performance metaphor
    150
National Arts Centre   45
Neptune Theatre   45, 206
New Play Centre   183
Newcastle Playhouse   17
Newsome, Jeremy   180
Next Year Country   30, 56, 57, 101, 110, 250
Nichols, Mike   199
Noble, Kevin   176
Notes from Quebec   28, 35, 250
Nottingham Playhouse   17
Nunn, Robert   66, 107

O.D. on Paradise   10, 11, 46, 223-228, 232, 234, 239, 254-255
O'Casey, Sean   31
    Purple Dust   31
O'Horgan, Tom   21
    Hair   21
    Jesus Christ Superstar
    21

O'Neill, Eugene 151
Oh, What a Lovely War! 16
Oil 44, 64, 94, 248, 251
Ondaatje, Michael 127
One Third of a Nation 16
Open Space Theatre (London) 18
Open Theatre, The 20, 23, 40, 46
  Chaikin, Joseph 19, 21
  Nightwalk 21
  Terminal 21
  The Mutation Show 21
Osborne, Marg 208
Our Town 205
Owens, Rochelle 34
  Futz 34

Pageant Players 23
  Michael Brown 23
Palmer, John 33, 34
  Memories for My Brother
    33, 34
Paper Wheat 11, 30, 46, 107,
  113, 216-218, 224, 226, 228,
  230, 247, 253
Parti Quebecois 134, 138
Peace Shall Destroy Many 115
Pearson, Bob 109
People of the Buffalo 233
Performance Group, The 19, 21,
  26, 35, 181
  Dionysus in 69 26
  Euripides' *The Bacchae*
    21
  Paradise Now 21
  Schechner, Richard 19,
    21
Peters, Henry 23
Peterson, Eric 45, 120, 127, 130,
  180, 181, 183, 186, 187, 210,
  215, 225
Piscator, Erwin 15, 16, 40
Pittman, Al 172, 173, 176

Planchon, Roger 31
Plater, Alan 17
Polish Laboratory Theatre, The
  Grotowski, Jerzy 19
Potter, Miles 68, 78, 129
*Prairie Landscape or...If You're
  So Good, Why Are You in
  Saskatoon?* 107

Radical Arts Troupes 23
Reaney, James 32, 36, 94, 106
  "Ten Years at Play" 36
  Listen to the Wind 32
  The Sun and the Moon 32
Red Ladder 18
  Taking Our Time 18
Regional Theatre
  Britain 17, 18
  Canada 24, 26
Richler, Mordecai 146
Rising Tide Theatre 8, 44, 135,
  136, 165, 254
Robinson, Dennis 120
Rochdale College 49, 50
Rock and Roll 10, 45, 180, 198-
  206, 210, 212, 214, 245, 254
  dramatic dimension 201, 202
  in-performance structure
    202, 203
  Screamin' John as
    performance and choral figure
    203
  target audiences 201, 214
Rogers, Clarke 46, 107, 217, 226,
  229, 232
Ryerson, Stanley 83

S: Portrait of a Spy (play)
134-136, 155, 161, 163
adaptation 156
depth of characterization
158
political aim 160
spy/thriller and political
polemic 161
S: Portrait of a Spy (novel) 10,
134-136, 155, 156, 161, 163,
244, 255
Sainer, Arthur 18
Salty Tears on a Hangnail Face
182
Salutin, Rick (see also for
individual titles) 15, 38, 40-43,
78, 82, 83, 87, 90, 92, 117, 129,
130, 133, 134, 136, 145, 146,
154, 156, 163-165, 167, 170,
171, 176, 179, 182, 186, 217
1837: The Farmers'
Revolt 40, 41, 43,
44
1837: William Lyon
Mackenzie and the
Canadian Revolution
38
ambivalence between
presentational and
mimetic 162
as source of idea and
ideology of *1837* 83
collective documentary
playmaking 165
contributions to *1837* 87,
90, 91
dramatic realism 163
Fanshen 43
in Newfoundland 164
mimetic dramatization
171
on drama of place 79
on timeliness of *1837* 81

The False Messiah 135
San Francisco Mime Troupe 22,
23
Davis, R.G. 22
Holden, Joan 22
Savage, Booth 183
Savath, Phil 53, 95
Schechner, Richard 46
Performance Group, The
180
School Show, The 221
Schreiber, Phil 100
Schwarz, Ernest J. 35
Studio Lab 35
Shank, Theodore 19
Shaw Festival 24
Smallwood, Joey 167
Spirit of '85, The 56
Sprung, Guy 135, 136, 139, 219
Stable Theatre (Manchester) 180
Stafford-Clark, Max 22
Joint Stock 22
Traverse Theatre 22
Staffordshire Rebels, The 41
Stankova, Mariska 33
I am Coming from Czech-
oslovakia 33
Stearns, Sharon 217
Steinhouse, Don 35
Stewart, Ellen 21, 34
La Mama Experimental
Theatre Club Troupe
21
Sticks & Stones 94, 98
Stratford Festival, The 24, 31,
151, 152
Studhorse Man, The 127, 229
Sullivan, Rosemary 147
Sweet Eros 34, 50

Tahn, Andras 45, 106, 218, 225
Tamahnous Theatre 180-182, 187

Bacchae, The 26
   ensemble interpretations 26, 180
   Shaman's Cure, The 26
Tarragon Theatre 13
Tartuffe 24, 32, 33
Taylor, David 31
Tempest, The 180
Ten Lost Years 28, 30, 57
Terror in the Name of God 51
Terry, Megan 20, 46
   Viet Rock 20
Theatre 3 30, 116, 253
Theatre Network 29, 120, 230
Theatre Passe Muraille 8, 9, 11, 13-15, 26, 28-36, 39, 40, 42-46, 49, 50, 56-59, 62, 63, 65-67, 74, 78, 79, 81- 83, 87, 92-97, 102, 106, 107-109, 113-116, 118, 120, 124, 126-130, 134, 135, 137, 146, 148, 153, 166, 179, 181-183, 185-188, 204, 207, 208, 210-212, 218, 220, 222, 224, 225, 227, 229-231, 236, 241, 242, 244-247, 250-255
   creative breakthrough in improvisational playmaking 93
   actor/writers 44, 45, 94, 128, 130
   Canadian folk history 59
   collective process of story-telling 126
   comic and folklore hero/politician 124
   creative performance at 67, 70, 75, 76, 84, 87, 120, 124, 128
   engaging audience 97
   expressive set components 57, 61, 69, 85, 97, 109, 113, 127
   influences of 30, 107, 113, 181-183, 185-186, 206, 210
   metaphoric theatricality 92
   Oil 44
   origins in counter-culture 26, 33-35, 50
   outreach 14, 29, 30, 42, 63, 78, 80, 94, 106, 113-114, 126-127, 179, 218, 226
   participating writers 31, 43, 45, 57, 82, 95, 114, 116, 179, 182, 183
   popular rural culture 96
   presentation of documentary material 148
   regional influence 63
   relationship to audience 78
   reliance on factual sources 39
   Shakespeare for Fun and Profit 46
   texts as notation 43, 51
   The Horsburgh Scandal 44
   The West Show 44
   Them Donnellys 44, 45
   Thompson, Paul 116
   touring 29, 30, 79, 93, 107
   Under the Greywacke 44
   Wiebe, Rudy
      a novelist 118
   Wylie, Betty Jane 116
Theatre Passe Muraille seed shows 29, 107
   Kelman, Paul 29
   Rogers, Clarke 30
   The Edmonton Show 29

Theatre Workshop 16, 28
Them Donnellys 9, 37, 44, 45, 63, 79, 93-99, 101-106, 109, 116, 126, 128, 243, 251
   contrast to Reaney 94, 95, 98
   expressive physicality 99, 128
   gothic supernaturalism 100
   pioneer folk romance 96
   rural popular culture 96
   staging (Homemade Theatre) 95, 98, 99
Thirty-Nine Steps 215
Thomas, Powys 32
Thompson, Paul (see also under Theatre Passe Muraille and individual titles) 13, 26, 28-33, 35-39, 41, 42, 45, 46, 51-53, 57, 59, 60, 64, 66, 67, 69, 71, 84, 95, 107, 108, 117, 118, 129, 130, 133, 135, 136, 146, 153, 181, 183, 217, 218, 220-222, 226, 228-231, 237
   1837 83
   approach to history 41, 49, 61, 83, 92, 94, 96, 107
   association with 25th Street Theatre 107, 218, 231
   association with Blyth Festival 94, 221
   association with Theatre 3 (Edmonton) 116
   association with Victoria Theatre Petrolia 93
   audience orientation 14, 27, 36, 50, 55, 65, 80, 93, 126, 222
   background and early career 31
   career at Theatre Passe Muraille 29, 35
   character through improvisation 84
   collaboration with Maria Campbell 229
   contrast to George Luscombe 28
   directing Linda Griffiths 219, 220, 230
   documentary tradition 26, 39
   Doukhobors 83
   Farm Show, The 63
   fascination with the west 56, 59, 61, 107, 127, 229
   free-form improvisation 28
   La Cenerentola (with Douglas Campbell) 32
   on documentary tradition 41
   playwright's role 15, 116
   Tartuffe (with Jean Gascon) 32
   texture work 37
   working methods 36, 38, 41, 42, 50-53, 56, 57, 60-62, 64, 65, 72, 82, 83, 88, 90, 91, 99, 115, 120, 127-130, 231
Ubu Raw 35
Thorsell, William 125
Toronto Workshop Productions 8, 28, 30, 32, 35, 43, 57, 82, 140, 250, 253
Transformational Acting Style 185
Triple-A Ploughed Under 16
Turnbull, Keith 31, 32

25th Street [House] Theatre 11,
    26, 29, 30, 45, 46, 107, 109,
    113, 130, 216-218, 223-225,
    227, 229, 231-232, 245, 253
  association with Theatre
    Passe Muraille 30,
    107, 130
  Generation and 1/2 46
  *If You're So Good, Why
    Are You in Saska-
    toon?* 30, 45
  Paper Wheat 30, 46
  Sibyl 27
Twigg, Alan 181
*Two Miles Off: Elnora Sunrise
  with a Twist of Lemon* 120

Unequal Union 83
Usmiani, Renata 26, 35

Valdez, Luis 22
  actos 22
  El Teatro Campesino 22
  huelgistas 23
  mito 23
van Itallie, Jean-Claude 21, 46
  America Hurrah 21
  The Serpent 21
Vancouver East Cultural Centre
  45, 182, 187
Vancouver Playhouse 215
Victoria Playhouse Petrolia 93
Vipond, Neil 87

Wallace, Robert 86, 186
War Measures Act 139
Weiss, Peter 40
West Show, The 30, 106-110,
  113-115, 120, 121, 126-128,
  218, 229
  an amalgam of
    established and new
    Theatre Passe
    Muraille procedures
    107
  compared to *1837* 108,
    112, 121
  compared to *The Farm
    Show* 107, 126
  flexible set 109
  innovation through set
    127
  myth of the west 108
  "Where is the Voice Coming
    From?" 107
Whittaker, Herbert 34, 79, 97
Wiebe, Rudy 30, 42, 44, 107,
  119, 120, 231
  Far As the Eye Can See
    30, 42, 44
Wilder, Thornton 205, 206
Williams, Paul 85
Winged Warfare 186, 189
Woodcock, George 112
Worthington, Peter 155
Wylie, Betty Jane 41, 42, 116,
  119, 182
  The Horsburgh Scandal
    42, 44

Yankowitz, Susan 21
  Terminal 21

Printed in Canada